THE CHALLENGE OF DAYCARE

The Challenge of Daycare

SALLY PROVENCE

AUDREY NAYLOR

JUNE PATTERSON

New Haven and London, Yale University Press, 1977

Published with assistance from the foundation established in memory of
Philip Hamilton McMillan of the Class of 1894, Yale College.

Designed by Sally Sullivan
and set in Times Roman type.
Printed in the United States of America by
Vail-Ballou Press, Inc., Binghamton, N.Y.

Published in Great Britain, Europe, Africa, and Asia
(except Japan) by Yale University Press, Ltd., London.
Distributed in Latin America by Kaiman & Polon, Inc.,
New York City; in Australia and New Zealand by Book & Film
Services, Artarmon, N.S.W., Australia; in Japan by John
Weatherhill, Inc., Tokyo.

Library of Congress Cataloging in Publication Data

Provence, Sally A
    The challenge of daycare.

    Bibliography: p.
    Includes index.
    1. Day care centers—United States—Case studies.
I. Naylor, Audrey, 1912–   joint author.
II. Patterson, June, 1924–   joint author.
III. Title.
HV854.P76   362.7'1   75-43331
ISBN 0-300-01964-5

I sincerely believe that for the child, and for the parent seeking to guide him, it is not half so important to know as to feel. If facts are the seeds that later produce knowledge and wisdom then the emotions and the impressions of the senses are the fertile soil in which the seeds must grow. Once the emotions have been aroused—a sense of the beautiful, the excitement of the new and unknown, a feeling of sympathy, pity, admiration, or love—then we wish for knowledge about the object of our emotional response. Once found, it has lasting meaning. It is more important to pave the way for the child to want to know than to put him on a diet of facts he is not ready to assimilate.—Rachel Carson, *The Sense of Wonder*.

Contents

Preface

The research and demonstration project from which this report was derived was supported by a grant from the United States Children's Bureau, Office of Child Development, Department of Health, Education and Welfare. We owe much to the encouragement and wise counsel of Charles Gershenson, who was Director of Research of the Children's Bureau. Dr. Gershenson's interest and support throughout the project were enormously helpful. His creativity and vision in stimulating a group of research projects in child welfare in the 1960s were in the highest tradition of the scholar-scientist concerned with the well-being of the nation's children. To Dr. Gershenson and the Office of Child Development we express our sincere appreciation.

The Grant Foundation, New York, gave generous support for the writing of this book.

Two directors of the Yale Child Study Center, Milton J. E. Senn, who sponsored the beginning of the project, and Albert J. Solnit, who sustained it in countless ways, have our special thanks. The material in the book has been typed and reproduced many times by three singularly devoted staff members: Betty Lubov, Demetra Parthenios, and Arlene Richter. Margaret Frank's library research has been invaluable.

We are grateful to the Yale University Press, especially to Jane Isay and Cathy Iino for guidance, expert editing, and concern for the quality of the manuscript. We acknowledge most fervently the contributions of the children and their parents and our colleagues on the staff. All the staff members of the project, listed at the end of this preface, were noteworthy for their energy, competence, and insight into the work. It was a developmental experience for us all—demanding, often frustrating, always fascinating and challenging. The children and parents are not identified but they, too, have become a permanent part of our lives.

We hope that this book will communicate to others a substantial part of what we have learned about daycare. It begins with general statements about current issues in daycare and the complexity of its challenge. We then describe our program in detail, illustrating how principles influenced practice. Finally, we make a series of suggestions and recommendations that should be applicable to community daycare programs in general and conclude with a hope for the future.

We have used the feminine pronoun throughout in referring to staff of daycare centers. This choice reflects the prevailing reality rather than our conviction about what is desirable for children in daycare. In our center, the children fortunately had daily experiences with one constant male staff member and intermittently with a number of men students in medicine, psychology, and child psychiatry, who gave generously of their time for the opportunity to learn more about young children. We gratefully acknowledge their contribution.

Sally Provence
Audrey Naylor
June Patterson

The Staff of Children's House

Atkins, Gladys	Lubov, Betty
Atkins, John	McGarry, Mary
Baldwin, Karen	McKenzie, Pamela
Booker, Mildred	McKiver, Karen
Colonna, Alice	McLellen, Virginia
Comer, Shirley	Martin, Susan
Cox, Catherine	Mulvaney, Helen
Dahl, Kirsten	Naylor, Audrey
Dye, Martha	Northup, Mary
Ealahan, Jeanne	Owens, Elizabeth
Frank, Margaret	Parthenios, Demetra
Gray, Marian	Patterson, June
Greiner, Rosemarie	Pickus, Regina
Kamano, Virginia	Provence, Sally
Keniston, Ellen	Rhymes, Julina
Kirschner, Shirley	Richter, Arlene
Kuhn, Mary	Stockton, Jane
Landy, Gail	Washington, Janis
Leonard, Martha	Zavitkovsky, Anne

The Challenge of Daycare

CHAPTER 1

Introduction: The Complexity of Daycare

The purpose of this book is to share with others our conviction about the complexity of providing daycare of high quality. We are not arguing either for or against daycare in general. Our belief is that daycare is here to stay; it has become a necessary service to many parents, and it is of great importance that daycare be a benefit to children and families, not a detriment. The ancient oath of physicians to do no harm should be the absolutely minimal promise of child daycare. We hope that more positively stated goals can also be accepted as essential to high-quality daycare.

In the research and demonstration project we conducted over a seven-year period we approached the complex issues and challenges in daycare through considering the functioning of the adults (parents and staff) as well as that of the children. We have drawn heavily on our experience in conducting a daycare program to define and illustrate significant issues for daycare in general.

After summarizing some of the factors in the current pressure for daycare, we present the basic concepts that guided us in planning and carrying out our program and briefly describe the project from which we have drawn our illustrations. We have chosen to focus next on adults in daycare because their vital role in the success or failure of plans for care is not usually emphasized and examined. Their personalities, motivations, and competencies as parents and as daycare providers are of crucial importance. In addition, the structure, policies, practices, and problem-solving methods that are implicitly or explicitly a part of any daycare program, by plan or by default, affect both parents and staff in ways that either help or hinder their ability to provide good care for children.

Programs for children in daycare have received much emphasis and attention in the past eight to ten years. Publications, conferences, and seminars range from those which take up broad conceptual approaches to those which provide details of curricula. Parts of this book will illustrate ways in which developmental principles and empirical knowledge are translated into programs for children. Following the description of the children's

programs, we take a more detailed look at selected aspects of administration, staffing, and consultation. Finally, we discuss considerations in the
use of daycare and a view of daycare as a significant part of a coordinated
system of human services. We wish to emphasize especially in this book our
strong conviction that daycare will never achieve the universally shared
goals of providing good care for children and supportive services to families
without much more careful attention to adults who plan and provide daycare and to those who seek daycare for their children.

The Pressure for Daycare

The more obvious reasons for the current emphasis on daycare include the
inflationary economy, which has markedly increased the number of families
needing income from more than one job; the fact that grandmothers have
gone to work outside the home and are no longer available to take care of
grandchildren as they did in the past; and the greater mobility of the
population, which separates extended family members and thus eliminates
one traditional source of help for young parents. The trend toward marriage
before completion of education is a factor—some young mothers seek daycare in order to complete their own educations; others support the family
while the father completes his. Another factor is a change in governmental
posture toward public support of dependent children: daycare plus training
programs have in recent years been seen as eventually lowering the drain on
the welfare budget. Further, the inadequacy of most, if not all, welfare
grants goads many recipients into trying to get off welfare or at least to
supplement the welfare allowance through part-time employment, either
of which is often impossible without a child-care plan. And all these reasons
are given support by the fact that professionals in social welfare, mental
health, pediatrics, and nursing have come in recent years to think increasingly of daycare as a partial solution in various problem-laden situations:
for children deprived in their home life of the kind of care and stimulation
that will prepare them for the demands of public school; for children who
are in danger of being abused; for children with special handicaps; for
children whose overburdened mothers need the relief of having them cared
for by someone else for part of the day; for children whose relationships
to their mothers are so stormy, for whatever reasons, that partial separation
is indicated while work on the problems proceeds; for young children ex-
hibiting various kinds of disturbances in behavior at home. Indeed, some
mothers are convinced that professionals are saying a group experience as
early as age two is vital to the later social adjustment of a child.

Recently, much pressure for daycare has come from the women's liberation movement. Demands center on a woman's right to develop and use

all of her capacities, not just those of homemaker, and on society's obligation to organize social services so as to make it possible for a woman to do so. These demands are, of course, valid; but danger lies in not recognizing the unique importance of the mother to her child. Many mothers believe, often correctly, that with stimulation from other activities and part-time relief from child care they function better as mothers. The more militant voices on the subject of the need for daycare, however, often express no awareness that the kind of care and experience children have in the early years influences the kind of adults they become. Broad statements about parental rights to daycare do not come to terms with the issue of *who is* to care for children of parents fulfilling other potentials. The answer implied by failure to deal with this vital issue is that child care can be turned over to almost anyone who agrees to do it. But experience has taught us that many of the willing people have minimal capacity to nurture children and provide them with experiences that promote sound development.

Economic need is an unfortunate source of pressure on families to turn a large part of the parenting role over to others. If good substitute care can be found, some of the disadvantages of diminished parental influences on the child may be offset. But since much of what is offered by daycare providers is still not of high quality, its use often reflects a compromise between parental standards of child rearing and economic pressures. Such a compromise should not be required of the large numbers of people who want to have children. Thus we ask whether more and more daycare facilities are the answer to a social need of our times or whether the increasing demand is not mainly symptomatic of an economic problem.

However one answers this question there will always be some need for daycare. Some parents will use it whether it is economically needed or not, and for some children, we acknowledge, reasonably good daycare can provide better experiences than would be available to them at home. Whether daycare is used from necessity, which may deprive certain parents of a role they prefer not to delegate, or used from individual preference, inferior daycare will mean severe disadvantages for the children involved.

Three Principles

Three basic principles guided planning and decision making about every aspect of the program we conducted. We believe that they are relevant to daycare in general. They are
• that the developmental approach is essential to understanding and planning for both children and adults;
• that human relationships play a central role in determining the success of the program for children and adults;

• that separation is a constant influence in the lives of parents and children in daycare.

The Developmental Approach

THE CHILD   The development of a child is a complex, dynamic interactional process in which the child's inborn characteristics and the many experiences that comprise his environment continuously influence one another. Maturation of inborn bodily and mental systems takes place in predictable sequences according to a timetable specific for the human child. This maturation occurs in constant interaction with environmental influences. As a result, various functions emerge and are differentiated, organized, and integrated with others at successively higher and more complex levels of development. Each child shares certain characteristics with all others, but is also unique. He has an individuality codetermined by his endowment and by his environment. In the development of the infant and young child by far the most potent environmental influences are the experiences in his interactions with the adults who nurture him.

Another part of developmental theory of special relevance in planning for children is the phase concept: that there are characteristics and needs that regularly occur in the developing child at certain ages; that there are specific tasks to be mastered during each phase if development is to proceed in an optimal manner; that there are phase-specific strengths and vulnerabilities. For example, the child learns to walk and to talk early in the second year; at the same time feelings of autonomy and independence occur that reflect the child's growing awareness of his abilities. This is also the period when the child is most vulnerable to anxiety associated with separation from parents, and is much more sharply aware of his relative helplessness than previously. The relevance of the phase concept for daycare is that the characteristic competencies, vulnerabilities, needs, and styles of interaction with the environment are very useful as guidelines and must be taken into account in planning and carrying out programs for children.

The developmental approach applied to the child in daycare, then, involves knowledge of children in general and acquaintance with a specific child. For the individual, we wish to know: What kind of child is he? What is his developmental status in such areas as motor competence, speech, problem solving, emotional development, and social skills? With what personality strengths does he come? What are his sensitivities and vulnerabilities? How does he use his abilities to cope with the demands of everyday life? How are general expectations and plans to be adjusted in accordance with his unique individuality?

In daily contact with the child and in communication with his parents we gradually add to the first impressions and take note of the changes that occur. Gradually also, there is enough contact with the parents to know how the child functions at home and in other settings, how he relates to family members, how he is perceived by them. Information accumulates about conditions and events in his past that also may be quite important in planning for him. In this way a body of knowledge can be translated into specific practices.

THE PARENTS   Parenthood, too, is a developmental process. It has also been called one of the normal developmental crises of life (Bibring 1961). There are new tasks associated with this phase of life and new stresses as well as new sources of strength, pleasure, and satisfaction (Benedek 1959; Erikson 1959; Naylor 1970). The parents' earlier experiences, particularly their experiences with their own parents and important others, are powerful influences in the way they adapt to, cope with, and enjoy parenthood. All parents need certain psychological and tangible supports, even those who have been well nurtured as children and whose current life situation is favorable. Child rearing is not easy in our complex society even for parents who are competent, reasonably healthy in mind and body, desirous of children, and able to work and earn a decent living. In those whose own nurturance has been grossly inadequate or traumatic and in those whose current life situation is unfavorable for any reason, the capacity for healthy development as a parent is impaired to varying degrees. These less fortunate parents need even more help.

Planners and daycare providers should acknowledge that parents can be expected to be at various levels of expertise as parents, that they, like their children, will have competencies and vulnerabilities. Appropriate responses to their needs as they experience them will provide support to them in coping with the tasks and stresses of parenthood and will enhance their pleasure and self-esteem. Daycare programs will never achieve high quality unless they provide soundly conceived and sensitively offered supportive services for the development of parents.

THE STAFF   The developmental approach means that those who provide the services must learn and grow also. As is true with parents, staff members are more or less ready for the task. They bring their personal qualities and varying amounts of relevant knowledge, and under favorable conditions develop increasing competence. The leaders of the program need to operate with the knowledge that daycare workers, whether highly trained or not, must acquire new skills and must adapt previously acquired knowledge to a new situation. Each staff member goes through a developmental process in becoming effective. As with children and parents there are tasks, stresses, vulnerabilities, and strengths that enter into this process.

Program leaders, while expecting good performance from staff, should create ways of enhancing the development of individuals.

But the developmental approach in this context has an additional dimension: there must also be growth toward effectiveness in working as a group. The staff of any new enterprise goes through various phases in becoming a cohesive, task-oriented unit. Some of the stresses encountered, some of the vulnerabilities as well as the satisfactions are similar to those encountered in any human developmental process.

An acceptance of this approach means that the leaders of the program must be prepared to go beyond helping staff with the knowledge base and practice. They must provide methods of dealing with the problems that arise among staff members as a result of the inevitable stresses involved in the challenging work of daycare.

The Central Role of Human Relationships

We held three central tenets concerning human relationships: first, that human relationships are of crucial importance in the development of the child; second, that the parent–staff relationships are a major determinant of the effectiveness of a daycare program; and third, that the relationships among staff members create an atmosphere in which the work is either facilitated or impeded.

The nature of a child's relationships with others, the quantity and quality of his experiences with people are basic and vital influences in determining the course of his development. This belief is a central one— the bedrock upon which the program was built. The formation of deep and abiding relationships with people in the earliest years of life is of crucial importance. We agree with those who hold that there should be one main person with whom the child's primary attachment is securely made. In family life the mother usually has this role. She is the person with whom the child establishes his first communications and makes his first emotional attachment, the person who loves and cares for him and whom he comes to love and trust. When this attachment is a firm and mutually satisfying one, it provides a viable and necessary root system for future growth and development. For the infant and toddler in daycare, it is important that a main caregiver be provided and that the number of other caregivers involved with him be kept small in order to support his development as much as possible. Even for the older preschool child, personalized, individualized care is essential to an optimal program. Frequent changes of caregivers, even when all the caregivers are talented, do not provide this important continuity.

Through his human relationships, from early on, the child receives not only the necessary physical nurturance but also the protection, stimulation, training, and organization that enhance his cognitive, social, and emotional capabilities. His way of discovering his world and opportunities to act in relation to it, his capacity to cope with the tasks of development and the demands of his membership in society, his ability to feel and to deal with pleasure and pain, his becoming a thinking, feeling, and communicating person—all are anchored in and draw their major thrust from his relationships. No matter how promising his innate capacities are, if he is to flourish he must be nurtured in various ways by his parents and others. The society into which he is born transmits its values and attitudes, exerts its influence, makes him a member primarily through his relationships with people.

This basic assumption influenced how many and what kind of people we had on the staff, the kinds of relationships we worked out among staff members, how child and parent were introduced into our common venture, how children were received each morning and what happened to them during the course of a day. It was the source of our commitment to work with the parents and our expectation—repeatedly confirmed—that any young child away from his parents for long hours a day would undergo some degree of stress with which we would have to try to help him cope. It influenced our recommendations on how to individualize the care and education of particular children. Many of these elements will be recognized in the descriptions of the children's programs.

Our focus on the role of human relationships led to many kinds of questions. When is it important for a staff member to encourage a specific child toward greater closeness? When does it support a child's general responsivity, or facilitate his learning or the mastery of some developmental task, for the affective atmosphere to be highly charged, animated, vivid? When is it better to tone things down, encourage impersonal activities, neutralize the situation in the interests of his progress? How does the personality of each staff member affect each child's development?

The second of our tenets was that the quality of the daycare experience for the child depends in crucial ways on the relationships between parents and staff members. The responsibility for developing a partnership with parents on behalf of the child lies initially with the daycare staff. The staff must recognize the basic significance of the parent to the child, respect the parents' feelings, recognize that turning the child over to others involves stress for the parents, and that most parents try to do the best they can for their children even when they fail them in some ways. The daycare staff must understand that they become meaningful persons in the life of a child not as replacements but as supplements or temporary substitutes for parents.

There needs also to be a reasonable degree of agreement between daycare staff and parent about what they want for the children, and how they arrive at the goals may require some discussion between them. The quality of the relationship will be influenced by the parents' perception of the extent to which the program is responsive to their needs and those of their child. They surrender each day many of their prerogatives as parents. It is important that they have some ability to influence the program through channels provided them. The most effective channels are the relationships with staff. Communication improves as mutual respect and trust are developed.

Good communication also helps the child to integrate his home and daycare experience. The child who is away from home and family for long hours of the day will feel less lonely and abandoned if he is helped to integrate his home, daycare, and, for the older preschooler, his neighborhood experiences. It helps the child in his adjustment if he knows or senses that his parents are in good communication with his caregivers at the center. Thus it is vital that staff make every effort to help parents feel welcome in the center and to earn their trust that the staff is interesed in their child and in them.

Furthermore, the staff must know enough about the child's life and family that his references to them can be appreciated, expanded in conversation, and made real for him during the day. Reminders of home and parents by the staff help even the toddler to build more stable memories of them. It should be emphasized, however, that the more limited capacities of infants and toddlers for understanding make it far more difficult to build these bridges for them than for older children.

The quality of the relationships among staff members is another important determinant of the quality of the program. Person-to-person relationships as well as group and intergroup dynamics strongly influence whether the program runs smoothly or is fraught with conflict and dissension. A frequent consequence of such very human dissension is a negative impact on children, because the adults function less well and the affective atmosphere is not conducive to learning and to feelings of security.

The leadership of the program must be able to recognize signs of tension and develop methods for helping staff resolve dissension and conflict. A problem-solving approach in which all staff members are active participants benefits children and parents, but there are other benefits as well. Staff morale is improved; staff members are freed to devote their energies and creativity to making the experience of children in daycare a positive one; the professional growth of individual staff members is enhanced through experience in negotiating difficult but common tensions. Finally, individual and shared satisfaction and feelings of self-esteem increase as staff members experience themselves as significant members of a mutually supportive group engaged in important work.

Separation as a Recurrent Problem for Adults and Children

That separation is a situation of stress for child and parent should be acknowledged by the daycare providers, who should then develop plans to alleviate the stress as much as possible. The young child is especially vulnerable to the discontinuity of care that accompanies daily separation from his home and the emotionally important persons in his life. How well he can cope with such stress depends upon a number of factors, including the quality of his relationship to his mother and other family members, his developmental status, and his previous experiences with separation. It also depends upon the quality of the daycare program: the competence and understanding of the staff, the success in carrying out developmentally valid plans for the child, the attention to the creation of bridges between home and center.

For the parent, too, separation from the child is almost always experienced as stressful in some way. Mothers who work outside the home from necessity articulate their feelings most clearly. But others have these feelings. Even when there are strongly positive attitudes about work and career, or when much of the daily care of a young child is less than fascinating, most mothers have feelings of dissatisfaction with themselves or guilt or a sense that they have lost significant parts of their child's life. Almost never are parents completely untroubled about turning their child over to others for care during long hours each day.

For the daycare program, this means that there must be recognition of the frequency of such feelings, although they will vary in intensity and the way they are expressed. Then there must be policies, shared attitudes, and skills among the staff to support parents in coping with these feelings. While much of this support is derived from the knowledge that the program contains good experiences for the child, more specific help is needed. As indicated earlier, parents, too, have needs as well as strengths, and time and effort must be devoted to helping them cope with the experience of separation from their child.

Separation is dealt with in greater detail in Chapter 5.

Basic Requirements for High-Quality Daycare

Our three basic principles can be expanded into the following list of fundamental requirements for high-quality daycare.
• a clearly defined administrative structure, which delineates areas of authority and responsibility
• selection and development of a staff that can carry out the goals of the program, with competent consultation as needed

• assistance to parents in evaluating available daycare services and making a choice for their child

• a commitment, translated into a workable plan, to a partnership with the parents on behalf of the child

• the development of a method of solving the problems that interfere with staff members working together effectively, i.e., alleviation of tensions in staff relationships through a clearly articulated set of policies and procedures

• the development of staff teamwork in helping parents and children with problems that become apparent in the daycare center

• a program of child care and education based upon the developmental characteristics and needs of children

• a systematic method, whether formal or informal, of assessing each child's functioning, i.e., his developmental progress

• flexibility, i.e., the practice of adapting policies, procedures, and staff performance in accordance with the needs of individual children and parents

CHAPTER 2

Children's House:
The Project and the Families

In October 1967 we opened a daycare center as one part of a service-centered program of research on child development in low-income families, supported by a grant from the United States Children's Bureau.* We had two major goals. First, through various kinds of intervention based on knowledge of human needs and development, we wanted to try to diminish the erosion of human potential often associated with conditions of poverty or inadequate care in the earliest years. We wanted to find effective ways of helping young children whose development was either already *at risk* or was likely to become so. We believed that intervention would be most effective if it began early in the life of the child and that helping young parents with child rearing and with the stresses that impinged upon them would increase their capacity to rear healthy children. We hoped that the quality of their own lives would be enhanced as well. Second, we hoped to develop data through the research that could lead in the future to more effective methods of preventing or alleviating the intellectual impairment and personality damage sustained especially in situations of low income— that is, situations in which parents are denied many of the resources available to others in our society.

The project was divided into two phases. Phase I was a study of twenty-three children, ages fourteen months to four years, which we called the pilot group. Phase II was a study of nineteen firstborn children whose parents joined the study during pregnancy. The objectives and general design of both projects were virtually the same. We recognized that the effectiveness of our intervention could best be evaluated if intervention began before various environmental influences had already affected development in different ways and to varying degrees—thus, during pregnancy or at least at birth. However, in order to be ready for Phase II, when our intervention would begin before birth, we needed a trial run. We therefore used the pilot program to recruit and train personnel, to practice working to-

* Project #PR900 of the United States Children's Bureau, Office of Child Development, Department of Health, Education and Welfare.

gether, to try out and refine our research methodology, and to gain the
benefits of experience in trying new methods and modifying traditional
ones.

Both phases of the project were located in a remodeled old former residence we called Children's House. It is located in one of the inner-city
slums of New Haven known as the Hill. The residential section of the
Hill is less than one square mile, into which, according to the 1970 census,
21,628 people are crowded. The district suffers from the blight common
to such areas all over urban America: overcrowding into deteriorated
buildings, lack of play space, littered streets, and a generally dreary appearance. The Hill is an old part of the city and one of the last for which
urban redevelopment is planned. There are large numbers of Italians,
blacks, Puerto Ricans, and Irish; a smaller number of other Anglo-Saxons,
Germans, Jews, and Slavs; and a few students from the nearby medical
center. The Hill is the main place in New Haven for settlement of migrants
from the southern United States and Puerto Rico. While there are, of
course, exceptions, residents of the Hill suffer the consequences of low
educational levels, low incomes, and unemployment.

The pilot group children were referred by social agencies, by pediatric
clinics, and by a program for young unmarried mothers; and several admissions resulted from self-referrals within the neighborhood. For a child
to be admitted, the family's income had to be at or near the poverty level;
the child's development had to appear to us to be at risk as described later
in this chapter; and the parent(s), knowing the goals of the study, had to
agree to accept the responsibilities that participation in the project imposed.
These were mainly bringing the child regularly to daycare, being present
for the child's physical and developmental examinations, and being available for regularly scheduled interviews either at home or at the center. All
the pilot group children were admitted to daycare when the center opened
in October 1967 and remained either until they reached kindergarten age
or until July 1970, when this phase of the study ended.

Of the twenty-three children in Phase I, eight were from fourteen
months to two years old, four were between two and three, seven between
three and four, and four between four and five years old at the time they
entered. Nine were boys; fourteen were girls. Nine were white; fourteen
were black. Eleven of the children were from one-parent families. Ten had
working mothers; three had mothers enrolled part-time in training programs. Ten children were supported in full or in part by public welfare.

The selection process for Phase II was somewhat more detailed. The
nineteen families in the second group were selected from those registered
for obstetrical care in the Women's Clinic of the Yale–New Haven Medical
Center prior to delivering the firstborn child. If the clinic record indicated

that a patient lived in the inner city, was within the poverty group socio-economically, was likely to deliver a normal infant, and was not markedly retarded or actively psychotic, she was selected for interviewing about her interest in joining the study. She was offered an opportunity to learn about the study, the services it would provide, and the obligations it would impose upon the family. Fathers of the infants, when available, were included in the explanatory process. We described in concrete terms the services the parents would receive—not free, but in return for the time they would be obliged to give throughout the study in bringing children for physical and developmental examinations and for daycare or for shorter periods similar to nursery school, in talking regularly with the staff, and in generally helping to promote their child's development. Each applicant was also given a brochure that stated in simple and direct terms the purpose of the study, the services it would provide, and the obligations of membership. The final agreement to join the project was, in effect, a contract between the parents and the project staff, and was so described. All but one Phase II family remained in the study throughout its duration.* We believe that this continuity was due at least in part to the care we took in the entire admission process, from first contact to final agreement, including the emphasis on the mutuality of the work to be done, on the importance of the parents' role in helping their child develop, and on obligations as well as services.

Of the nineteen newborn children in Phase II, thirteen were black, three were white, two were mixed—white mothers and black fathers, and one was Puerto Rican. The last family had a second child during the study, so the total number of children admitted was twenty. Of these, twelve were boys and eight were girls. The number of intact and one parent families was about equal. In all the latter either the father or another man was a more or less regular member of the household. At the point of admission, not quite half of the families were supported by the fathers. Of the single young women, one was entirely self-supporting, one was supported by her parents, and eight were supported by public welfare.

The families selected for Phase II were admitted to the study between the fall of 1968 and the spring of 1970, gradually replacing the Phase I families as the children in the pilot group moved on to kindergarten or, in the case of the youngest two, to nursery school elsewhere. Our contacts with each Phase II family continued during the period before the infant was born, but increased greatly from birth on. Thirteen of the nineteen children were in the daycare program part of the time during Phase II. All but one of those not in daycare came to Children's House more or less

* The program ended in June 1972 because funding was no longer available. The youngest child was 2½ years old.

regularly with their mothers or other family members twice a week from the age of fifteen months, to participate in a part of the morning program called Toddler School.

The total daycare group reported on from both phases consists of thirty-six children ranging in age at the time of entry into daycare from three weeks to four years.

Our thesis was that if good services were provided, disadvantaged young parents could be helped to rear their children in a way that supported the child's development. Services were designed to alleviate the risk factors associated with one-parent families, insufficient income to provide for basic needs for food and shelter, discrimination faced in obtaining employment and in earning a living wage, problems in child care stemming from immaturity of parents or psychosocial pathology and loss of societal supports for child rearing. The services helped to alleviate stresses that were disrupting, chronically degrading, and disorganizing. Comparison of the development of the children in Phase II and the improved situation of their parents to those of unserved families reveals the enhanced ability of the project families to cope with stress and to improve the quality of their lives.

The specific details of the development of the children and families—i.e., the research data—are the subject of other publications. It is our conclusion, however, based on the study of these children and parents, and years of experience with young children and parents in a variety of settings, that the concerns and problems of our daycare population in Phase II were for the most part representative of those of children and parents from all socioeconomic groups. The children's needs were those of all children; parental concerns, tensions, and need for psychological support were those seen in all social groups; what parents brought to the tasks of child rearing—their personal strengths and weaknesses—were those that characterize human beings in general. Even those who had particular difficulties, as will be reported, had no problems unique to race or to social class. We are thus confident that our experience with the two groups permits some generalizations about the care of children outside their families.

Children at Risk Illustrated

To give a more vivid picture of the families and of our concept of children at risk we present below vignettes of ten Phase I children. At the point of admission, these children had already lived for periods ranging from one to four years in situations that in one way or another were not conducive to sound development. Thus, one sees in them some of the same deficits and problems we hoped to prevent or at least lessen in the children with whom we would later deal from birth.

The majority of the pilot group children lived in the inner city in circumstances of more or less severe poverty. Most of the illustrations of children at risk were chosen from this majority group: six children of four sets of parents. Yet it will become apparent that even in this grossly homogeneous group there were variations in family characteristics and in the kind and degree of functional impairments in the children, demonstrating once again that there is no such thing as a typical inner-city family.

In Phase I we were under less constraint that we were in Phase II to admit only those who lived within the so-called culture of poverty. For that reason it was possible to include several who did not, and who thus fit even less than the majority group the stereotype of slum children, though three lived in the inner city.They, also, were children at risk. Four of them are described here in order to demonstrate that deprivation with respect to the developmental needs of young children can exist in a variety of circumstances. We wish to make clear our conviction that while poverty of course deprives children of some of the advantages money can buy, it does not, in itself, deprive them of being loved and well cared for by their parents. Many children of the poor are not at risk, and many children not materially disadvantaged are at risk, because they are not well nurtured.

Callie Jones   Callie was 24 months old when her mother, then 45, asked to enroll her at Children's House. Callie's mother had heard about Children's House when her first daughter, Maydean, 19, was referred there for help with her own two out-of-wedlock children, Jane, 32 months, and Josephine, 15 months. At the point of application this extended black family, sharing a typically bleak, tumbledown, inadequately furnished slum apartment, consisted of those already mentioned and Mrs. Jones's three other children: Jennifer, 16, Samuel, 14, and John, 12. Mrs. Jones's first three children were fathered in a common-law relationship with the same man, who supported them until his death in 1952. John was the product of a more temporary relationship with a man who acknowledged his paternity but at no time lived with the family. Callie's father, a married man, promised support but wasn't working; at no time did he live with Mrs. Jones and nothing more is known of him. There appeared to be no adult male living in the household when Callie came to Children's House. Mrs. Jones wanted her to be there because "it would be good for her and I might get out of the house a little and find some work."

Mrs. Jones had been supported by public welfare for fifteen years, first in New York, where she had moved from a southern town in 1941, and then in New Haven since 1961. Her mother had died when she was too young to remember her. One of the youngest of eight children, Mrs. Jones was probably cared for in some fashion by her siblings since her father did not remarry until she was an adolescent. Mrs. Jones had only a third-grade education, and when we first knew her she was sporadically going to night school classes in order to learn reading and writing. She had worked and continued to work occasionally a few days at a time at various unskilled jobs.

Dizzy spells, which began to occur in 1951, were among the most frequently recurring of many symptoms Mrs. Jones had; others included headaches, general body aches, weakness, vomiting, and abdominal pain. She was obese, as were her three older children, and at times her blood pressure was high. Family records in the Yale–New Haven Medical Center were extensive, characterized by many visits to the emergency room. It was difficult to know how much of Mrs. Jones's poor health was physical in origin and how much was attributable to her phobic reaction to illness. Asked in an interview at Children's House about the cause of her mother's death, she said she did not know, became very upset, and later that day suffered from dizziness and headache.

At her best, Mrs. Jones had a kind of native good sense and was capable of playfulness and warmth toward Callie and her young grandchildren. However, she experienced frequent brief psychotic episodes characterized by auditory and visual hallucinations, and when not actively psychotic she was chronically depressed. At times the house was dark and the children silent as she wept quietly. Yet in spite of her handicaps Mrs. Jones was able to put some energy into taking care of her children, feeding and clothing them reasonably well and especially mobilizing herself to provide for their physical safety and for medical care in emergencies.

The extent to which the older children supplemented Mrs. Jones's care of Callie and her grandchildren, and the way they all "rallied around" in any emergency suggested an impressive amount of family solidarity and cohesiveness in this situation of multiple mothering. Nevertheless, Callie suffered from discontinuity of care and from a particularly unfortunate kind of inconsistency that jeopardized opportunities to develop logical reasoning and abstract thought processes. Mrs. Jones's playfulness could easily shift to punishment, or punishment to playfulnes in a most confusing way. Limit setting was dictated by the mother's mood, need, or comfort of the moment. Opportunities for a young child to learn in this environment thus were not only meager but inappropriate. At 24 months Callie's chance to develop her obviously normal potential was already seriously threatened.

Jane and Josephine Jones   Jane, 32 months, and Josephine, 15 months at the time of enrollment at Children's House, were the grandchildren of Mrs. Jones, described above, and the daughters of Maydean, Mrs. Jones's 19-year-old unmarried daughter. Since all lived under the same roof when we first knew the Jones family, living conditions and the kinds of nurturance Jane and Josephine received were in general the same as those described for Callie. However, in many ways Maydean was a less adequate mother for Jane and Josephine than Mrs. Jones was for Callie. While Mrs. Jones had some capacity between psychotic episodes and periods of relatively more depression to protect, play with, and talk to children, Maydean's way of relating to her children was almost totally limited to interfering with their behavior when it annoyed her. Unlike her mother, she was bland, apathetic, and intellectually dull—probably not by endowment but as the result of her own deprivation. She had finished high school in a special class, but she had no usable skills, amazingly little information about the simplest everyday things, and could read but seldom understood what she read. She was a severely impoverished person in every way, with resultant marked incapacity to nurture her children. Often she seemed to respond to them as if they were things, not human beings with needs and feelings; and even more than her mother she tended to respond to the children's behavior in ways totally inconsistent with usual cause and effect sequences. They were often punished, with no explanation, for the same behavior that was accepted or responded to playfully moments before.

Jane and Josephine had different fathers, and perhaps partly for this reason Maydean responded to the two little girls somewhat differently, with her limited nurturing efforts going mainly to Josephine, whom she sometimes seemed to enjoy holding. There was almost no verbal or physical contact between Jane and her mother except in connection with punishment, and we had reason to believe that Jane's care during the first year was more severely depriving than Josephine's during her first year. Since, in addition to the difference in quality, the noxious elements in Jane's life had continued over almost three years, she was a severely damaged child— the most impoverished in the pilot group, just as her mother was the most impoverished parent. Although early developmental assessment at Children's House indicated probably native capacity for normal learning, Jane was so disorganized, unfocused, and distractable, her investment in people and activities so tenuous, her range of affect so limited, that she was unable to use her intellectual capacity effectively, and thus we feared her chances for substantial improvement were highly questionable.

In the Jones family we see graphically illustrated this perpetuation of environmentally determined impairment from one generation to another, and the consequent waste of human potential.

Susan and David Page   Susan, 50 months, and David, 23 months, were the children of an attractive, unmarried 21-year-old black high school graduate. Miss Page had completed training as a keypunch operator and, though supported by public welfare, hoped to find full-time employment. Her two children were the issue of a relationship that had begun when she was 16 and still continued. The father was employed and paid for the children's support. Although he and Miss Page saw one another frequently, he did not spend any substantial amount of time with the children. Miss Page said she could not get interested in any other man, that she wanted to marry him but knew he wasn't ready for marriage and didn't want to trap him into it.

At the time of Miss Page's application to Children's House, she had just moved out of her parents' home and was attempting in other ways as well to establish independence of them; but she still very much needed help, especially with child care. Although her mother had taken care of the children in the past, she was now unwilling to continue, and therefore Miss Page sought our help. She was a self-respecting, fairly well functioning young woman striving toward improving her economic status, and her children were devolping reasonably well, with only mild impairment of speech and cognitive functions. However, it appeared that Miss Page was at a point in her life when establishing her independence from her parents and working to improve her standard of living were going to take precedence over her children's welfare. This was not because she was unconcerned about her children, but rather because she was not fully aware of what had gone into bringing them to their present level of functioning and what would be involved in protecting their future development. With all of the uncertainties that lay ahead for this young woman and her children, we felt justified in deciding that without the kind of care and education we could provide them, their development might well suffer setbacks. Admission to Children's House was seen mainly as supporting and facilitating rather than actually remedial.

Cindy Edwards   Cindy, 3 years and 9 months old, was admitted to Children's House when it was opened. She was the oldest of four children in an intact white family. She had two brothers, ages 27 months and 16 months, and a sister who was born one month before Cindy began daycare, which was requested for her only. Thus, she was the one child in the family not at home all day with her mother and father. Mr. Edwards had been severely physically handicapped since age 16, shortly after dropping out of the eighth grade. He was at age 25 an emaciated, pale man, unable to use his upper extremities and one leg. Between frequent hospitalizations due to pneumonia, his life was spent confined to his wheelchair or bed. The many attempts by public welfare and rehabilitation agencies to help him develop a vocation had failed since they were always interrupted by his recurring respiratory problems.

Mrs. Edwards had met her husband prior to his disabling illness. After finishing high school she worked for two or three years as an aide in a convalescent home before marrying Mr. Edwards a year before Cindy's birth. When we first met Mrs. Edwards, she was, at age 24, a thin, pale, careworn looking woman with various physical ailments. Several missing front teeth added to the impression that she was herself a neglected person.

Supported by Aid to the Disabled, the family lived in a typical run down, inner-city apartment, which was poorly heated and drafty. Mrs. Edwards was a good housekeeper and attempted to make the rooms more attractive, but they were still dark, barren, and shabby.

Mr. and Mrs. Edwards were poorly prepared for parenthood, since both had experienced various kinds of deprivation as children. Mr. Edwards was one of seven children of an alcoholic mother. Mrs. Edwards was one of five children whose mother had abandoned them. Her father had remarried and several more children had been added to the family. Even for parents who had been more adequately nurtured in childhood, the stresses the Edwardses faced might have been overwhelming: the physical and emotional problems related to the father's severe impairment, four children in as many years, the mother's poor health, an inadequate income with consequent struggles to make do, poor housing, poor food, and lack of any but the most dire necessities. The Edwards family was known to many health and social agencies in the community, and while they had had a good deal of tangible help—for example, homemaker service at various times—they were quite understandably also resentful of the need for such help and angry about the intrusion into their privacy that was involved.

Cindy, for many reasons, was the child in the family who received much of the parents' expressions of frustration and anger. This situation had many determinants. Cindy had certain constitutional vulnerabilities that probably caused her to be a difficult child to deal with. Also, her particular meaning to her mother greatly accentuated the problems between them. In addition, because she was the oldest child, maturity of behavior far beyond her competence was expected.

Born at full term, Cindy was premature by weight, 3 pounds, 5 ounces. She spent the first five weeks of life in an incubator, and was discharged at seven weeks as a healthy baby. From the beginning of their life together her mother found her difficult to feed, and gradually an angry, fighting relationship developed between them especially in evidence in relation to the giving and withholding of food. Because of Cindy's slow weight and growth gains and slow motor development, she was studied extensively in various clinics of the Yale–New Haven Medical Center from the time she was a year old, without explicit explanatory findings. By the time she was two, her gross motor skills were still somewhat delayed with no evidence of specific neurological abnormality. She was also still extremely tiny for her age, below the third percentile for both weight and height. Our impression was that her failure to thrive was at least in part experientially determined. Cindy's brothers, who weighed five pounds at birth, though pale and pasty looking were now plump little boys of average size for their age. Even after thorough study, we were not able to be certain as to possible constitutional factors, other than her small size at birth, that may have contributed to her problems and to her mother's feelings about her. We saw her as unusually vulnerable and oversensitive to many ordinary life experiences, a characteristic which added to her discomfort and to staff difficulty in helping her.

One did not have to look deeply into the family life, however, to find ample evidence that whatever inborn tendencies were present in Cindy were indeed accentuated not only by the many stresses on the entire family but by Mrs. Edwards's feelings about her first child. Mrs. Edwards could be quite protective of Cindy if those outside the family behaved unfavorably toward her. However, her mother's prevailing attitude was a negative one in which she saw Cindy as hostile, jealous, selfish, and stubborn—as a child who could have talked adequately if she wanted to and been kind and generous toward her brothers. Whether consciously or not, Mrs. Edwards seemed to confuse Cindy with her own "selfish sisters who got away with anything they wanted" and were favored by her mother at the expense of Mrs. Edwards and her two brothers.

At the point of admission we had much less information about Cindy and her environment than we have given here. Nevertheless, in view of her intrinsic disadvantages and her highly unfavorable life situation, we saw Cindy as a child whose future development was unquestionably at risk.

Tim Lambert *   Tim was 37 months of age on admission to Children's House; his only sibling, Sharon, was 13 months. They were the children of a white couple who lived some distance from the center, sharing the small but comfortable house of Mrs. Lambert's aged foster father in a middle-class neighborhood. Tim's father had had two years of technical training after high school; his mother was a high school graduate. Mr. Lambert was employed as a skilled technician in a small manufacturing firm. Income was modest but above the poverty level and a small fee was paid for Children's House services.

Although he was of above average intelligence, Tim's development was at risk. We learned from our contacts with this family in our child-development clinic, where the parents had sought help with Tim's sleep

* Some of the material on this case appeared in Naylor, "Some Determinants of Parent–Infant Relationships" in Dittman (1970). *What We Can Learn From Infants.*

disturbance, that he and his mother, and to some extent his father, were engaged in a furious retaliatory struggle with one another, beginning with parental expectations of behavior far beyond a three-year-old's capacity. The mother experienced the child as fearless and defiant, with no recognition of the terror he felt at the same time that he taunted her into screaming at him and punishing him. The father was somewhat more tolerant of the child, somewhat better able to help him, through clear and firm, even if too strict, limits, but he, too, was short-tempered and harsh. The parents also tried to undercut one another's disciplinary efforts with Tim. Mrs. Lambert kept Tim beautifully clean and handsomely dressed, but exposed him to physical danger, again through unrealistic expectations of what situations a child his age could handle.

In spite of the vicious cycle of mutually retaliatory behavior between mother and child, areas of Tim's learning, especially the cognitive, had not yet been invaded by the conflict, and in fact the mother was a very good teacher in areas that had nothing to do with their feelings. Tim was thus a child with a good deal of information and intellectual curiosity, a child who could be a delightful companion one moment but a severely disruptive child the next. However, because he was not helped by his parents to develop the capacity for self-regulation and control of impulses, his social adaptation was already impaired, and without intervention learning problems appeared to be inevitable, as did intensification of behavior problems he already had. (Tim and his mother are discussed in more detail starting on page 37).

Stanley Capello   Stanley was 42 months old when he came to Children's House, initially for the morning period only. He and his sister, age 7, were the only children of a white couple, the mother of Polish extraction, the father, Italian. They lived in a well-kept duplex near Children's House, in an area fast becoming mainly black in population. Mrs. Capello had strong wishes to move out of the neighborhood into the suburbs. Both Mr. and Mrs. Capello were high school graduates, but he, at his wife's urging, had had to finish high school after their marriage, going to night school over a four-year period. After working in factories for many years, he had recently become a carpet salesman, but low income ostensibly kept the family in a neighborhood they had come to fear and feel was not a proper place for child rearing.

Mr. Capello, preoccupied with earning a living, appeared to be relatively uninvolved with Stanley, leaving the boy's upbringing to his wife. Mrs. Capello, ashamed of her own background, which involved poverty and an alcoholic father, was ambitious for middle-class status, disliked herself, tried to escape her past with a facade of masklike makeup, elaborate hair styles, bandbox dress for herself and her children, and a meticulously kept house devoid of books, magazines, and toys. Impetuous, short-tempered, and unable to understand a child's feelings or point of view, she wanted her son to be always clean, polite, compliant. Mr. Capello, who remembered being a coward at age seven, wasn't sure how he wanted Stanley to behave. At age 2 Stanley's precocious back talk and somewhat aggressive exploring of his environment had evoked his mother's severe disapproval and physical punishment. Her attitude toward these normal exploits and her harshness appears to have interfered with the development of curiosity, enjoyment in learning, and healthy aggression.

When Stanley first came to Children's House, at 42 months of age, he was a large boy with fair, very scrubbed-looking skin and extremely neat and clean clothing; his poise and conversational ability were unusual for his age. But he was unspontaneous and inhibited, both in the use of his body and in the use of his good intelligence for imaginative play and enjoyment of his achievements. He was unable to use toys and materials without the continuous support of a teacher. He frequently blushed in situations of social stress, a trait unusual in a child of his age. His passive-aggressive and manipulative tendencies and his somewhat feminine characteristics soon became apparent. Without intervention Stanley was headed for trouble in a number of ways.

Jennifer and Linda Davis   Jennifer, 53 months, and her only sibling, Linda, 15 months, were both admitted to full daycare at Children's House when it opened. Their parents—white, intelligent, articulate college graduates—were living on the mother's small salary as a research assistant and occasional contributions from the paternal grandfather while the father completed his graduate education in a professional school. The necessity to work and to maintain a household for four people interfered with Mrs. Davis' ambition to be a writer. The Davises lived in substandard housing on the edge of the inner city; their apartment was sparsely and uncomfortably furnished; the attempts at interior decoration were rather bizarre. There was ample evidence in the form of books and periodicals of the parents' intellectual interests and of their involvement in protest movements and demonstrations, for example, for civil rights and against the Vietnam war. In their dress, their scorn of the "materialistic" values of their parents, and their zeal to find the good life, they were similar to many of the nonviolent young intellectuals in the protest movements of the sixties.

The Davises were fairly compatible in their interests and in the causes to which they devoted themselves. However, there seemed to be little place in their lives for children. Mrs. Davis, in particular, had little awareness of or patience with the dependency needs of children, and little ability to give emotional nurturance to them. In addition, she inappropriately applied to her young children her ideas about individual freedom and self-determination.

Jennifer and Linda looked as waifish as any children in the pilot group and more so than most. They were pale, thin, poorly dressed, sad-faced, and often not clean. More important, each presented many symptoms of deprivation, in spite of the intellectual superiority of their parents. Their development was, indeed, at risk.

These, then, are some of the children we considered to be at risk with whom we began our program of intervention.

CHAPTER 3

Developing an Effective Staff

It has long been recognized that in any social service program, the physical setting, equipment, and plan of the program can all be excellent, but if the staff members who carry out the plan are not well qualified for the work, or if they do not work well together, little change occurs. To insure that staff members work together effectively, administrative structure, including lines of authority and responsibility, must be clear, and there must be ways of resolving the inevitable staff tensions. To illustrate this conviction we look first at the staff of Children's House and how it was administratively organized. The problems in working together and some of the solutions are described, and then we give examples of successful staff collaboration on behalf of children and parents.

The Staff and Administrative Structure

We began with a staff made up of both well-qualified professionals and promising paraprofessionals. The staff was organized into four major work groups, or units: (1) teaching, nursing and childcare: responsibility for a program of childcare and education that we regarded as a unified function; (2) social work: responsibility for working with parents and for home–daycare liason; (3) medicine: responsibility for pediatric care of children in the center (during phase II, for their total medical care); (4) developmental examination: physicians and psychologists responsible for periodic assessment of each child's development. One person from each of these four units made up the team working with each family. Each team was responsible for coordinating all aspects of the child's and parents' experience in the program.

Each of the four major units was headed by a supervisor, who was responsible to the director or, in some instances, to the assistant director. All staff members within each work group were responsible to their respective supervisors. Two subsidiary units served the internal needs of the organization: the secretarial and clerical staff were responsible to the director and assistant director; the food-service and building-maintenance personnel were attached to the child-care and education unit.

24

Responsibility for performance of each unit's primary task was vertical, from staff to supervisor to director. Communication had to take place not only vertically but across lines, however, from one work unit to another. Some of these communications took place in regularly scheduled meetings under administrative sponsorship. There was also much informal, spontaneous communication, but even this kind followed certain patterns.

To be sure, our staffing pattern was not typical because of the large number of different disciplines represented. This undoubtedly complicated relationships. Furthermore, some roles performed by staff in our program would usually be performed by consultants. However, our work with other community daycare programs convinces us that most administrative structures are no less complicated. The role of both board of directors and parents in policy formulation and decision making add different dimensions of complications. In community daycare there is equally great need for clarity about roles and about authority and about responsibility.

Even the best-conceived plan at the beginning of a program exists only in theory. When things begin to happen, confusion and problems arise.

The Administrative Structure

For purposes of clarity we found it useful to think of our organizational structure as follows. The director, who has responsibility for the overall primary task of the organization, delegates an area of responsibility or territory to each unit supervisor. The supervisor has authority over that territory and the staff assigned to it by virtue not simply of administrative choice but by virtue of the authority born of special knowledge and skill. The territory has boundaries that designate the limits of both authority and responsibility, and, as with geographical and political boundaries, there are both legal and illegal or authorized and unauthorized ways of crossing the boundaries. To carry this analogy further, not everyone assigned to a given territory may be the spokesman for it in communication with another work unit or territory, and not everyone may be the recipient of communications from another unit. Rather, the supervisor of each unit determines whether she alone receives the communications, whether other designated members of the work group do so, and, if so, whether they receive only certain kinds of communications. In a similar way, the director determines who besides herself sends and receives communications to and from the territories beyond the boundary of the agency.*

The director can limit or extend the supervisor's authority, but even

* We borrowed from Rice (1965) some ideas and terminology that helped us to conceptualize and systemize our administrative procedures, especially those related to problems in working together.

the director does not, unless requested by the supervisor, listen to complaints from, or exert direct authority over, a work-unit staff member. To do so would be to undermine the administrative authority of the supervisor and to interfere with task performance. Of course, if the supervisor is not carrying out her responsibilities in a way that is effectively serving the goals of the program, the director has the right to take the necessary action.

The constraints on the director's firsthand dealing with those in a supervisor's work group refer only to a particular kind of communication between the director and the various members of her staff. Many kinds of communications need to go from her to all staff members. As the director, she must represent the goals of the program in their most ideal form and seek the implementation, as far as possible, of that ideal. Much of the *esprit de corps* must come from her enthusiastic leadership, from her efforts to maintain excellence in all aspects of the program, and from the very real help she gives the staff. In order for her to exert influence of this kind, she must have access to all staff both directly, in various kinds of staff meetings, and indirectly, through supervisory personnel. Thus, when we speak of constraints on the director's activity, we refer to purely task-oriented problem situations within a work unit that a director ordinarily expects the supervisor to handle.

Thus, if the director gives instructions to, listens to the complaints of, or deals in a disciplinary way with a worker, bypassing the supervisor, an unauthorized transaction across the boundary has taken place. If one unit supervisor tries to tell a worker in another unit how to do her job, an unauthorized transaction has taken place. Such actions cause confusion, undermine authority, invite intrigue, and work against achievement of the program's goals. The director, then, works through the supervisor.

Since good communication is vital to the program, the work groups cannot operate as closed systems. Their members do not relate only in a vertical way. Information must flow horizontally, and—more difficult— there must always be a monitoring function within work groups and between them. This can be done in a constructive way only if an organization has proceeded far enough in its development to put excellence in task performance above personal feelings and needs.

Horizontal communication that is not monitoring but simply conveys needed information is the least problematic. Regularly scheduled conferences of various kinds provide channels for intergroup communication. But there must be provision also for nearly instantaneous transmission of certain information between work groups if that information is to be as useful as possible. For example, if on a home visit a social worker learns of a family crisis that will almost surely affect the behavior and mood of the child brought to the center that morning, to whom does the social worker give the information? If a teacher learns when a mother brings her child to the center that the mother is very upset because of a quarrel with her husband the night before that ended with his leaving, threatening never to come back, to whom is this information given? The answers to these questions can vary a good deal; many different ways of channeling information will work, so long as those involved know and use them. For example, in the early days of our pilot group there was much confusion, teachers and others caring for children were overburdened, and we were all inexperienced in working together. Information from the social-work and medicine work units, for example, to the child-care and education units went only to the appropriate supervisor. If she was unavailable, a written message was left for her and, if urgent, the information was also given to the teacher with a reminder to inform her supervisor. After a few months, as we progressed in working together, information was regularly given either to the supervisor or to whomever she designated in her absence. Still later, after everyone learned the importance of sharing and using information, any member of the child-care and education work group could be given the information, if in the rush of the day's work that was most convenient, with the assurance that it would reach those who needed it, including, of course, the supervisor.

It was easier to move away from a rigid method of channeling information when the information involved was factual than when it involved judgments on the quality of the work being done. Clearly it isn't the role of staff in one work group to evaluate the functioning of another work group. However, we believe that task-oriented workers can take responsibility for monitoring the organizational system to be sure it is working in the best possible way. Following are some examples of situations in which monitoring is involved or could be, depending on what action is or is not taken.
• From her contact with a parent, the social worker knows that the parent does not understand instructions given by the staff nurse and will not be able to follow them.
• A teacher finds that information that could have been highly useful in helping a child cope with his feelings on a particular morning was not shared by the social worker until it was much less useful.
• From a parent, the social worker learns that the teacher who was responsible for doing so did not inform the parent in advance of a specific outing, though it is important to respect the parent's right to know where the child is when not at the center.
• A teacher's discussion with the parent suggests that the social worker has misjudged the parent's capacity to tolerate the anxiety aroused by discussion of a particular subject.

In each situation a staff member of one work group learns something about the functioning of a member of another group that suggests the need for change, correction, or shift of emphasis. These examples pertain to everyday issues in the program's functioning. Yet if one of the workers is still at an early stage in development as a staff member, or if one of the workers is insecure about her competence and feels competitive with her colleagues, then direct communication about the substance of any of these four examples might result in friction, for the more highly developed stage of task orientation has not been reached. Even for very experienced and competent staff, regression from this stage can occur as a result of crisis, and monitoring may temporarily need to take place indirectly. The worker then gives information to her supervisor, who will tell the other worker's supervisor, who discusses whatever the issue is with the person concerned (we assume the two supervisors are beyond the point of intergroup competitiveness). The cumbersomeness, extra staff time, and delay in the indirect communication emphasize the importance of reaching the stage when excellence of service is the highest priority, so that monitoring can take place across work-group boundaries. It is a sign of growing competence when a staff member can analyze a situation judiciously and decide when it is appropriate to speak directly to the person concerned and when not to. Of course, those in leadership roles must also point out the value of good work, for we learn from being helped to see what in our work is effective. Furthermore, judicious praise may make more tolerable the pain of learning about mistakes.

Our thesis is that one must first create and learn to function within a system in which lines of authority and responsibility are clear and roles are as fully defined as possible; only when this task is accomplished can one make the spontaneous, on-the-spot analyses of situations that allow departure from the rigidities of the structure.

Problems

It might appear relatively simple for individual staff members who are genuinely interested in and committed to the objectives of the project to do their assigned work and share their thoughts and ideas with others. But this is not easy for any group.

There are certain kinds of problems that arise frequently in most new programs, though they are seldom publicly acknowledged and often are not even recognized. Staff confusion and dissension and the situations that cause them are what make many programs falter. Failure to recognize and deal with tensions in staff relationships is a major threat to the success of any group venture. Such tensions are rarely due to bad humor or personal malice but rather occur in the *absence* of two essential elements:

administrative policy and structure in which lines of authority and responsibility are unambiguous; and the existence and implementation of problem-solving methods.

We encountered many difficulties in becoming an effective working team. The first days were frenetic and exhausting. We overestimated the amount of time even a young, energetic teacher could spend with small children each day without becoming extremely tired. Illness among staff and children depleted us. Many of the children regressed more rapidly, were more excitable and impulsive, needed more attention, and were less verbal than our teachers had expected. Ways of working with children and parents had to be modified; staffing plans had to be changed; experienced people began to feel unsure and incompetent. The necessity to expose oneself and one's work to colleagues in research documents and weekly staff discussions caused anxiety to mount. (We suspect that the demands of the research component in our situation—a new experience for many of us—added greatly to the normal tension and distress.) Threatened thus, the staff developed special sensitivities and became confused about roles; jealousy, competitiveness and anger grew. Although roles and responsibilities were delineated and discussed during the period of planning and orientation, once the real work began, uncertainty set in and problems of autonomy flourished. Some functions of each work group were perfectly clear; in the less well defined border areas, where functions could logically overlap, territorial disputes arose. If, for example, a child had a sleep disturbance that manifested itself both in the center and at home, who was to counsel the mother about it—the person in charge of the children's program, the teacher who worked with the child and saw the mother briefly each day, the mother's staff social worker, who had weekly interviews with her, or the pediatrician who saw the child and mother occasionally? Each might have something to contribute. But the staff must reach the stage of development at which it is task oriented and at which satisfaction is found in excellence of service rather than in individual exploits for the necessary collaboration to occur. In the beginning we were far from this goal.

Another kind of problem we had to solve concerned the appropriate use of information we were developing about families—information that was sensitive and would have been treated as confidential by mental health professionals. Many of our staff members had no previous training in this field. Therefore, not all staff members were initially included in some conferences about particular children and their parents, and this, understandably, was one source of tension among those who were excluded. We did provide a training program for them, based on the premise that the development of professional ethics and judgment in matters of confidentiality have to do not with the information per se but with attitudes toward it and discipline in its use. By the end of the first year we included all staff in meetings about children they worked with, and sensitive information was freely shared. We suspect, however, that the increasingly professional attitude of our paraprofessional staff about use of sensitive information came not entirely from the training program; a process of identification with attitudes of the professional staff was probably of even greater importance.

Problem-Solving Methods

Leaders need to take initiative and develop processes through which all kinds of staff problems can be resolved. Otherwise, staff tensions will be expressed in acting-out behavior, and differences of opinion in questions of policy will be expressed in grumbling.

Once we recognized that our problems threatened the effectiveness of our work, the motivation to solve them was high. In the stress of each day's demands, however, there was no orderly development of problem-solving methods. We lived from crisis to crisis, relying on past experience, which wasn't always helpful. We were not aware of changes we were making as we went along, and it was only after the most difficult problems were behind us that we could begin to order our experience and extract principles for future use.

Of the human problems that arise in an organization, not all grow out of difficulties in working together. The clinicians among us sometimes listen to staff members who bring in personal problems. Employees certainly are not patients and should not be treated as such. But people in a leadership role can appropriately spend time with staff members who wish to discuss personal problems. Sometimes a few minutes of sympathetic listening is all that is wanted. If the problem is personal, a staff member should be free to consult whomever on the staff she wishes, as long as she is not avoiding discussing with her supervisor aspects of the problem that affect her work significantly. In any case, she may need help to be able to talk with her supervisor about the effect of the problem on her work.

If the problem the individual brings to the supervisor is difficulty with another staff member, hearing out the complainant can be a mistake, because the implication is that the supervisor will then do something about the offender. After consenting to hear the nature but not the details of the complaint, the supervisor ought to ask whether an attempt has been made to work out the issue directly with the other person. If this has not been done, the supervisor may suggest that the problem is the worker's, not the supervisor's. The aggrieved person can usually be helped to recognize her responsibility to try to resolve the issue with her colleague. The supervisor may wish to offer the option that if the effort is unsuccessful, she will be willing to meet with both. If friction continues, and no meeting with the supervisor is requested, she will, of course, need to insist on one. The guiding principle for such a meeting, which must be understood by the participants, is that the primary task of those involved comes first, and that staff behavior is viewed in terms of what the task is and whether or not the behavior of each person aids or interferes with its performance.

Plans for problem solving must include recourse for the staff member who has trouble with a supervisor. If the staff member and supervisor have made a conscientious effort to work out the difficulties themselves and have not succeeded, then either one may ask that both discuss the problem with the director or next person in line of administrative authority. In this discussion, as in those among any other combination of staff members, emphasis is given to the task. What often intereferes with performance is not misunderstanding about duties or lack of skill, but the personal feelings involved. Therefore, part of the role of the arbiter may be to help those involved recognize the effect of their feelings on their work. Often this is the only way the real problem can be identified. Once it is out in the open, it can be more easily dealt with. When a project is new, its participants tend to be frightened of one another and of their own feelings. The emotion that is involved for each person and the courage that it takes to say what is felt are all-important factors involved in such problem-solving situations.

The makeup of problem-solving groups changes depending on who is having trouble. We first became aware of severe tension among members of the professional staff at work-group meetings in discussing the research aspects of the program. For a period we had to abandon these discussions and devote our time to what was happening among the participants. These meetings were highly charged and often painful, as we struggled to look as openly as we could at our feelings about each other, our jealousies and fears, our sense of inadequacy, and each person's belief that "her part" of the project alone would accomplish whatever good came out of it and, paradoxically, that the only failure would be hers. Through the frightening process of looking at ourselves and at what kept us working well together, we learned that we could survive honesty, we could survive strong feelings, and that we were not alone with our fears of incompetence. At such group meetings rumors were laid to rest, misunderstood behavior was clarified, and we began to see one another less as threats than as common sufferers. As tensions lessened, energies could be focused on the primary task, and participants began to feel some enjoyment.

The meetings with the staff were the first of a series that continued throughout the project, with various combinations of staff members. Such meetings were not group therapy, sensitivity training, or any of the other fashionable group methods.*

As we progressed in our development as a task-oriented staff, the emotional currents tended to be reduced, and content directly related to the work increased. The success of our problem-solving efforts probably depended on the method's being sponsored by the director and other leaders, on the respect the program leaders had for the participants, and on staff confidence that the leaders were benevolent toward everyone and would not allow anyone to be victimized. Our staff at all levels found such meetings helpful. Paraprofessionals as well as professional staff asked for meetings when needed. A new person joining the staff or a new demand upon the staff can arouse some of the same initial anxiety. However, it is our experience that after once working out many of the initial tensions, problem solving is more quickly instituted. Also, over time, as individual skills are valued, as fear of failure lessens, mutual respect develops and ability increases to relinquish some autonomy in the interest of better serving families.

These problems in working together are inevitable when one starts a new program with highly motivated people who have strong convictions about giving good service. If such problems are not dealt with, if they are swept under the rug of surface civility, the underlying tensions accumulate and the degree of staff collaboration necessary for creative work cannot evolve.† As we changed from a collection of individuals with various uncoordinated skills into an effective task-oriented team, we could question and challenge each other in a way that stimulated thought and helped us better serve the children and parents in the program.

Problem Solving on Behalf of Families

There were various levels of problem solving in situations where we became concerned about a child and/or his family. Sometimes a staff member simply shared a piece of information with another person, helping to

* See *Preparing Teachers to Work with Disturbed Children* by Braun and Lasher (1970). Chapter 9, "Sensitivity Training in a Teacher Training Program" describes with refreshing candor the problems encountered when staff and trainees were involved together in sensitivity training sessions.
† That this is true in all situations where cooperative work is necessary was demonstrated by Argyris in *Interpersonal Confidence and Organizational Effectiveness* (1962). Argyris reports a study of leadership of a large industry. He found a group of technically and intellectually competent executives relatively poor in interpersonal confidence. There was a tendency to want to exclude in decision-making conferences anything that was considered to be emotional as opposed to strictly rational. "Let's keep feelings out of this" was frequently heard. Argyris also found that as feelings were suppressed and openness in discussion decreased, caution and suspiciousness increased, willingness to experiment with new ideas decreased with resultant decrease in the vitality and creativity of the organization (pp. 38–42, 272–74).

resolve a problem at an early stage or even preventing it. Sometimes a hastily called informal discussion among members of the family's "team" took place. The potential for quick response to staff distress about a problem benefits the child and family and has a favorable effect on staff morale, which in turn influences the quality of service. Most frequently, however, major problems and concerns were brought to regularly scheduled meetings of the entire staff.

As Children's House opened, the staff met for purpose of discussing in turn each child and family in the pilot group. At first our purpose was to gather all the information and impressions we had about the family and to inform the research staff as well as those giving direct services. Discussions at first were more theoretical than practical on problem solving. They were useful as staff training for ongoing service and research. As our experience and our data about both children and parents accumulated, and as patterns and trends began to emerge, our research goals prompted us to attempt theoretical formulations, to develop hypotheses, and to make predictions. This allowed us over time to test both the adequacy of our data and the validity of our formulations. Gradually, as we became concerned about particular children, our discussions took on more immediacy and urgency. Sometimes as we pooled our data and began to put together a picture of a child's functioning in the center, compiling information from episodic material, assessments prepared by the teacher, the results of developmental testing, descriptions of his functioning at home, and assessments of the current home environment, concern was aroused. After the first few months, comparisons with earlier assesments of each child allowed us to be aware of his progress or lack of it in various areas of development. After the first round of scheduled discussions of each child, our plans to continue them regularly gave way to the more urgent discussions of children about whom we were concerned at a given moment.

Whatever the problem, the procedure was approximatey as follows. The concerns about the child and questions about solutions were presented, usually by the teacher who worked most closely with him. If she had quite recently prepared a formal assessment of him, it was reviewed, along with her current detailed observations, focusing on the areas of concern. Her supervisor and other teachers presented their observations and impressions, usually supplementing but sometimes in various details disagreeing with one another. The rest of the family team—developmental examiner, pediatrician, social worker—presented whatever seemed relevant from their recent dealings with the child and parents. Others then contributed whatever they could from their own observations and impressions. Usually the material presented stimulated the director and others to ask questions that brought out additional information.

In addition to what the usual good consultant brings to the problem-solving situation by hearing data supplied by the staff, our director-consultant often brought her own firsthand impressions of children and their parents. Such firsthand knowledge was valuable not only for its own sake but because it enabled her to focus the discussion in more profitable areas and to ask questions more incisively than would otherwise have been possible. Often her questions drew from the staff more information, more clinical wisdom, and more resourcefulness about solutions than they knew they possessed. There were also times when she could diagnose the problem and define the therapeutic task but called on the expertise, for example, of the educational director for the details of implementation—another consultative contribution to promoting the self-respect and professional development of staff members. Sometimes meetings ended with no plan having been arrived at. Sometimes the pooling of information served only to make us aware of contradictions—to confuse, not to clarify. Usually, however, we were clearer than before about what we needed to know, what we needed to observe more carefully, listen for, and try to be aware of in preparation for further discussion later. Often, too, our meetings ended without a clear diagnostic formulation and problem-solving plan but with a tentative idea for a procedure to be tried.

Examples to follow reflect the efforts of the total staff in consultation with the director and the cooperation of individual staff members. They illustrate the complexity of human behavior in a daycare setting. If intervention is to be effective, this complexity must be confronted with the most detailed knowledge possible about each child or adult.

Lynn Rogers   Mrs. Rogers enrolled her 32-month-old daughter, Lynn, the youngest of seven, at Children's House the moment the doors opened. Mrs. Rogers was not working but wanted her child to have a good preschool experience as she was convinced that education, which she hadn't had, was most important.

At the time of one staff discussion Lynn was 54 months old. Her teachers were concerned about her language development and certain emerging personality problems. In order to confirm the impression that this natively competent child was falling behind in her language skills, the developmental examiner was asked to review some aspects of test results compiled during Lynn's enrollment at Children's House. On first developmental testing at 34–35 months, her overall performance was slightly below age. Language skills were six to seven months delayed, but on problem-solving tasks that have particular relevance for later eschool learning, she was at age level. When Lynn was retested at 40 months her overall score was also at age level. Gross and fine motor skills were well above average, and problem-

solving skills were at age level, but language skills had not shown anticipated improvement. In fact, they were slightly lower relative to age than
before, now being approximately eight months behind. The 52–53 month
test revealed that although there were gains in a number of areas, language
development was still not consistent with other areas, approximately five
and a half months below her age, and children whose language skills were
much poorer than hers on admission had passed her by.

Lynn's teacher, AZ, then presented selected material from a recent
assessment, bringing before the group her perceptive, skillful, minutely
detailed observations of Lynn. This information, together with the spontaneous contributions of other teachers and the information that emerged
as a result of the director's questions, gave us a picture of Lynn's behavior
in the group: the kinds of material she selected to play with, those she
avoided, what she did well, what she had trouble with, her typical emotional reactions in various situations with other children and staff. A pattern
appeared: she did well with materials that did not require much initiative.
What was missing from her play and her emotional reactions was aggressive
content, which was instead being turned inward in the form of hurt feelings,
sadness, and resignation.

When these diagnostic impressions of Lynn were put together, the social
worker, CC, pointed out a connection between what she knew of the family
traits and what the teachers were seeing in Lynn. CC described the
mother's periodic depressions and her withdrawal from situations that required her to take a stand. She had become a participant in and then
dropped out of a series of citizen-action groups, repelled by the infighting
and undoubtedly made anxious by her own unacceptable counteraggressive
feelings. So pervasive was the prohibition against aggression in the Rogers
home that although the family lived on a welfare budget, Lynn's teenage
brother sometimes took a taxi home from school to avoid a possible en-
counter in the street.

Lynn's behavior was now somewhat more understandable; it reflected
what was both implicitly and explicitly expected of her at home. Lynn was
unable to mobilize the energy that should have gone into initiative and
self-expression. Her aggressive feelings often seemed to be turned against
herself, resulting in periods of sadness and pouting. Speech, as the most
complex and most recently acquired skill, was the most vulnerable—the
one in which her development was delayed. We were as concerned about
Lynn's personality development as about her lag in language, but reasoned
that help in one area would help in the other.

The treatment plan was to continue to help Lynn differentiate among
her feeling states and especially to show her acceptable ways of expressing
anger; to choose for Lynn stories with aggressive, heroic content, especially

ones that she and other children could dramatize. Implementation was left to the ingenuity of the teaching staff. They were to continue, of course, the kind of language stimulation which was a part of every child's experience at Children's House.

We then took up the problem of how to help Lynn without creating difficulty for her at home, making her mother a partner in the effort to promote Lynn's development. We did not hope to bring about significant modification in Mrs. Rogers of a deep-seated, long-standing personality trait; however, as we appraised her relationship to her social worker and her favorable attitude toward Children's House, we thought it would be possible to influence her to accept some shift in Lynn's behavior away from what Mrs. Rogers preferred. We would begin with the mother's conviction about the value of education, and explain our view that Lynn's problem in dealing with aggression would interfere with learning.

Lynn's final developmental examination, at 63 months of age, showed some successes in language at the six-year level but averaged at sixty months, only three months below age, a greater relative gain than she had made during any other interval between tests. Perhaps more impressive than the actual gain in language competence was a general qualitative change in her test performance and behavior. During the 52–53 month test the examiner, MK, had noted the tendency for Lynn's moods to swing widely between depression and feeling "high" and becoming "carried away," a trend that could interfere with future test performance and good learning. MK's summary impression of Lynn at 63 months reads, "Lynn functions in all areas at an age-adequate level; the relative gains in the language area . . . are especially impressive. Qualitatively her performance is also impressive: she now appears to be a relatively well organized child who is interested in many of the materials for their own sake and evaluates, perseveres, and corrects her own performance. She appears to be more realistic about and confident of her abilities; she seems capable of pleasure without displaying wide mood swings."

In addition to the test findings, teachers reported that Lynn seemed more aware of her feelings, especially angry ones, expressed them more appropriately, seemed to have more energy for learning, and was generally a happier child.

Although the overall gains Lynn made were not dramatic, they were still important for her future development. Since Lynn continues to live very close to Children's House, we see her often and know that she is doing well in grade school. Her mother continues a friendly relationship particularly with her social worker. Perhaps Mrs. Rogers, too, gained something from our efforts to help her permit Lynn to know more about her feelings and to be a bit more aggressive: she is taking an active part in political action in her ward and holds elective office.

The next example illustrates the gathering and use of observations and information on the part of two senior staff members, their collaborative diagnostic thinking and consequent planning.

Tim Lambert   Tim, introduced first in Chapter 2, had been known to us first in our Child Development Clinic, where he was brought when he was not yet three because of a sleep disturbance: he awoke frequently at night screaming. By day he seemed to his parents a fearless and defiant child. Mrs. Lambert, a conscientious mother in many ways, had been deprived of her mother during her first year, when she was removed from home because of parental neglect and placed in a foster home. While we suspected that her treatment of Tim was determined in part by an unconscious identification with a mother she considered bad, we had no evidence of that beyond the paradoxical fact that while she kept him immaculately clean and handsomely dressed, she also exposed him to danger, incited him to tantrums, and then retaliated in ways that made her feel a bad mother. Perhaps Mrs. Lambert's behavior was due to the simple fact that she herself had not experienced a sustained, protective, and nurturing relationship with her own mother. A home visit made it clear just how desperate the situation was for both mother and child. Even with the social worker present, the mother could not control her behavior. The full force of her fury at the child was observed. Several times the mother made a demand for maturity far beyond Tim's years, and when he could not comply, began to move toward him screaming angrily. His eyes wide, Tim picked up a toy golf club and made threatening gestures at her. In a rough, menacing way, the mother grabbed the toy club away from him. He threw himself on the floor, crying and kicking. His mother then grabbed him by his wrists and threw him on the bed. He continued to cry and scream incoherently but with intonations suggesting threat. It was evident that though Tim was terrified, he had to incite his mother just as she incited him. His mother said to the social worker, "You see what he's like?" A few minutes later Tim was told that if he could stop crying he could have a cookie. He began to recover from his disorganization and was about to get the cookie when his mother insisted he stop his whimpering first. When he could could not, she shook him, setting off another cycle.

From interviews with the mother, the social worker was aware that Mrs. Lambert was acutely anxious about her violence with Tim and avoided being alone with him as much as possible. Much of their time together was spent visiting friends or going shopping. Her behavior with Tim appeared to grow out of a depression, in which she felt alive only when she was fighting with the child; for that reason, Mrs. Lambert was equally uncomfortable without him. In an effort to protect both mother and child, we suggested daycare when Tim was just over three and continued our casework with the mother. Though somewhat relieved, she at first could accept the separation for only half a day. At Children's House, Tim's behavior was soon a source of concern to the teachers.

At this point, detailed knowledge of what went on between Tim and his mother, together with careful observations of his behavior with teachers, made it possible to see clearly the counterphobic aspects of Tim's highly provocative behavior. Although surface bravado very nearly concealed his terror, Tim tried to reproduce with his teachers the same excitement and violence he experienced with his mother. Awareness of the terror that accompanied his aggressive attempts to arouse his teachers to anger and retaliation, and realization that this was an attempt to reenact scenes with his mother helped the teachers to deal with their own feelings about Tim. Part of the teaching task that required patient work, day after day, was to help Tim recognize his fear and find better ways of coping with it and controlling his impulses.

When Mrs. Lambert appeared ready to tolerate a longer separation, Tim's stay at Children's House was extended to a full day. By then he was 4. At that point a somewhat different kind of staff teamwork was called for. The increased separation was difficult for Mrs. Lambert. Feeling that Tim would think that she was trying to get rid of him, she could not handle his daily protest about the longer stay at Children's House. Although his trust in the staff was helping him to tolerate the day quite well, he was preoccupied with fears of abandonment. He used his highly developed verbal skills to torture his mother with words and as his daily reproaches exacerbated her guilt, the daycare plan threatened to break down.

Mrs. Lambert shared with the social worker her reluctance about the daycare plan. She talked about her love for Tim and her suffering at the idea that he thought she wanted to get rid of him. Their relationship was so conflict-laden that Mrs. Lambert could not talk to Tim about why she wanted him to be at Children's House all day, and Tim could not listen. But the social worker thought that in the calming presence of his teacher, JP, to whom he was close, he could begin to listen to his mother. After a preparatory session in which the social worker helped the mother find some words for what she wanted to convey to Tim, Mrs. Lambert, JP, and Tim met. When all three were seated, JP asked Mrs. Lambert if she would tell Tim why she wanted him to stay through the nap period and for a play period in the afternoon. Mrs. Lambert looked at a loss for words, started, stopped when Tim got up out of his chair, and looked as if she were about to cry. JP helped Tim come back and sit down. Tim drew up his knees, crossed his ankles, and was very still. Mrs. Lambert had recovered enough to begin, and said to Tim, "You know how Mommie and you fight at home. I don't like to fight with you. If you come to school all afternoon we don't fight so much. You learn how not to fight with Mommie and Mommie is learning how not to fight with you. I'll always come for you—you know I always have. I love you and I want you to come home."

Mrs. Lambert's words, of course, did not entirely solve the separation problem; it was too complex in its origin and meaning. But Tim's longer day at the center became more manageable, and at home his mother found it easier to talk to Tim when he protested, often referring to the conversation at Children's House. The teachers, too, reminded Tim of what his mother had said when he became anxious that she would not come for him. In the context of the serious problems existing between Tim and his mother, easing the separation problem was a minor accomplishment. Yet if it had not been done, the therapeutic efforts on behalf of both would have been delayed or irrevocably disrupted. This apparently simple plan, of having the mother talk to Tim in the presence of the teacher, involved many long-standing and complex relationships. Mrs. Lambert's readiness to speak to Tim was made possible by her explorations with her social worker of her own feelings of being abandoned as a child, her ambivalent feelings toward Tim, and her vulnerability to Tim's taunts. The child, as well, needed to feel the protection of his teacher, who had shared with him countless moments when speech was shown to be more helpful than blows or screams. For all, the timing of the session was crucial, and that decision was based on precise and complete information shared by the staff.

Our last example illustrates the case-conference situation, in which the information, impressions, and diagnostic hunches of the staff come together and, with the director's help, develop into a plan of action.

Annette Thomas   Annette, 30 months of age on admission to Children's House, was a delicately featured, bright, alert, perky little girl who at times became very sober and even apprehensive. Inventive in dramatic play with or without props, she quickly became a leader in the group and on the whole made good progress. However, a sequence of events that reached a kind of crisis 18 months after admission threatened to interfere with her development and required the combined efforts of the pediatrician, the social worker, and the teacher to be resolved.

Annette was the fifth child and first girl in a family of six children. There was no father in the home. Mrs. Thomas told the social worker, SK, that her four boys were the sons of her husband, from whom she was now separated. The paternity of Annette and a younger girl remained for us uncertain, and Mrs. Thomas seemed to feel some guilt about these extra-marital conceptions. Our impression that the relationship between Annette and her mother was generally positive was supported by the quality of

Annette's functioning, both in formal testing and in the Children's House program.

Three months after Annette came to Children's House she had a febrile convulsion over a weekend, was rushed to the hospital emergency room, and was discharged when her fever dropped rapidly. Mrs. Thomas telephoned the following Monday to report what had happened and required a good deal of reassurance from our pediatrician. Mrs. Thomas told the social worker that she had been terribly frightened by the convulsion. She raised questions about aftereffects, and a month later reported that Annette "jumped" in her sleep since the convulsion.

Evidence of concern gradually disappeared, and Annette progressed much as before. The crisis arose when the child, now age 4, had a viral infection and another febrile convulsion. During Annette's week-long absence from the center, the social worker had several telephone conversations with the mother. In the last of these, Mrs. Thomas appeared to be very frightened about Annette, saying she looked bad and describing a pronounced repetitive facial grimace or tic. The pediatrician and social worker visited Mrs. Thomas and Annette. Annette seemed only a bit peaked, like any other child recovering from an infection, but Mrs. Thomas was not reassured. When the child puckered her mouth a bit, her mother in an alarmed manner pointed to her saying, "There, that's what she's doing now that I told you about on the phone." It was clear to all—probably including Annette—that her mother saw her as a damaged child. The pediatrician used Mrs. Thomas's revelation that she had had some similar illness-connected seizures as a young child to reassure her that they were not uncommon in early childhood and usually disappeared without sequellae.

By the end of April, when any aftereffects of Annette's infection should have disappeared, she was still behaving like a convalescent. The lively, active, assertive little girl was now cautious, apathetic, and overly concerned about herself.

As the staff in conference puzzled over how best to help Mrs. Thomas and Annette, we reviewed the following information that had been known to us but that now took on added significance. Part of the time during Annette's first two years Mrs. Thomas had worked, and Annette was cared for by day in the home of an acquaintance. When Annette was 22 months old the babysitter's own child was admitted to the hospital with lead poisoning. Frightened, Mrs. Thomas took Annette to the outpatient clinic, where she acknowledged that the child had been eating plaster for five months. A high blood-lead level was found, but Annette was without symptoms except for a mild iron-deficiency anemia. When hospitalization to lower the lead level was suggested, Mrs. Thomas resisted, saying she was afraid of hospitals and reporting that the whole family was so upset they had stopped eating. Only on threat of police action had she admitted Annette to the hospital. After discharge, one followup clinic appointment had been kept but two had not. We concluded that her overreaction to Annette's convulsions was rooted in her guilt about the pica, guilt about her resistance to the hospitalization and failure to keep followup appointments, and guilt about Annette's paternity. This hypothesis became more tenable when Mrs. Thomas's social worker reminded us that she had been reporting for some time a gradually increasing aura of depression about the mother. We felt that Mrs. Thomas's disappointment in herself, her own sense of defect, and her guilt about Annette all had contributed to the changes we saw in Annette and in her mother's view of her. We planned, then, that the social worker would first try to help Mrs. Thomas to identify some of the components in her own mood of discouragement. Since some of her most significant comments about Annette had been in the educational director's presence at Children's House, we planned that the educational director would also be involved in the work with Mrs. Thomas.

It was fairly easy to help Mrs. Thomas see the change in Annette as the result of the child's view of herself as a sick child. In a discussion, Mrs. Thomas reported an incident of a scuffle between Annette and her brother in which a tiny scratch caused Annette to reproach him for hitting her because she was a "sick girl." It was more difficult to help Mrs. Thomas understand her part in bringing about this change. Whether or not Mrs. Thomas's view of Annette really changed as a result of our work with her we were not sure, but she was able to control expression of her feelings enough to permit Annette to resume her progress.

CHAPTER 4

Working with Parents

Here we present a comprehensive account of our rationale for working with parents, the principles that guided us, the responsibilities we assumed, and examples of the process. The following conceptualization of work with parents reflects our common goals and theory of behavior, emphasizing some of the principles and methods of social casework.*

The atmosphere of an institution does not develop quickly. It is created bit by bit through each interaction among parents, children, and staff; the receptionist, the secretary, the director, the cook, and the teacher all help to create the atmosphere of the enterprise. Each parent may have perceived Children's House differently, but we tried to develop an atmosphere in which they felt respected as a vital part of the center and sensed the benevolent interest of the staff in them and their children. Without this trust, the parents' feelings about the program would interfere with their full use of its services, and each staff member would find her specific task harder. No amount of skillful work on the part of any staff member can offset problems created by an atmosphere in which the parent does not feel a full partner in the undertaking of promoting his child's development.

One way to convey to the parents their vital importance to the achievement of our mutually accepted goals (though this was not the basic reason for the policy) was to require, from the start of the admission process, regularly scheduled interviews, either home or office visits, with a member of the social work staff. Because we were offering desired services, parents accepted more or less graciously and with varying degrees of anxiety the necessity for meeting with their social workers, whether or not they had any conception of the purpose. Even though some parents were understandably ambivalent about this requirement, it gave us the best possible opportunity to be of help both to parents and children.

Are the skills of clinical social workers needed in all daycare programs, or only in those with research components or those serving certain popula-

---

* This emphasis exists because the writer is able to conceptualize the work with parents best in terms of her own professional discipline, clinical social work. Thus throughout the chapter there is reference to the social work role, whereas the responsibilities of that role were carried in several instances by others as well.

tions? It would be foolish to assume that all parents using daycare need professional help. However, even for well-functioning and well-adjusted parents, turning over a substantial part of the parenting role to someone else is, in itself, a situation in which distrust, jealousy, and guilt can flourish. Asking a young child to separate from his mother and to adapt to a second environment can also create problems. Thus, no matter how competent the parent may be, there is a need for a trusting relationship and good communication on a regular basis between staff and parent, so that problems can be dealt with readily.

But special training is required for skill in working with parents, and the less aware the parent is of his problems in child rearing, the more skill is required to involve him in a process of exploration that may lead to improvement in the child's situation. While a few daycare directors or teachers may have special training that allows them to be experts both in childcare and education and in work with parents, this is not usually the case. One can be both an excellent teacher of young children and an excellent parent without having the skill to help another parent. In fact, excellent parents sometimes feel self-righteous indignation toward less effective parents; teachers and others caring for children may alienate the parents in their zeal to improve life for the child.

As reasonably experienced and competent practitioners in a clinical setting dealing with developmental problems of preschool children, we had worked with parents from almost every socioeconomic level and racial group in the community. But the clinic presented us problem situations, in which parents came, albeit often reluctantly, because they thought they had a problem. While we knew that daycare parents were not so oriented, and realized that we had to be prepared to modify our traditional ways of working, our basic convictions about working with parents would stand:

• While the ultimate goal is the welfare of the child, the worker must begin with the welfare of the parent as an individual. Every person has his own unique experiences, assets, liabilities, and needs. This consideration has validity with reference to all parents but is of special importance for those who are psychologically handicapped. Their children are often referred to daycare by persons other than the parents. Unless the center offers something the parent considers helpful besides childcare, such referrals often fail.

• Parenthood brings its own problems even to the person functioning well. Erikson (1950, 1959) has extended the concept of childhood developmental phases and tasks throughout the life cycle. Both Erikson and Benedek (1969) have written about parenthood as a developmental phase, and it is important to recognize parenthood's own peculiar vulnerabilities and stresses. Every adult still has within him the potential for feeling or even acting like the young child he once was. One cannot expect mature behavior with his child from the parent whose own nurturing was poor and whose development was full of conflict. Well-meaning but misguided efforts on behalf of the child that asks more of the parent than he is able to give are likely to provoke anger in the parent, and may even cause him to retaliate against the very child one seeks to help (Naylor 1970).

• Out of respect for each parent's individuality and in response to our conviction that no one fits the stereotype of the inner-city, the suburban, or the culturally deprived parent, we would try to be aware of and respect each parent's value system and look for assets and strengths even as we sought to alleviate deficits and needs. The basic casework principle, "Begin where the client is," is a deceptively simple idea that applies to everything from understanding the obvious manifest content of communication to the most complex and sophisticated understanding of individual psychodynamics, leading to a clinical judgment as to the person's readiness to accept an interpretation about his behavior or to take a step forward.

• In our planning to meet with parents routinely and at frequent intervals, we recognized that the traditional casework principle, develop a relationship with the parent before attempting to influence his behavior, would be useful.

The initial contact with the parent involved gathering information about the child and sharing information about the daycare center. The point came, however, and often quite soon, when a parent could no longer maintain an interest in the discussion of the child, how he was reacting to the center, how he was doing at home, and so on. In developing a relationship this is a crucial point: where does the conversation go from there? If, in an effort to keep the parent engaged, the worker continues to focus on the child, genuine contact may not occur. If, on the other hand, in her zeal to convey her interest in the parent, the worker becomes overly intrusive, the parent may also flee. This is bound to happen, for example, if the first item on the agenda is an attempt to change behavior toward the child.

In the context of a developing relationship, both practical assistance and psychological help can be offered. However, skill is necessary to decide when each will be found useful. Only gradually did we learn what each parent would consider "help." And this process of learning involved sensitivity to the nuances of both direct and indirect communication. In the daycare setting the person who sees the parent cannot assume the relatively more passive role that would be appropriate in a child guidance clinic or in a family service agency. Initiative is needed in developing the basic relationship. We had expected to be active in home visits; for example, if a mother was ill we would change and feed the baby for her or provide some other help. But particularly where the cultural gap is wide, the family worker may need to volunteer information and to answer more questions about herself than in the usual clinical setting. Although we had not anticipated such a shift, early in our pilot-group experience, we found ourselves making significant modifications.

Earlier we referred to stereotypes. We tried to be aware of racial and sociocultural factors as they might affect parenting. But we found few child-rearing practices in our population that we could explain on these grounds. Our families had a somewhat greater tendency to toilet train early, to use physical punishment, and to think that very young children would be "spoiled" if they were picked up when they cried. But there were significant exceptions. It may ease our anxiety as we enter a new world if we seek a cultural explanation, but recognition of the cultural pattern even when it does account for individual behavior (and it often doesn't) solves nothing and is often a rationalization for accepting the status quo. One must still determine whether or not the behavior is adaptive or maladaptive, and what its effects are. If the behavior is maladaptive, one must carefully assess the chances of modifying it and the method most likely to succeed.

But what about the cultural gap and racial tensions, between the white, middle-class daycare worker and, for example, the deprived black? Can they work together? This question was being asked in many places as we began in 1967. Frequently the answer was no. But from our experiences since 1967, we believe that there is no clinical validity to the idea that only black can work with black. An example from our experience illustrates the reverse. In the early days at Children's House, our black paraprofessionals had trouble with their feelings about black parents who were not, in their judgment, doing right by their children. One mother in particular, Miss Jones, referred to in Chapter 2 and about whom more will be said later, aroused their disapproval and dislike, which sometimes extended to her children. Her white family worker, CC, found ways to inject her own more positive reactions into discussions of the Jones family. After many such discussions, a staff member who had been among the disapproving said, "I used to not be able to stand the Joneses, but Miss C went right on liking them and I finally decided there must be something there to like."

If the worker is willing initially to assume most of the responsibility for the relationship and is willing to try to meet the parents psychologically wherever they are, if she can respond to the parents on the basis of their common humanity, then the problems of communication across backgrounds and races do not develop. We did not avoid or minimize the real differences between us; instead we commented on them, confessed our ignorance, and conveyed that we had much to learn from our families—

perhaps more than they from us. Our experience, then, is that the quality of interchange between two human beings is still a more important determinant of their relationship than whether one is poor and one is not and whether one is black and one is white.

We stressed earlier that the relationship is the medium through which we hoped to help parents. But the relationship is only a beginning, not an end in itself. The parents in our project needed the kind of help that goes beyond good communication. We found no substitute for respectfully individualizing each parent and no substitute for the professional knowledge and skill this requires. Such individualizing, at best, calls for knowledge of both the person's outer world—his concrete situation—and of the inner world of his thoughts, feelings, and aspirations. It requires knowledge of his past as well as his present. Personality characteristics, competence, ways of coping can vary as much among the underprivileged as among the privileged.

In the period before admission of the child into daycare and during the early weeks of enrollment much information that will help the staff to know something about the child is gathered. While there is relatively more information developed in the beginning than later, there is a continuing need to try to integrate the child's home experiences with those at the center, so the person who works with parents continues to be in the strategic liason position. This function, however, does not and should not be allowed to substitute for direct communications of many kinds between teachers and parents. In the beginning, parents usually try to present themselves, their child, and their ideas and practices of child rearing in the best light. These are frequently idealized versions. Later, as trust gradually develops, something closer to the real picture begins to emerge. Usually, too, a great deal of trust must develop before most people can talk about their feelings. Thus continued, regular contact with parents is essential to the effectiveness of the daycare service.

In the early days, before the parents felt comfortable enough with us to express directly their disagreements with our philosophy of care and education, the worker was alert to the sometimes obscure hints of doubt or disapproval and tried to help the parents express reservations more fully. Other issues also had to be made explicit, in order to be resolved. For example, one worker became aware of and dealt with a white mother's subtly expressed ambivalence about her child being in a daycare center with black children. There were less subtly expressed complaints: Tim came home wearing someone else's sock; Yvonne wouldn't sleep last night—did you let her nap all afternoon? Ricky is learning to hit other children because you don't hit him back. As parents got acquainted with the child-care and education staff, complaints and questions also came to them.

Sometimes they were dealt with on the spot, but when they were not, it was suggested that the subject be discussed with the person whom they saw regularly, who was informed by the teacher of the question or complaint. Sometimes a complaint was a disguised expression of the parent's pain over separation from the child and had to be understood as such before the parent could be helped to deal with the feelings. Sometimes parents' complaints about the program were valid and resulted in modifications. Whatever the outcome, staff members' responses to parents' questions and complaints are crucial. It can be a satisfying experience to talk to someone who really listens with interest and without defensiveness, who helps one articulate complaints one was not fully aware of, and who acts on the belief that one's reactions are a vital factor in improving services.

Sometimes discussions that began in relation to complaints or questions led to changes in parental attitude and behavior toward the child. The responsibility for giving advice about child rearing and handling of problem behavior was shared by our pediatricians specializing in child development and the social workers. Most of this was done by the social workers, however, because they had more access to the parents. Such advice was not given gratuitously, but only as part of a dynamic process in the context of the relationship.

Still another role of the worker was to help parents realize some of their own goals for better housing, jobs, education, birth control counseling, or health care. Usually these hopes and aspirations were not shared until trust had developed. Once that happened, we could help parents to use other community resources fully. Their first, sometimes frightened and faltering applications had our enthusiastic sponsorship (often with our physical presence). Sometimes we had smoothed the way by advanced contact with the agencies, and always we gave our moral support. Even with a reasonably well-functioning legal rights association in the community, our voice was sometimes needed to speed the course of justice—for example, in the case of a stolen welfare check not replaced for weeks. Sometimes what was hoped for could not be accomplished or was long delayed because of limited resources. This was true in relation to housing. However, with families eligible for housing paid for by public welfare, persistence eventually brought results, and we *could* help the discouraged applicant to be persistent.

One objective was to work in such a way as to increase each person's capacity to function effectively on his own behalf, instead of becoming the passive recipient of our activity. Valuable as the tangible results of helping people to help themselves are, the most valuable result is the internal change, when people stop seeing themselves as helpless victims of urban bureaucracy or of society's inhumanity, and start to rcognize themselves as forces for change.

The following cases show the highly variable individual characteristics of those within a superficially homogeneous population and, thus, the need for flexibility as to the methods of intervention. We have not chosen to present "success" cases. Three out of four are ones in which our gains had to be extremely limited and the results were modest indeed. One case, less dramatic and difficult than the others, is representative of a group within our population in which the work was more effective.*

The Joneses   Reference has already been made to Miss Jones and her children. She was the most psychologically handicapped parent in our pilot group. When we first knew her she was a 19-year-old, obese, black mother of two out-of-wedlock girls, 32 months and 15 months, supported by Aid to Families of Dependent Children. Although she had a high school diploma, Miss Jones was of no more than dull normal intelligence, probably functionally retarded as a result of her deprived background. Her psychological and intellectual limitations were manifested in a number of ways. She was unclean, as were her children; she neither said good-bye to them nor greeted them on reunion; she sent her little girls to Children's House when they were ill, brought them late, or kept them home without notice or explanation; she could not follow through on a course of action, for example, to clear up their recurrent impetigo.

She had a severely limited knowledge of or experience with anything beyond the narrow confines of her drab life lived always on public welfare. Her social worker, CC, must initially have seemed to Miss Jones like someone from another planet. Everyday aspects of the worker's life became for this young woman a source of amazing new information, and, thus an important part of the contact. Many of Miss Jones's questions were personal—where did you buy your coat? How long have you had it?—but for her the answers were educational, introducing her to the idea that a coat could be dry-cleaned, repaired, or shortened, that, in fact, the social worker had worn the same coat for three years. Through hundreds of similar questions and answers over the weeks and months, Miss Jones's

---

* Since the following examples do not make clear the extent of our work with fathers, it should be explained that out of ten families in Phase I in which the father was in the home, we had fairly active contact with six and some contact with one more. Of the eight families in Phase II in which the father was in the home, we had fairly active contact with six. Some fathers were difficult to see because they worked at more than one job, but some regularly either brought the child to daycare or picked him up. Even this kind of peripheral contact was helpful. Something of what the daycare program was like and something about the staff could not help but be known to these fathers. Thus, when a problem arose that needed discussion and the father was asked to participate, he was not suddenly on strange ground with strange people.

world widened. Many questions arose out of what she had heard on television or what she tried to read but could not understand. Her worker read to her the magazine article she had been struggling with, read and simplified for her the recipe she was attempting to use. When Miss Jones was hospitalized for a tonsillectomy and was confused by the doctor's explanation of what would happen, her worker was there to translate for her.

This case exemplifies how the worker had to start "where Miss Jones was," had to build the kind of relationship with her that would eventually help her make use of suggestions. This deprived young woman had to be nurtured before she could become more nurturing to her own children. When the relationship was strong enough, the worker was able literally to teach Miss Jones that it was important to the children that she say good-bye to them and greet them on her return. At another point the worker was able—using information from observation of her child's play at Children's House—to discuss why it was not a good idea for the child to witness intercourse. From changes in the child's play we are reasonably sure Miss Jones did change the sleeping arrangements. She may not have fully understood why this was important, but her relationship with the Children's House staff by then was sufficiently trusting that she did some things simply because we asked her to.

After eighteen months of work with Miss Jones, her social worker summarized the gains:

> She has become very invested in Children's House, sees it as a good place for her and for her children and has moved from bringing the children late and sporadically to bringing them regularly and calling when they are not coming or when she cannot keep an appointment. Her physical appearance has improved; she takes more care in dressing herself and the children. She is very pleased with our interest in her and is less passive and bland. She also has moved from being unaware of the children's illnesses to taking them to the doctor or asking our advice. She is now able to follow through on medical treatment at home. Miss Jones has also become much more independent. She does not see or talk with her mother daily as she used to, makes decisions on her own, and has in a sense become head of her own household. She continues, however, to be impulsive and inconsistent in her dealings with her children.

The idea of being a "good mother" to a deprived person before she can be a better mother herself is not new, but this case illustrates the flexibility of approach that made it possible for this young woman to accept a model for identification. In the usual daycare context, the busy teachers could not have given this parent, in the few minutes' contact involved in arrival and departure, what she needed in order to grow. She could not have tolerated the fact that only her children were given to, and the contact would have continued to be highly sporadic or would have broken down.

Real communication began with another mother of similar background, who was older, depressed, and subject to psychotic episodes, when her worker sat with her all through a long, anxious morning in the hospital waiting room with her sick child.

The Bairds   The Bairds were an intact, self-supporting black family with two children, Alex, who was 5 years old, and Yvonne, who was 17 months old when they joined Children's House. Our contacts were mainly with the mother. From the beginning one of our chief concerns about the Bairds was that in order for them to be self-supporting, Mrs. Baird supplemented her husband's income by working the night shift in a nursing home and doing housework in private homes by day, giving her very little time for rest and sleep. Mrs. Baird impressed us as a competent, intelligent person struggling under the burden of holding two jobs and taking care of her household. Initially, she reacted to the proposed social work contact politely, and dutifully, but with some puzzlement and anxiety. Her initial account of her current life, as well as of her childhood, was somewhat idealized. It was with discomfort, then, that she later revealed she had a grown son born out of wedlock. At age 13, sent away from home to go to school and be a part-time domestic, she had become pregnant and dropped out of school to support her child. She later married, though not the baby's father, and that marriage ended in divorce. Gradually, Mrs. Baird trusted the social worker with a more realistic version of her current life, especially the problems in the second marriage, including her husband's chronic alcoholism. After working with Mrs. Baird for over a year, her social worker wrote

> Almost from the beginning, impressions of Mrs. Baird's personality characteristics, her strengths, her defenses, were consistent with the fuller picture that developed over time. We saw Mrs. Baird as overly polite, conscientious, compliant, anxious, and fearful. Despite the breaking through of sexual and aggressive impulses during early adolescence and behavior that was forbidden by her family's moral code, Mrs. Baird impressed us as a constricted and inhibited adult. The self-punishment built into her early acting out may have foreshadowed the somewhat masochistic organization of her adult life. Any slightly hostile thought or action had to be very passively expressed or disguised with moralistically tinged rationalizations. Mrs. Baird occasionally allowed herself some passive form of aggression but on the whole either suffered from backaches and rather vague illnesses that suggested somatization of conflicts

or she externalized her unconscious anger in a self-punishing way, suffering from many fears and anxieties.

It took five months of contact with Mrs. Baird before she could tell us of her anger at her husband for failing to do more than bring home a paycheck, and more until she told us about his drinking and that she was considering separation. Fairly early and throughout the contact, however, Mrs. Baird had ways of seeking help indirectly that preserved her appearance of self-sufficiency. After a few months of contact with Mrs. Baird, the social worker wrote, "In the course of most interviews Mrs. Baird brings up something on which she appears to be wanting a reaction from me, an opportunity to expose her own ideas to scrutiny. Almost every time I see her she reveals something that can be considered a psychological problem, though without any explicit indication that she's doing so in order to get help with it. Yet at the end of our appointment she decides on a course of action that reveals her use of my contribution to the discussion and later carries out her decision."

In this way, Mrs. Baird used the contact over a two-year period to get help with such problems as Yvonne's loss of appetite, her sleep disturbance, her temporary preference for her father and wish to be in his bed, Alex's involvement in sex play with an older boy, Yvonne's sudden interest in her brother's penis, Alex's insistence on privacy in the bathroom, and Yvonne's separation problem. Mrs. Baird also used interviews to deal with her feelings about such things as unfair treatment at work and her husband's passivity. Gradually she became a little freer in expressing anger. She also used her appointments to evaluate her marriage. After deciding to talk again with her husband about his drinking, she announced that things were better and she thought she could live with the problem.

After seven months of work with Mrs. Baird her social worker recorded, "In these last five interviews she has obviously felt freer to talk about family problems and about her own aspirations. I would like to think that this reflects a growing trust and that her willingness to talk of her hope for more training means that I've been able to convey not only an interest in her welfare but belief in her potential." At about this time Mrs. Baird's wish for better housing and for training as a licensed practical nurse came up regularly. At first the social worker's role was to support her in her hopes and to supply information about ways to apply for better housing and the high school equivalency exam she would have to pass before acceptance for LPN training. To have been more active on Mrs. Baird's behalf at that time would have suggested to her that her worker saw her as inadequate. Almost a year later, when the relationship was stronger and the trust greater, and Mrs. Baird felt herself valued and her abilities respected, the worker's judgment was that the time had come when Mrs. Baird could allow herself to be helped in a practical way. When Mrs. Baird brought up the possibility of taking the high school equivalency exam as she had the year before, the worker drove her to the registration office, helped her register, several days later presented her with a book to help her prepare for the exam, and offered to arrange for tutoring. Following this period, Mrs. Baird for the first time became active in using the information about housing she had been given months before. She also took the exam.

On one occasion the social worker was trying to help Mrs. Baird understand—not intellectually, but emotionally—that Yvonne could both want to come to Children's House every morning and still at points in the day miss her mother and want to be home. At first Mrs. Baird found this too contradictory to accept. The worker tried asking her if she could not recall some similar experience in her own life, past or present. She could not. Then the worker referred with some feeling to her own memory of wanting as a young child to stay several days with a much-loved aunt and uncle, to the overpowering homesickness that flooded her during the visit, to the fact this did not prevent her from going the next time she was invited. Mrs. Baird then not only recalled with vivid detail a similar experience in her own childhood but spoke of relatively current feelings of both enjoying an out-of-town trip without her husband and missing him and home. This bit of insight was perhaps a simple accomplishment, and yet it was a necessary step in her ability to understand and deal with her child's separation problem.

Some of the ways of working with this verbally adequate woman were not appreciably different from methods used in traditional casework. While daycare was the felt need that brought Mrs. Baird to us, and a few other practical services were supplied as well, she was a woman who also needed and could use help to change her self-image. Practical services alone—no matter how numerous—would not have given her all she needed. Mrs. Baird also illustrates our thesis that there is often little homogeneity within the "culture of poverty," that intervention must be based on detailed knowledge of each person, that such knowledge can be developed only in the context of an ongoing relationship.

The Keelers Sometimes our experience with a person forced us to modify our early diagnostic impressions and to accept limitations about the extent of our intervention. In the Keeler case, from Phase II, a pervasive limitation on intervention gradually became apparent. Miss Keeler, a severely deprived young black woman, an apathetic, displaced person, longing, it seemed to us, for the loving family she had never had, at first seemed to have the potential for responding to a mothering concern for her. But what initially appeared as a depression that might lighten with sensitive support on longer acquaintance was understood as a kind of psychological hollowness. Psychological pain, which we had assumed to be present, and on which hopes of improvement were predicated, was not a major component of Miss Keeler's awareness. It would perhaps be correct to say that she is one of those persons, well known to clinicians, who is depressed but does not know it. Despite conscientious efforts to maintain a regular contact with her, there was great irregularity not only in her use of the worker but also in bringing her child to daycare. There was from time to time a partially self-initiated flurry of contact. On taking a closer look at what appeared to make it possible for Miss Keeler to use casework on these occasions, we learned that her greatest responsiveness was always around periods of concern about her physical condition or the death of acquaintances. We had recognized early that she had a good deal of anxiety about her own illnesses and those of her child, and her response to our helping her get and use medical care had been an important reason for our initial hope to involve her in a therapeutic contact. On that occasion Miss Keeler had not been eating well, had become so thin that she worried greatly about what was wrong, and the worry upset her so that she ate even less. She was showing some signs of depression: eating little, losing weight, and sleeping a great deal. Although we felt that Miss Keeler's weight loss was due to her psychological rather than her physical state, two factors influenced the plan we made: one was that repeated efforts to help her identify what she might be depressed or worried about had not been productive; the other was that her marked weight loss made imperative the evaluation of physical causes. As the social worker, JS, began inquiring about her medical history, she learned that Miss Keeler had never been able to give a full account of her symptoms and concerns or eating habits to any physician, and her infrequent visits to doctors had always been unsatisfactory.

Guided by a consultation with the pediatrician, the worker went over with Miss Keeler the relevant facts of her health history, her current complaints, past and current eating habits, and other matters a physician might want to know about a patient with her presenting symptoms. Following this general preparation the caseworker involved her in some simple role playing: "I'm the doctor at the clinic; let's rehearse what he's probably going to ask you and how you are going to answer his questions." In preparation for the appointment, which she helped Miss Keeler arrange, the worker wrote the physician a letter outlining relevant information about her and conveying our interest in her having a thorough examination, telling about her inability to get good medical care in the past and the preparatory work we were doing with her to try to assure that she would be able to help in the diagnostic process. On the appointed day the worker agreed to accompany Miss Keeler to the clinic, to stay with her through the history taking, and after the physical examination to rejoin her and the doctor to hear his diagnostic impressions and recommendations. The entire process required about four hours—a totally new experience of thoroughness for Miss Keeler. The physical findings were negative. An antidepressant was prescribed and dietary advice was given. Her relief on being convinced for the first time that she had no mysterious disease allowed her to eat better, to gain weight, and to appear more animated. Several such crises occurred later centering around different bodily concerns or death, and each time she made good use of similar casework intervention.

In addition to helping Miss Keeler at times of concern about her health, it was possible to help her improve her housing. Motivated to find better living quarters by our discovering that her child had a slightly elevated blood lead level due to eating paint chips, Miss Keeler still required enormous amounts of help over many months to persist in making and following up on an application for admittance to a new housing project. When the move was finally made from a typically dingy, tumbledown slum flat to the sparkling new apartment, Miss Keeler said she felt better than she had in her whole life.

Nevertheless, she remained uninfluenced by attempts to bring her to insight about her substitution of physical symptoms for psychic pains. We concluded that she used us so selectively because she could not tolerate awareness of the feelings she would have had to experience in order to achieve a better adjustment. She also remained relatively intractable in any area of childcare except her son's physical health. But there was marked improvements in her health, her housing, and her social life. Since we ended our official contact with her, Miss Keeler has frequently telephoned her worker, presumably because the contact was meaningful to her in spite of its limitations. She calls to keep in touch and never makes a request for any kind of service.

Miss Keeler demonstrates that while such limited results are troubling when one's hopes are high, their value should not be minimized. The help made an important difference in her life and that of her child during his early years. Without our policy of requiring continuing contact with the worker, we would not have had access to Miss Keeler in a way that would have made possible our work with her. She is not the kind of person who would have presented herself at a family service agency or mental health clinic or who would have accepted a referral to such a service. We retain a strong bias in favor of our daycare model, one staffed in a way that offers a variety of services to parents given by a staff familiar to them through almost daily contact. While this versatility may appear to be an extravagance, we are convinced that is just the opposite.

The Andruses The Andrus case, described here only briefly, illustrates in another way the multiple services daycare can offer if it is not conceived of simply as a place to house and educate children. In order to understand the relevant aspect of the Andrus case, it is necessary to know that the contract we originally made with Phase II families did not include daycare services until the child reached the age of two. Though we were prepared to offer daycare if other plans for the child seemed harmful, parents were not made aware of this possibility unless the need arose. Thus when the question of the mother's going to work came up shortly after Jackie Andrus's birth, the parents had no expectation that we would furnish daycare; they planned to hire a baby-sitter. Mr. Andrus, 22, and his wife, 19, were a white couple describing themselves, and especially Mrs. Andrus, as having every problem in the book. This was no exaggeration. A high school graduate, Mrs. Andrus was an intelligent but disturbed young woman with a highly pathological history, which included a sexual relationship with her father. She was aware of the long chain of social pathology in her family, and on joining the study during her pregnancy wondered aloud whether she would be "strong enough to break the chain." At times she was a maddening person to work with because of her flighty, often silly, sometimes sarcastic, sometimes obscene and tough way of talking, but she was also shrewdly insightful and even at times pathetically appealing. Although Mrs. Andrus made many efforts during the two and a half years of our acquaintance to find employment and to take training courses, she did not succeed in either effort for almost two years. Even after much work with her, we doubted that she was employable and were pleasantly surprised when she managed to get and hold a job.

Mr. Andrus, who had completed tenth grade, was somewhat better put together than his wife. He was employed as a construction worker during six to seven months of the year. However, partly because of the seasonal nature of his work and partly because of the couple's childlike use of money, the Andruses were always deeply in debt. Mr. Andrus was an expert at seeking out all the help the community had to offer to the economically besieged, and he was not unwilling to involve himself in misrepresentation and fraud in order to improve his financial situation. Thus, had we offered daycare when Mrs. Andrus first mentioned going to work, it would have been eagerly accepted.

We did offer daycare when child abuse occurred when the infant was just under 4 weeks of age. The mother, in a state she described as "becoming unglued" over his crying, had hit Jackie on the head with his bottle.

She acknowledged also having spanked him once and said that the father did so regularly when the child cried at night. One must be able to visualize the size, fragility, and vulnerability of a three-to-four week old infant to appreciate fully the gravity of the situation. This parental behavior and our initial impression of the parents' severe disturbances greatly alarmed us, and we decided to convey to them our sense of crisis and the need to protect both them and the child. Our urgency was heightened by evidence that the interval between feedings for this very young infant was sometimes as long as seven hours, that he was dressed on cold days, when all windows in the house were open, in only a shirt and sodden diaper, that he was alternately left for long periods hungry, wet, and cold and then overstimulated when his parents felt like playing with him. On one occasion, when the baby was two months old, Mrs. Andrus said that if she fed him whenever he was hungry now, later he wouldn't come to supper when called.

The day Mrs. Andrus hit Jackie on the head with the bottle, she was frightened enough to telephone our pediatrician, PM, though when PM returned the call, the mother gave another explanation for wanting to talk and only later acknowledged hitting the baby. At this point we had known the family for only two months, but they had rather quickly and enthusiastically made use of all offers of socialwork contact. We recommended daycare with the explanation that many people could not give a child good care twenty-four hours a day but could do so for shorter periods, that we wanted to relieve them of the baby's care a part of each day and thus help them with a situation that was creating too much stress for them to handle. Their reaction indicated that there had not been enough time for a feeling of trust in us to develop; they thought the recommendation of daycare was an attempt to take the baby from them. Our further recommendation of intensive counseling with their worker, MG, was accepted, however. Their fear and distrust of us was not so great as to cause them to avoid us. They continued to welcome the social worker into their home, and when they came to the center for interviews, they left the baby in our nursery. For several days he was with us part of the time, once from early morning until well after closing time. Still they could not agree to bring the baby regularly, though Mrs. Andrus began to talk of bringing him if she got a job.

For a period of about six weeks, during which our contacts were frequent enough to give us some assurance of the baby's safety, we pondered legal aspects of the situation and the pros and cons of referral to the overburdened protective service branch of the Welfare Department. We decided to try to keep the Andruses in the study and to maintain a stance that conveyed our determination to protect their child at the same time that we protected them from their own impulses, and hence from possible arrest. Such a course of action appeared to offer more protection to the child than would a more precipitous course, which might cause them to run away, as they occasionally threatened to do. We thought we saw the beginnings of positive feelings toward the social worker, and that this would be lost if, in a panic, we invoked the law.

Mr. and Mrs. Andrus did not bring the baby to the center during the period immediately after we learned of the baby's being spanked and hit on the head. As a precaution and a means of helping the mother to care for her baby, we offered the services of our pediatric nurse, JR, at the Andruses' home. This offer was not accepted with overwhelming enthusiasm: the mother said she didn't need any help with baby care, but the visits would provide her with company. While comments or suggestions the nurse made during the series of visits were almost always ignored or disputed at the time, some were later incorporated into Mrs. Andrus's care of the baby and presented as her own ideas. On the whole, however, she remained flighty and unpredictable in child care as in everything else.

When Jackie was 10 to 16 weeks old, he was brought sporadically to daycare—sometimes when his mother simply wanted baby-sitting, sometimes when she was angry because he vomited what she fed him (he did not do this in our care), and sometimes because she felt too "uptight" to take care of him. On days when the baby was not at Children's House, either the social worker or pediatrician was in contact with the mother and baby. The fear that we wanted to take the baby away was subsiding. When Mrs. Andrus enrolled in a training course when Jackie was 6 months old, he came regularly to daycare. During the six to seven weeks she remained in the course he was with us every day. Then she began to deteriorate in her functioning. She continued to bring him after she dropped out of school. By now her trust in us was such that she let us know when she began to behave abusively with Jackie. On one occasion during this period she called her social worker to "come take Jackie off my hands." We did not usually pick up children coming to daycare, but we always responded to Mrs. Andrus's request since she was a poor driver and was dangerous to herself and others when she was more upset than usual. In the telephone call for help she reported that Jackie, now 7 months old, had not taken all of his food and had cried and refused the bottle. Then she had tried to change his diaper. "He was so wiggly, it got under my skin, and I said, 'Listen, kid, I'm not changing your pants for my benefit!' Then I hit him a few times, to put it mildly!" When the social worker and nurse arrived to pick up Jackie, Mrs. Andrus said, "I hit him on the ass and threw him on the bed!"

As a result of Mrs. Andrus's deteriorating self-control, it was agreed in a family team meeting to refer her for psychiatric evaluation. Convinced that she was now dangerous to Jackie and in general feeling upset, she accepted the referral. This resulted in a five-day hospitalization, during which she said that the only two people important in her life were her husband and MG, her social worker.

The hospitalization was disappointing to us in its brevity and the absence of any realistic plan for aftercare. Soon both parents began reporting their anger about the child doing a lot of crying and their spanking of him. (At the center Jackie cried very little after we once got him settled down from whatever distressing experiences he had had at home.) Mrs. Andrus said she was thinking of giving him up, but she had no serious intentions of doing so, and knew her husband would object. However, after commenting that she and Mr. Andrus didn't have simultaneous impulses to spank Jackie, she added, "If we should ever be up tight at the same time, it might be fatal." She added that if she killed the baby, she would then kill herself. Even after such an acknowledgment neither parent could come to terms with the need for Jackie to be protected from their dangerous impulses through foster home placement or even, when it was first offered, through going at night to the home of his familiar caregiver at Children's House. So Jackie continued to come to the center by day. Mr. Andrus was warned that he must not leave his wife alone with the baby even briefly.

After several more crises in which the parents complained bitterly of the baby's crying and we suspected further physical assaults on him, we asked both parents to see a psychiatrist on the staff of the Child Study Center. With him, both acknowledged their spanking of the infant for crying. The psychiatrist noted, "Reflectively, Mrs. Andrus said, '. . . I might throw him down on the floor or out of the window someday.' When I wondered if that was a feeling or more of a conviction that she might do it, she said she felt somewhat better now but still thought she might do it."

As a result of the psychiatric consultation, we were able to convince the Andruses that they should allow us temporarily to care for Jackie at night as well as during the day. After several days of this arrangement, Jackie was allowed to go home at night in response to his father's pleas and strong assertion that they could stop one another from hurting Jackie. The next morning another crisis occurred. Jackie was now 8 months old. In response to an early morning call from Mrs. Andrus, the social worker and nurse went to the home to bring both mother and child to the center. They found both in distress, the baby especially so. In contrast to his usual tendency to stop crying and become calm in the arms of a familiar staff member, he continued to cry very hard almost all the way to the Children's House, finally tapering off into sobs that wracked his body. Gradually he became at least outwardly calm in the comforting arms of his most familiar caregiver. His mother had acknowledged on the way to the center another episode of his crying and of her getting angry at him, but it was only when he was carefully examined at Children's House that we discovered a bruise over one eye, red hand marks on his abdomen, and severe bruises in several places where his mother had bitten him. Summoned from his work to the center, Mr. Andrus was appropriately distressed, and also angry at his wife. The parents gave us their written permission for an indefinite period of total responsibility for Jackie, knowing that otherwise we would have no choice but to report them to the police.

Very early in our acquaintance with the Andruses, when Jackie was less than a month old, we feared that Mrs. Andrus would probably always be a threat to a small child, the father somewhat less so. Thus, as soon as we felt their relationship to their family worker was good enough, the worker began discussing with the parents the advisability of permanent placement for Jackie. The mother at times seemed to welcome the idea and, as we have indicated, at points of stress warned us that she was dangerous to Jackie. The father, however, could not agree to any kind of placement except temporary placement with our staff. "If he goes, you go," was his ultimatum to his wife. In our minds at all times was the fact that we had no case that would stand up in court if we pressed for revocation of parental rights. Jackie, a highly adaptable and resilient child, was doing well—perhaps largely because of the unusually devoted and skillful work of his caregiver—in spite of his experiences with his parents. At times they were able to behave playfully and lovingly toward him. We were providing closer surveillance of the situation than the official protective agency could have. Thus, when the father's seasonal layoff meant that he could be with the child before and after his stay at the center, our night care was discontinued.

After the period of night care, Mr. Andrus was unable to find full-time employment and he was available to be with Jackie at home. Then Mrs. Andrus found full-time employment. With the parental roles reversed there continued to be crises in the family life, but none involving serious physical abuse of the child. The bodily care, while highly inconsistent, was somewhat better. After weekends, however, Jackie continued to arrive at Children's House wet, unclean, fatigued, and often highly irritable. The parents, despite continuing intensive work, remained unable to modify their ideas about children or their behavior toward their son.

The Andrus story shows that daycare with quality auxiliary services such as social work, nursing, and pediatric consultation can be a first line of defense for children against abuse and neglect. The built in surveillance that daycare provides can be a kind of early-warning system, but without these additional services the daycare staff can do little more than report the suspected abuse to the appropriate authority, running the risk of alienating the parents and thus separating them from a needed service. The developing relationship between the parents and their worker made it possible for us to keep the parents involved during the first critical confrontation about abuse and at the same time to substitute our care for the legal authority. That they came to perceive our watchfulness and even our occasional ultimatums as protection was reflected in several ways: during one of her psychiatric interviews, Mrs. Andrus said with pride in her voice, "Our social worker has had us under surveillance for some time now." On the occasion of her striking and biting Jackie, Mrs. Andrus told her mother that we could have thrown her to the cops, but were going to help her instead. Our director, whose authority as well as clinical skills were used directly with the Andruses occasionally, seemed to be perceived for the most part as a benign and protective mother because at times she placed firm requirements upon them. Thus we were able to be both benevolent parent and "policeman" to this troubled couple.

Some parents who use daycare have little or no need for the services described. However, many do. Those who have responsibility for planning and carrying out programs for large numbers of children may feel that we are proposing the impossible. While we acknowledge the enormous problems involved in funding and staffing daycare centers so that the various services parents need can be provided, we want to emphasize the need; for unless the need is recognized, the services will never be provided.

CHAPTER 5

The Problem of Separation

One of the most problematic aspects of daycare is the separation it requires between a child and the people to whom he is most closely attached, usually for six to nine hours five days out of every seven. They may be reunited at four or five P.M., and ordinarily have only a few hours together before the child goes to sleep for the night. The early morning hours characteristically are rushed, if the parents begin work at eight or nine. This usually leaves only a small number of the child's waking hours when he and his parents are together. Moreover, if the parents must rush through them to shop, prepare meals, and take care of the rest of the family, their time together can also be qualitatively endangered. These realities impose stresses upon both the young child and his parents that have an impact on their functioning, on their relationship, on the parents' development as parents and on the child's own development.

Among the determinants of the impact of the separation experience for the child in daycare are the following:

• THE QUALITY OF THE RELATIONSHIP TO THE MOTHER AND TO OTHER FAMILY MEMBERS—i.e., the strength of the tie, the degree of trust the child has in the continuity of affectionate interest and concern of his parents, the preponderance of positive over negative feelings. Quality is determined by the intensity and nature of specific experiences between parent and child, in combination with the child's innate characteristics. If the child has not established firm bonds with his parents he may show little reaction to separation from them, though he may still react to a strange new place. If the bonds are strong and healthy he will react in a variety of ways, some of which will be illustrated in pages to follow. If his relationships are highly conflicted, separation may lead to behavior symptomatic of a pathological process.

• THE DEVELOPMENTAL STATUS OF THE CHILD. Age specific competencies and age specific vulnerabilities are important determinants of the child's ability to cope with separation and what the separation experience means to him. There are developmental periods in the life of the normal child when separation is particularly stressful and is painfully experienced.

• PREVIOUS EXPERIENCES WITH SEPARATION. When these have been well

61

handled and the child has been supported in coping with them, his resources are strengthened; but when previous separation experiences have
been intensely traumatic, they make him more vulnerable to the impact of
subsequent separation.

•THE QUALITY OF THE DAYCARE PROGRAM. The presence of competent staff
members who understand and can respond to the childs interests and needs
will ease the stress of separation. So too will a developmentally sound program that includes appropriate concrete experiences in which the child can
become involved.

• THE CREATION OF BRIDGES BETWEEN THE HOME (PARENTS) AND THE
CENTER in the mind of the child through a variety of measures.

What Separation Means to the Child

Before discussing separation in respect to daycare, we will turn our attention to some of what is known about the meaning of separation from home
and loved ones to young children, and the special vulnerability of the young
child to this experience. There is by now a fairly solidly established body
of knowledge about children's reactions to separation, from observations
of behavior in a variety of settings and from clinical experience (Freud and
Burlingham 1944; Provence and Lipton 1962; Yarrow 1964). The most
relevant aspects of the theory that guided our attitudes and practice are
condensed in the following paragraphs.

Through being cared for in ways that meet at least his most important
needs, the infant comes to recognize and form an attachment to the nurturing person. This attachment is facilitated when the caregiver is mainly one
person, though others share in giving care. It appears that not only the
amount of care but the quality of care, which is strongly influenced by the
nurturing person's feeling for the child, is an important determinant of
the closeness of the attachment. Most infants considered to be developing
normally discriminate between their mothers and other persons by not
later than four to five months, and one usually sees their strongest reactions of pleasure and greatest contentment in interaction with the mother.
Gradually, since the mother is both the source of greatest pleasure and
the one who necessarily regulates and frustrates the infant in some way,
she becomes the object of his most intense feelings, both positive and negative. In a mother–child relationship that is healthy, the positive feelings far
outweigh the negative ones.

Under favorable conditions of nurturing, a baby by eight to nine months
of age shows awareness of the mother's absence and may seek in some way
to call her back, even though he may be quite accepting of social contact
and the care of substitute caregivers. By eleven to twelve months, it is be-

lieved, the child's growing intelligence makes him realize that this person to whom he is so attached is not always available and can be lost. The mental images he has of her may serve to sustain him with reasonable comfort for brief periods of time, but not for very long. Since his needs for food, for rest, for comfort and social interaction are compelling, he will accept physical care and social approaches from others and, at least part of the time, will be playful and involved in activities. This acceptance and responsiveness can be observed in infants of this age in the daycare setting. Such behavior, however, should not lead one to the conclusion that separation from his mother has no effect on him.

An infant or young toddler probably has difficulty keeping firm in his mind the idea of the permanence of his parent throughout the long day. For the child at home frequent though discontinuous exposure makes stronger the ability to keep the mother in mind when she is out of sight. Even recognitory memory—that is, memory that operates when the familiar person reappears—is probably more precarious as time away from the parent lengthens, and evocative memory—that is, the child's ability to call up the image of the familiar person through his own mental activity— surely must be more difficult to maintain in the absence of fairly frequent reinforcement. Ideas about the subjective experience of very young children away from their mothers for a whole day are conjecture, but when with them, one can see that their feelings range from a sense of bewilderment to acute longing for mother and home and that their adaptive capacities are increasingly overtaxed as the hours lengthen. This seems to be true for most young children even when the staff/child ratio is favorable and the program is of high quality.

Time is a significant factor in determining the effect of separation. From observations over the five-year period of our study, we are convinced that for most children stress increases markedly with the number of hours away from home and family. A four-hour separation for young children calls for a substantial adaptation, but it is vastly different from an eight-hour separation.

We are not overlooking the end-of-the-day fatigue and disorganization that is common to young children, and adults, too, for that matter. We are well aware that late afternoon in most households is the time when everything can get out of hand. In our center, knowing that fatigue of children and staff was to be expected, we planned that the end of the children's day with us should be relaxed and undemanding but not empty. It was a time when small groups enjoyed quiet activities together and children often had individual attention. However, what we refer to about the impact of the length of day is a different phenomenon, and our concern arose from our observations that the children who seemed to us to use the program best were those who spent shorter though regular days in the center. For all the children, whose homes varied widely in the extent to which they met developmental needs, the first love was their own home, and the relief they felt at going back to it was vivid and palpable. This does not mean that reunions with parents or other relatives were always pleasant and gratifying; indeed, it was not rare for children to become quite difficult when their parents came for them, an occurrence parents needed help to understand and handle. Some days we had the impression that the child, obviously relieved, was thinking, "Well, I made it back to mommy one more time," as though he had been in great danger. On other days a child might behave angrily toward his mother or might ignore her, suggesting that he was thinking, "Here she is and now that I know I've got her back again I'll get even." These behaviors occurred even when the child had been having happy times during part of the day and was gaining a great deal from the program in many respects.

There is another universal component of the separation experience, which comes to the fore as the child reaches the age at which he becomes aware that he has both positive and negative feelings toward his mother and other emotionally significant people. This, of course, is a gradual process, and apparently a child expresses pleasure, displeasure, affection, and anger, long before he has more than a hazy awareness of these feelings. By sometime in the second year, however, most toddlers have enough awareness of self and others to have some thoughts about their own feelings, to reflect, however briefly, upon them. From this time on, the child's fear of loss and abandonment have an added dimension. Not only is he in danger because he might lose the persons he has come to love, but also he begins to believe that he may lose them because he has been bad; that is, in his mind he may be abandoned because he has misbehaved or has had angry, aggressive feelings. Thus the child's reaction to separation becomes more complex. He develops anxiety at first involving a fear of loss of the parent in reality, then involving a fear of loss of love and approval, which at times, he may conclude he deserves to lose. When one observes the reactions of a six month old and of a three year old who are brought into the daycare center, one is immediately aware of the enormously greater complexity of the mind of the older child. The body tension and irritability of the six-month-old infant brought in by a tense, angry mother must be responded to with appropriate measures by the caregiver, but are of short duration compared with the persistent or recurring concern during any one day of a three year old who has had a fight with his mother over eating or toileting or has been punished for hitting his baby brother. It is well known that the desire for love and approval and the fear of losing them exist in any normally developing child and are powerful factors in his socialization and successful adaptation to family and others. However, when these fears are greatly heightened, as they appear to be when the young child must wait all day to receive the assurance that his parents do love him after all, the stress becomes very difficult for him and may be beyond his capacity to cope with it.

Reactions to Separation Stress—Individual and Age-Specific

From about the beginning of the second year on, then, the normally developing child increasingly reveals his awareness of the importance of his parents, his pleasure in being part of a family and his pain and confusion when separated from them for long hours. In our daycare center, where every effort was made to provide individualized, personalized care, we still saw these reactions. In some children there were clear indications of anxiety or anger. Others reacted to separation by losing their liveliness and becoming apathetic and slow moving. Some displayed loss of previously acquired skills; some restricted their contacts and activities in various ways.

Infants under ten to eleven months who entered daycare showed less vivid reactions than those who were older. With individual variations among them they generally adjusted more easily at first, with fewer signs of distress, than did the children who entered between ten and twenty-four months. This is *not* to say that it is better for the infant to come into daycare before nine or ten months. In infants placed in full daycare at an early age there is likely to be some interference or delay in the formation of a close attachment to the parent.

What, then, can daycare staff do to assist child and parent with the separation problem? How can they support the child in such a way that the feelings of anxiety and loss are reduced? What can they do to help the child develop methods of coping with his concerns? Some general suggestions are listed below. These are followed by examples drawn from our experience with children whose behavior reflects various types and aspects of the separation experience and how we attempted to handle them.

How to Alleviate the Intensity of the Separation Experience

Experiences should be arranged that specifically enhance the child's ability to cope with separation. In principle, this is no more than part of arranging a program that meets the child's developmental needs as a whole. But the length of the day deepens the developmentally normal concern with separation characteristic of young children, so the staff needs to take special supportive measures.

• Ask parents to stay with children at the time of entry and at other points when the child is having a difficult time. Try to get them to come at midday, if they can, or at other times, to be with the child in the center. This will help the child feel safe at the center and give him a break in the long day.

• Try to know enough about the child's home life and family to talk with him about them during the day or acknowledge them in his experience through the use of familiar objects, food, and so on.

• Encourage the parent to give the child something to bring from home that could connect home and center in the child's mind and help him to be more comfortable away from home. This might be something with which the child plays or on which he depends, such as a toy or a blanket, or some possession of the mother or father. Such things appear to give the child tangible representations of the parents, which are reassuring to him.

In one highly individualized example of this kind of tangible reminder, several mothers in our group worked in or near the medical center and found it possible to leave their cars parked on our street where the child could see them. At various times during the day we would find a child going to the window, looking at the car, saying "mommy," or when a little older, "mommy's car" and being reassured by its presence. There is no doubt that in these instances the car stood for the mother and, while it might have increased the longing at some times, it seemed most of the time to remind the child that his mother would return. Sometimes even for other children such a symbol was reassuring. The fact that Linda's mommy's car was there seemed to mean to other children that their mothers would return for them too.

• Obtain pictures of parents or of parents with the child, which the child can look at during the day. One child for a period of about two months between the ages of 18 and 20 months went to his locker periodically to get a picture of his mother and himself, which he would then carry around, sometimes commenting on it, sometimes simply keeping it with him as he did other things. All children had free access to their lockers, where they could keep things that they had brought from home.

• Use the telephone as a support for the child. After the age of eighteen months or so many children are familiar enough with the telephone that it has meaning as a line between themselves and a parent. We found it of greatest usefulness with children who were over two and a half, but occasionally it was helpful also for younger ones to call and talk with a parent.

• Help the child to acknowledge his feelings about separation by helping him to say hello and good-bye—that is, to acknowledge actively by word or gesture the events of leave-taking and reunion. During the day, encourage the child to remember and talk about his parents and home.

• Include many basic learning experiences in the daycare program, in order to help the child build his resources for dealing with feelings such as those he will have on separation from his family. Acquiring a variety of new skills gives a child feelings of self-direction, competence, and enjoyment, which serve to alleviate feelings of helplessness and need. Mastery of cognitive and social skills in particular enchances a child's adaptive capacity, including his ability to cope with stress. Thus, while learning activities are desirable for a number of reasons, they are important aspects of an effort to reduce the stress of separation.

• Provide situations, too, in which the child can actively master his feelings specifically about separation. Games in which the child controls his own coming and going and directs the coming and going of others, games of hiding and rediscovering, and games of losing and finding are all activities in which he can find and perfect methods for dealing with separation, disappearance, and rediscovery, even when there is no direct reference to his being away from home or parents. Play may also include the child's actively repeating with a teacher, another child, or dolls the themes of parting and reunion, in their fragmentary or complete form and with or without direct reference to his own situation.

The Adjustment for Parents

Parents, too, need help in adjusting to the separation daycare imposes. When parents bring their infant or young child to daycare, leaving him with strangers, they will have mixed emotions. Some mothers who regret the necessity of going to work will be fully aware of feelings of loss at missing so much of their baby's day. But even those who strongly wish to return to school, to work, or to a career often have feelings of sadness or guilt at giving the baby into the care of others. Parent surrogates should be aware of this complexity, no matter what the mother's surface behavior may suggest.

In every instance parents need to be fully informed about the center, its staff, its policies, and so on. They should know with whom they should exchange information about the child. In the beginning, it is best if this can be one person. Later, when parents are familiar with the place and personnel, it is natural that other staff also exchange information with them.

However, there should always be one main person to whom a parent can talk when there is a need to discuss things that may be upsetting or problems that have arisen at home or in the center. The parent should be encouraged to call the center during the day to ask about the child, and the staff should know how to reach the parent at home, work, or school.

It is important that parent and child spend some time in the center together. This helps the parent to know the setting, and also helps the child feel comfortable and safe there. Feelings of tension and anxiety or of relaxation and contentment are often communicated from mother to child in quite subtle ways. The tense, anxious, or angry feelings with which she hands over her baby to his caregiver may speak more directly to him than the smile on her face or the words she uses, and will make more difficult his adjustment to the staff and program. Conversely, if the parent feels the interest and respect of the staff and his confidence in the staff and the program, the child will feel this too. At Children's House we required that parents come with the child for a visit prior to entry, and asked that they arrange to stay for a while each day during the child's initial adjustment period. In addition, the parent's presence is needed to help the child with those periodic upsets that are an expectable part of his life. The more a parent can be helped to feel welcome in the center, and the more she feels a part of her child's life, the more continuity there will be in the child's care and the less stressful the situation will be.

Some Case Histories

Terry Young   Terry Young entered daycare at the age of 9 weeks so that his 19-year-old mother could complete her senior year in high school. His mother was tense and unsure of herself with the baby, frightened, and often hostile. She was driven by a desire to get ahead in the world, to have a nice apartment, to finish school and get a good job. Her husband regretted having left school and encouraged her to finish her schooling. When Mrs. Young first brought Terry to the nursery, she was invited by the daycare staff to spend as much time as she could with him there. There was a rocking chair available where she could relax and observe how MB, the child-care worker, held the baby, fed him, talked and played with him. She was invited to participate as much as she wished, but was not asked to assume responsibility for the baby's care. She took a liking to the child-care worker, asked her questions of the sort an adolescent might ask her own mother. She handled the baby awkwardly and was often intense, serious, and silent in her interaction with him. She smiled with pleasure, however, as she watched the staff talk to the baby and coax responsive vocalizations from him. It was not long before she started to talk with him and smile in response to his reactions.

At the time of admission Terry was a visually alert baby with a great deal of muscle tension and an allergic skin rash. He frequently seemed uncomfortable and cried lustily with a loud, shrill, penetrating, insistent cry, which was invariably accompanied by heightened muscle tension and jerky movements. When comfortable he could respond to people by smiling broadly and using a variety of vocalizations. From the beginning we recognized that his sensitivity and tension would require particularly careful handling by the child-care staff. We also recognized that his mother's tension and ineptness often heightened his own tension and discomfort, making him cry more, flail his arms, and become difficult to feed, bathe, change, and so on. His father had an easier way with him, and was quite warm and gentle when he held him.

Here is a brief record of our observations on a certain day, followed by our commentary on the events described, in italic.

Terry, age 13 weeks, was brought to the center by his mother, who seemed harassed and in a hurry to be on her way. She reported that he had a cold and that he had vomited in the cab on the way over. He was crying loudly and kicking with stiff, jerky movements as his diaper was changed and as his nose was suctioned with a bulb syringe to assist his breathing. He quieted down when held and rocked, but his musculature remained tense and he seemed unable to relax. He did not respond to the adults' attempts to get him to smile and vocalize, and during the feeding he seemed to be just staring into space, in contrast to his usual visual alertness. Gradually his eyes closed and his arms and legs relaxed as he sucked on the bottle.

Terry was handled by three people within the first hour after waking this morning. First, a harassed mother who was in a hurry to drop him off and get to school, second, SC, who changed his diaper and aspirated his nose, and third, MB, who rocked and fed him. He was also approached by the observer and possibly other staff members as he entered the building. It appears that the diminished social responsiveness and body tension were indicators of the stress he must have felt. His crying eventually subsided in response to the care given him.

Departure (age 19 weeks): when Terry's father came for him he was awake and in a happy mood. He looked at his father, smiled a big smile and squealed a loud, happy squeal. His father laughed aloud in response. It was quite clear that Terry recognized his father and was delighted to see him.

At this time Terry's father was coming for him every afternoon. The staff was impressed with the father's interest, gentleness, and fondness for the baby. Both at this stage and later he had an easier, more relaxed way with Terry than did the mother.

Terry, age 19 months, was brought by his mother. He clung to her, crying when she tried to put him down, so she stayed for half an hour and he began to play. When she left he started to cry and MB took him to the window to wave to her and watch her go. He quieted, and remained there looking out the window for several minutes. He hailed GM from the window as she arrived, calling "Hi!" and came to the door to meet her.

Terry had been in the program from early infancy and was entirely familiar with the place and with the staff. Nonetheless, one sees in this example that it was not easy at this time for him to be left by his parents.

Terry, age 21 months, was sitting on the floor playing with the toy trucks when he heard the door open. He got up and went to the gate as if expecting his father, and found him. Mr. Young came in, leaned on the gate, and smiled at Terry, who returned the smile and ran the toy car up and down the gate with appropriate accompanying car sounds. When Greg approached the gate and Mr. Young said "Hello, Greg," Terry hit out at Greg, obviously not wanting to share his father with him.

Terry's expectant behavior regarding his father's arrival, his pleasure at seeing him, his showing his father the car he liked, and his annoyance at Greg's intrusion are all expectable and normal behaviors.

David Ferris   David's mother had been his only caregiver, except for a rare sitter, until she accepted a job and asked for daycare when he was 8 months of age. From our contact with them through the home visitor and the monthly visits to the center for pediatric care and developmental evaluation, we knew David to be a healthy baby who received good care and was developing well. The relationship between mother and infant was good, they seemed well adapted to each other, and he appeared to be a secure baby who had come to trust adults to take care of him.

When he was admitted to daycare, one of our child-care staff was KM, a soft-spoken young woman who though she did not look like David's mother had certain similarities of voice and ways of moving. We made her David's special person to help him adjust to this new and potentially difficult experience, but were prepared to modify this plan if he proved to be more comfortable with another staff member. This time, our expectation was correct, and on the first day he accepted being turned over to her by his mother without active protest, though with some solemnity. As was our custom, we encouraged Miss Ferris to stay for as long as she could, but she saw no reason for staying beyond a few minutes and was confident that he would adapt without upset. KM took full responsibility for his care and the first day was a relatively smooth one. David cried two or three times when KM left the room and was reassurred when she returned.

Second day (age 8 months, 7 days): David's mother brought him in a carriage from her home a few blocks away. The staff and children were in the yard and she picked David up and handed him to KM, chatted briefly and left soon, without saying good-bye to him. He did not appear to notice her departure and looked at KM but did not smile. As she held him he studied her face intently and then looked at JR (observer) with a solemn, puzzled expression on his face. She spoke to him; he gave her a fleeting smile before looking solemnly around the yard at the several strange (to him) people. Thinking to make him more comfortable, KM put him in a walker, but he immediately began to cry, so she picked him up again and he stopped. She carried him around the yard talking soothingly to him for a few minutes and again put him in the walker. This time he did not cry, but picked up a bell from the tray, rang and then mouthed it, and began to look around the yard at the activities of adults and children. He played quite industriously for a long time by grasping the bell clapper, mouthing both handle and bowl, chewing, biting, and licking it. When KM, who stayed near him, brought a large ball and rolled it toward him on the ground, he lost interest in the bell and attended the ball, trying to move the walker toward it. He stood up, reached out toward it excitedly with an interested expression on his face. The rest of the outdoor period was spent in the walker or on KM's lap, where he remained silent and watchful. He smiled for the first time when she carried him into the house and set him on the counter where he could see his image and hers in the mirror. He watched her as she took things from the bag his mother had brought from home and as she handed him his bottle he recognized it, up-ended it promptly, and put the nipple in his mouth. It was a new, hard nipple purchased by his mother for his entry into daycare and was unlike the soft nipple he was accustomed to. When the milk did not immediately come out, he made a protesting sound and threw the bottle to the floor and continued to make complaining sounds. As soon as he was placed in the high chair and saw the food, he became excited and accepted it eagerly. After several spoonfuls he smiled, vocalized, and seemed happy for the first time today. As he ate he looked at and "talked" to KM happily and tried to grasp the food dish.

David had several reactions worth emphasizing. We interpreted his pervasive soberness and watchfulness as indicating at least some degree of uneasiness and perplexity about the new situation. We were careful to respect what we felt was his need to receive all of his bodily care and most other interactions from KM, expecting that if we did so he would more quickly become secure in the new setting. The first evidence of real pleasure and relaxation came as he ate his lunch, a familiar and enjoyable event. Just before lunch, when KM, thinking to comfort him, had offered his bottle brought from home, he found it alien and unsatisfactory, apparently because of the new, hard nipple. Indeed, he may have felt especially betrayed! This was no disaster and may seem a minor point, but it suggests it is important to think about how such things might be experienced by a child.

In addition to providing him with a constant person we tried to provide also during these first days interesting things to look at and manipulate and opportunities for movement, reasoning that his being able to be active in perceiving, manipulating, and moving would increase his feelings of well-being and help him deal with the long hours of separation from his mother.

Over the next two or three days, during which KM continued to take care of him, David no longer reacted as though the center was a strange place that needed to be checked out each time he came. He seemed increasingly comfortable and often smiled and vocalized in a happy way. He was content to sit in one spot on the floor playing with various small toys, and responded to all the nursery staff with smiles and vocalizations. He remained most responsive to KM and was most easily comforted by her. He quickly became characterized by the staff as a pleasant, easy-going, and tolerant baby, responsive to people, accepting of toys but not especially interested in going after things that were not within reach. He rarely cried in distress but would grit his teeth and look serious when anxious.

David was a more comfortable baby than some of the others. While discriminating among people in terms of degree of responsiveness, he seemed to assume that everyone meant well and could be trusted to take care of him.

Three weeks later (age 9 months): When David's mother carried him into the room, KM greeted him and held out her arms in a come-to-me gesture. He smiled at her, then playfully turned back to his mother. He did this two or three times, as though playing a little game before he went to KM. All three of them seemed to enjoy it, and afterward he seemed ready to let his mother leave. When Eileen, his sitter, came for him in the afternoon he recognized her immediately, smiled, and began to crawl toward her.

Turning first to KM and then back to his mother was a kind of game frequently seen in babies of this age. At one level it can be regarded as social play, which flourishes when adults are responsive to it. Like the peek-a-boo game, it is one of the active ways of a baby's coping with the transition from mother to mother substitute. This transaction was helped also by David's perception of the friendly feelings between his mother and KM and their approval of him. Note also the functioning of recognitory memory in his greeting of Eileen.

Age 40 weeks (after a week's absence): David, in his mother's arms, was unresponsive to KM and other staff, in contrast to his usual behavior. It was as though he needed several minutes to get his bearings. When his mother put him down on the floor he cruised a bit, using the wall for support, and then smiled for the first time when HM, the cook, came into the hallway. She was a great favorite with the children. They spent time in her kitchen and she saw most of them many times during a day.

Note the difference in David's behavior on arrival after a week's absence from KM and the center. Only after several minutes of being there did he begin to feel at home again. This is a good example of how quickly, in the mind of a baby, the mental images of a person or place become dim when they are not strengthened by frequent exposure.

Following is a record of observations made during a stressful period in David's life. It presents a good example of one of the typical ways in which young children react to stress. It also shows the way we used the observations of the staff, discussions with parents, and consultation to solve problems.

When David was 14½ months old his mother took him out of town on a visit for two weeks. On his return, the daycare staff became concerned about what they considered a dramatic change in his behavior. He now cried and clung to his mother every morning when she brought him in, and when she left was solemn, preoccupied, and uninterested in his surroundings, and unresponsive to the adults. He seemed to have entirely lost his cheerfulness and spontaneity. He had virtually stopped using the words and jargon we had heard before. He played with toys in a desultory way and was passive, compliant, and undemanding. He would cry when put down for a nap and no longer seemed comforted by KM. His liveliness and animation would return briefly on occasion when his mother came to pick him up.

This situation went on for about two weeks before the staff asked for assistance, having tried without success to help him. A plan was instituted immediately, to which he responded with reasonable promptness; after two to three weeks he was again in much better shape. An observation recorded on the second day of the plan illustrates the change: Ms. Ferris was asked to stay with David for a while and he smiled and laughed happily while she pushed him in a swing. When the children and staff moved into the small backyard he played on the slide with obvious pleasure while she sat nearby. When Greg went over to her and tried to take her pocketbook, David moved to his mother at once, pushed his way between her and Greg, and would not leave her for two or three minutes. With her help he then played in the sandbox, looking at her occasionally. At one point he climbed out of the sandbox and started toward her, but before he reached her seemed to change his mind and returned to the sandbox to play happily again. When she was ready to go she spoke to him but he did not respond. She told him good-bye and said that she was going now but would be back later and he toddled in her direction. KM took his hand and walked him to the gate with his mother and then picked him up as his mother left, waving good-bye to him. He did not object to her leaving and resumed his play in the yard, pushing the stroller, after she had left.

This routine was continued for about two weeks, his mother gradually diminishing the amount of time that she stayed until he was able to let her go immediately when she brought him in. He became happier, more talkative and responsive, more involved in play and regained most his spontaneity.

The consultant who visited the nursery to observe David when the staff expressed concern and perplexity about his change in behavior was of the opinion that David was, at this point, suffering while away from his mother and that the center, which he had formerly enjoyed and felt safe in, no longer was a place of comfort, security, and interest for him. Instead, he went through the day with a woodenness and diminished responsiveness that suggested his mind was elsewhere. We learned from his mother that while he had been with her throughout the trip and had apparently tolerated it well enough, on their return home, because she was exhausted and somewhat upset herself, his mother was less able than usual to be aware of his needs. She must have seemed quite different to him. It was fortunate for David that his mother could understand, when it was discussed with her, that he might be feeling unsure of her and that she was able to accept our request that she arrange to come early each day and stay with him for a time prior to going to work.

David's unresponsiveness to staff in spite of their best efforts to make things attractive and enjoyable for him after a week or so resulted in their feeling rejected by him. They said they no longer found him appealing and expressed some annoyance because they were indeed working very hard to make things all right for him. However, they were gratified at the promptness with which David began to respond to the plan. (We would not have been surprised had it taken somewhat longer.) His mother's presence both in the rooms and on the playground with him had a very salutary effect not only on David's behavior but, not surprisingly, on her and the daycare staff. Her being around in this informal way gave staff an opportunity to know her better and for her to know them better, and it clearly enhanced feelings of mutual understanding and friendliness.

This episode shows the importance of trying to keep on top of such situations and acting to correct difficulties before they get worse. In this case not only might David have suffered for a longer period had there not been some attempt to solve the problem, but his behavior, if not understood by the staff, could also have given rise to prolonged difficulties between himself and the staff. Such difficulties interfere with the alleviation of the problem just as set patterns of behavior make it difficult to improve the relationship between a child and his own parent.

Two children, Linda Davis and Yvonne Baird, entered daycare early in their second year. Each showed typical, though different, responses of toddlers.

Linda entered daycare at the age of 14 months, when she had just begun to walk and was still moderately unsteady. She had a few single words and fairly well developed jargon. She brought her blanket every day and it seemed to comfort her when she was unhappy. In the beginning, she would drag her blanket around after her crying dolefully a great deal. When not crying she often had a bewildered expression on her face and mouthed, rather than played with, most of the toys. She was responsive to affection and interest from adults and, indeed, seemed hungry for affection. About the third week she became ill with diarrhea and during that period cried even more and wanted to be held almost constantly. Even so, it was difficult to comfort her. While she gradually adapted, for many weeks she seemed confused, and her mood was either somber or actively miserable, though there were periods of enjoyment of some of the activities and particularly of interaction with adults. It was easy to recognize when Linda felt under stress because she reacted usually by crying and often crying very loudly. Other children reacted to stress more silently and their anxiety was as a result more difficult to discern.

Yvonne entered the Center at the age of 16 months. Because her mother, Mrs. Baird, needed to work, she had had four or five different caretakers prior to that time. She seemed to be generally a rather sober and thoughtful child who, however, would respond with smiling animation when especially pleased about something. She was usually very responsive to physical demonstrations of affection from a person with whom she was comfortable. She never cried when her mother left but was quite solemn and would not respond to her mother's good-bye. She would not even look at her. For several months, when her mother came for her in the afternoon Yvonne ignored her and made no move toward her, although we gradually became aware that she became freer and happier in later afternoon, as if anticipating her mother's arrival. Yvonne's ignoring her was distressing to her mother and made her feel that her child did not miss her. At the beginning of the year Yvonne took extremely long naps (three or four hours) and after a time we realized that the excessive sleeping probably was Yvonne's way of trying to cope with the long day away from home. Her security in our setting grew gradually, and at about three months after admission Yvonne would watch her mother leave in the morning, say good-bye to her, and greet her in the afternoon by running to her and reaching out her arms and smiling.

The following observations were all made on the same day early in September when the children were returning to the center after a month's vacation. The children described are Joan, age 20 months; Paul, 21 months; Larry, 22 months; and Curtis, 24 months. Their reactions are all considered normal for the age and situation, but one also sees their highly individual styles of responding both to the stress and to efforts to help them.

Joan, age 20 months, returned after a month's vacation. Her mother remained with her for forty-five minutes. Joan seemed shy. She made several little forays into various parts of the room where there were toys and other children and teachers, frequently looking back at her mother or speaking to her. Occasionally she went back to lean against her or crawl up on her lap. Then she and her mother sat at a table with one of the teachers, who helped Joan play with a toy mailbox and some other toys. She watched the other children and adults and occasionally called the name of a toy she held or saw. Her mother told her after about forty-five minutes that she had to go to work and would see her later. Joan and MD walked her to the door; MD picked Joan up and said, "Say good-bye to mommy." Joan whined, "Oh, mommy," as her mother said good-bye. MD said, "Mommy will be back; let's go find something to play with." Joan looked sober for a few moments but was soon captured by the sight of Curtis enjoying the rocking boat and went to join him.

Joan's mothers was one who often stayed around for ten or fifteen minutes in the morning chatting or watching the children, partly because she en-

joyed doing so. On this occasion, however, realizing that after a month away from the center Joan would need more of her time, she had arranged to stay longer. The observation shows Joan's gradual coping with her return to the center. For several minutes she regulated her own coming and going to and away from her mother. When her mother had to go, a teacher went with Joan and her mother to the door and helped them say goodbye to each other. She repeated what Joan's mother said, assuring Joan that her mother would be back, and helped her find something to do. As she became actively involved in the rocking boat, her pleasure in the rhythmical movement was apparent and she had apparently successfully coped with the mother's leaving.

Larry, age 22 months, was crying as he entered the room with his mother. His crying subsided as they were greeted by MD, but was resumed as his mother left rather abruptly. MD succeeded in getting him briefly interested in the housekeeping corner, but when he resumed crying she took him on her lap, talking to him comfortingly. He appeared limp and apathetic. He became very quiet and attentive for about fifteen minutes as she read to him. Then she helped him get interested in a table with dishes and pots, and as he began to play he asked, "Where's mommy?" MD responded, "She has gone to work, Larry; she'll come back after you have played and had your lunch and your nap." Larry asked again immediately, "Where's mommy?" The teacher repeated what she had just said. Larry, seeming a bit more free now, became involved in playing with the pots and pans and dishes in the housekeeping corner quite busily, smiling to himself occasionally. At this point he was able to play with apparent enjoyment without needing the teacher. When he heard another child cry, he stopped playing to look at him, walked across the room to pick up a play lunch box, and went back to the housekeeping corner to what he was doing.

From the time Larry first entered, at age 16½ months, he showed more signs of distress than any of the other children at separation from his mother. Part of his difficulty in adjusting appeared to be related to the irregularity of his attendance. However, more important was the fact that Larry's mother, who had taken a part-time job, had almost as much trouble separating from him as he did from her. In her behavior she gave him mixed signals: one message said she wanted to be at the center and make use of the program and that she was angry when he cried about it, another message said she didn't want to leave him and could hardly bear his becoming attached to someone else. Note that Larry was at first unable to be interested in any of the opportunities for playing actively and needed the lap and comforting talk of the teacher. As she read to him, he gradually regained his equilibrium, and showed some readiness for more active play.

She stayed nearby, however, sensing that he was still in need of a good deal of support, and when very soon he asked about his mother he was able to listen to the answer, though he needed to be told twice. The teacher's behavior was determined by her judgment of his needs from moment to moment.

On the same day, Curtis Banks, age 24 months, arrived with his grandfather and immediately sought out KB, his favorite teacher, who was there to greet him. Though he had not seen her for a month he seemed to recognize her promptly and stuck close to her much of the morning. With her help he played with some of the toys, choosing to remain uninvolved with the other children, and not talking much. When Paul began to cry at his mother's leaving and MD tried to comfort him, Curtis watched closely, stopping what he was doing. KB, noting Curtis's soberness, explained to him, "Paul is crying because he didn't want his mommy to go. Mrs. D will help him feel better." Curtis played for a while on the rug with several toys and then took KB over to the rocking boat. She sang to him as he rocked with a pleased expression on his face. Curtis now seemed quite cheerful, got a hat and suitcase from the dress-up corner, put on the hat and some gloves and said "hat." Joan also put on a hat; they looked at each other and giggled.

Curtis had first entered daycare at age 13 months. He had reacted with silence and apathy, which took several months to alleviate. Gradually, and primarily through establishing a close relationship with KB, he became more lively, more animated, more comfortable, and more actively involved in learning and in interaction with others. Note that on this morning he seemed to recognize KB immediately after the month's absence and that she made herself available to him as long as he needed her. This sequence illustrates our belief that having a person whom the child knows and trusts free to spend time with him reduces the stress of separation from home and readjustment to the center.

At the end of the day, Jackie, age 19 months, along with Steven and Paul, was happily dancing and swaying to the music of a lively record. Jackie also periodically approached JR, playfully touching or tapping her lightly, then backing away, giggling and laughing when she responded to him. All this time he was holding a bottle and drinking juice from it. When his father arrived and greeted him, Jackie smiled with delight, then turned his back and playfully ran toward JR. Giggling excitedly, he clutched her around the knees; she laughingly boosted him over the gate to his father, who greeted him warmly. Soon they were smiling and enjoying each other.

Jackie's reactions are familiar ones, both his pleasure at seeing his father and his running away, which was clearly a game in which part of the fun was being caught. Note that both the father and the staff member were able to enter with pleasure into Jackie's way of handling the reunion. Had they become angry at his game, the occasion might well have become one for tears.

In conclusion, we hold that the adults in daycare as well as the children must in a continuous way work at the central issue of separation. For parent and child the psychological work to be done centers around hundreds of experiences of parting and reunion, of being separate and together. Their personal vulnerabilities and capacities for mastery and their relationships to each other influence how they will deal with the feelings engendered. The work of the daycare staff is to assist parents and children in this ongoing, many-faceted adaptive effort. In so doing they too bring varying capacities and vulnerabilities. They require from the leaders of the program a structure, an orientation, a plan of action, and expertise, which facilitate the use of human relationships in providing a helpful service.

CHAPTER 6

Providing a Nurturing Environment

In planning the children's programs we began with a conception of the specific developmental needs of young children, as set out below. We defined what we would have to do or provide in order to meet those needs. The central importance of the adult's relationship to the child is inherent in all of the statements to follow.

Physical Care

Physical care first of all involves protecting the child from dangers in the environment—from accidents, from exposure to physically dangerous agents. It involves careful nutritional planning, the prevention and treatment of illness, and a concern for the child's state of health. There should be a carefully worked out plan for medical and nursing assistance in the center. One or more staff members should be familiar with first aid measures. It is important that illnesses be recognized as promptly as possible, and this can be best assured through responsible observation of each child by his major caregiver. The center should have a policy and a mechanism about handling illnesses and accidents, including communication with parents. Most people are well aware of the need to protect the child's physical health and most daycare centers are required to conform with local or state standards for space, and proper sanitation, and the building code and fire laws governing children's facilities.

The kind of physical care the child receives affects much more than his bodily health. First of all, his psychosocial development is also affected by the nature of this care. For the infant and the very young child, feeding, bathing, cleaning, diapering, and dressing are events around which many communications come to him from the caregiver. He hears her voice, sees her face, feels her touch. Very early, her interest in him, her concern for his comfort, her pleasure in being with him begin to be transmitted in these ordinary caring situations. Her handling may be gentle or rough, intrusive or adaptive to the child; it may reflect the mutuality of the relationship or its opposite. His body and its boundaries, its feelings and sensations, and the person and actions of the caregiver are the most constant and influential sources of his earliest learning. As he grows a little older his development is influenced either favorably or unfavorably by adult attitudes and behavior in regard to self-feeding and sphincter control. The first stages in the development of a sense of self, of a personal identity, involve awareness of the body self. The care the child receives and the attitudes of the caregivers toward his body strongly influence his later sense of identity and his feelings of self-worth.

When the child is old enough to talk, to run, to climb, to move out toward his environment, he at first has little judgment about realistic dangers, and he may protest the adult's limiting and protecting him when he is pursuing some attractive but dangerous object or activity. But so protected, he learns eventually to distinguish between what is safe and what is dangerous. The expectation that the important adults will keep him from harm is a characteristic of the well-cared-for young child and is one important aspect of his feeling valued.

The young child also benefits from seeing others being cared for. When another child is ill or hurt, young children feel concerned and are reassured when he is comforted or his injury is taken care of—even while they may also feel jealous of the added attention he receives. Moreover, such experiences help them to learn both to feel empathic with the child and to identify with the actions and attitudes of the caregiver.

Another part of caring for the child's body has to do with his encounters with the aggressive behavior of others and with his own hostile feelings as they emerge. Protection of the child's body from the aggressions of others and in turn preventing him from aggressing too strongly against others conveys interest in him. It also conveys an attitude that favorably influences his development toward control of his own impulses.

Finally, the concern for the child's physical well-being has great meaning for his parents. There is no doubt that a staff's commitment to good physical care goes far toward alleviating parental anxiety about the long hours they are separated from their children. It is a tangible demonstration of interest and concern that has great meaning for parent and child.

A Supportive Physical Environment

The physical environment of the facility for children must, first of all, be a safe one, and one in which parents can feel confidence. Much more than that, however, is included in what we consider a good physical environment. That environment either limits or facilitates the children's programs. The rooms may be too large, too small, too barren, too cluttered, too open, too chopped up, too noisy, or in other ways inappropriate. If the physical facility is grossly inadequate, staff cannot function well, and making the children's experiences rich and appropriate will be very difficult. But one can improve the environment, even if it is, as most such places are and as ours surely was, far from ideal. Space, materials, colors, and equipment in the children's room can be arranged to support learning, to optimize opportunities for perceiving, for acting, for having a good day, according to what that means for children of varying ages. Outdoor space or the neighborhood outside the center can be used to expand horizons, to vary experiences in a beneficial manner. The kitchen, the laundry, the workshop, the secretary's office, and other rooms that are mainly the domain of adults can be incorporated into the child's experience. The physical environment can be used flexibly to individualize a child's program.

Two opposite attitudes are often seen as more daycare centers are planned. One is that almost any building will do. Many buildings that are seriously offered, and seriously considered by harassed planners, are about as favorable for a good child-care program as the moon is as a home for mankind. The other attitude is that if the physical environment is a good one, the people who provide the care are relatively unimportant. Nothing could be further from the truth. The facilitating physical environment only enables a good staff to plan and carry out good programs for children with greater effectiveness.

Responsiveness to Individual Needs

In theory, individualized care is a noncontroversial point. Good parents and good teachers have always been aware of the need for it. Good clinicians expect that treatment will have to be individualized in accordance with the age, the health, the idiosyncrasies of the patient. But in practice, it takes a very strong belief in its importance to provide a favorable amount of individualization for children in group daycare. The staff of a daycare center must find ways to respond to the needs of individual children and families as they arise; such responsiveness is absolutely indispensable in conducting programs geared to developmental needs.

A commitment to individualized care is an important determinant of the number and kind of staff: Most of the daycare directors with whom we have spoken know that they do not have enough staff to allow for needed individualization—indeed, there are often not enough adults to conduct much more than a protection-from-physical-danger program. The concern they have expressed is abundantly confirmed in many visits we have made to a variety of centers. But individualization requires more than a favorable staff/child ratio; it requires a readiness to be flexible, a high regard for the individuality of the child, a willingness and ability to observe, reflect, and plan anew, and the availability of staff with a variety of competencies. It places enormous stress on the adaptive capacities of the staff.

Opportunities to Act upon His Environment

The child's acting upon his environment is one of the processes through which physical, intellectual, and psychosocial development occur. The significance of activity in the development of motor competence, the importance of the active repetition of the passive experience as a psychic mechanism, the manipulation of objects as a condition for the development of sensorimotor intelligence, the ability to mobilize physical and mental initiative—all these reflect the role of activity as an essential factor in development and learning. The capacity to initiate motor and mental activity is partly determined by the basic biochemical and structural organization of the central nervous system; it is also influenced in crucially important ways by experience.

This need influences program planning in many ways, ranging from providing opportunities that allow the child to act according to his preferences of a given moment to the planning of quite detailed experiences that are meant to evoke specific intellectual, social, emotional, or motoric activity. At a particular time, for example, a space might be arranged in which a child can creep about the floor, practicing this skill while going toward whatever object or person might look attractive to him; a child might be helped to say a word clearly or to complete a puzzle or to think his way through a problem; he might be helped to make connections between body language and spoken language or thought, to say he is afraid or sad or happy, or to make a social overture to another child. Responsive people who value the child stimulate increased competence. They help him invest physical and mental energy in the kinds of skills, communication, expression of feelings, and ways of coping that are especially useful to his developmental progress.

The ability to be active in relation to his external world influences and is closely related to his increasingly complex internal world of thought and feeling. Gradually he comes to learn that he has choices to make, options to exercise, activities to initiate; he realizes that not only the powerful adult, but he, too, can choose and influence the environment of which he is a part. Some things he must be taught or told; many others he must be allowed to discover for himself.

An Enriching Affective Atmosphere

Not only the presence and behavior of adults, but also their feelings and the atmosphere of the daycare center are enormously important in their effect upon the children and their parents. The atmosphere can be expected to be at times serene, at others light and playful; at times demanding and at others tolerant; mixtures of joyful noise and unhappy crying are not unusual. The room may hum with the sounds and appearance of children seriously absorbed in an interesting activity; at other times it may be filled with excitement that is both frightening and exhilarating to the child. Anxiety and hostility can be so thick as to pervade the room; conversely an atmosphere of friendliness and good will is just as apparent.

The affective atmosphere cannot be planned or scheduled. However, it *can* be thought about and even worked on as staff members live their days with children and with each other. The responsibility for the atmosphere resides in large part in the leadership of the program. It is of enormous importance that the leaders make a conscious and continuous effort to be aware of, to take frequent readings of the emotional atmosphere. When staff members have been chosen for their personality characteristics as well as their knowledge of children, when there are agreed-upon ways of working out the difficulties among adults that are bound to arise, when the staff are supported by their supervisors and the director in their work with the children, and when most of the time they like what they are doing, then the atmosphere is usually favorable. In such a setting the amount of spillover from the adults' private lives, especially in times of stress, can be lessened, so that staff do not frighten or mystify the children by inappropriately making them the target of intense feelings that belong elsewhere. What is done when the balance shifts from a supportive to a tense and anxiety-producing atmosphere depends, of course, upon whether the source of trouble, as expressed in adult behavior, can be identified and alleviated.

In emphasizing the importance of the affective atmosphere we do not separate the cognitive and emotional aspects of the child's life. There is always an important element of perception and cognition in the child's feelings and in his relationships. Similarly, there are affective influences on all his intellectual activities. Cognitive and affective development occur as a result of an integrated process of development. In general, the younger the child the more apparent is the interdependence of emotion and intellect, and neither should be neglected in supporting the child's best development.

A Speaking Social Partner

Speech development occurs as a result of the interaction between the child's innate biological equipment and his experiences. It is quite important that children not only hear adults and older children talking, but that adults speak directly to them. The speech of the adult is one of the principal channels through which information comes to the infant and young child about himself and his world, who he is, how he feels, what he is doing, who others are, and so on. Even in early infancy being talked to is important, because it reinforces and stimulates the child's inherent tendency to vocalize and babble and increases his social responsiveness and interest. A little later, being spoken to is one of the important elements in his attaching meaning to the sounds he makes. The speech of the adult is one of the important carriers of feelings through its inflection, tone, and rhythm as well as its informational content.

It is generally recognized that in daycare settings children over a year old need to be helped to talk, largely through speaking with them. Even earlier, however, long before children are expected to give verbal responses, adults in such a setting need to develop the habit of talking to them, for all the reasons mentioned above. Nonverbal communications that are expressed in holding or touching a child, through gestures, eye contact, and facial expressions are important, too, and it should be acknowledged that one can be a good communicator with babies without a great deal of talk. However, when adults do not speak with children in their care, they tend to become distracted or preoccupied with thoughts unconnected with the child, and he loses some of the feeling of the adult's interest and involvement. Thus, it is well to encourage adults to talk with children, and not to remain silent or talk exclusively to one another. Infants and especially toddlers become silent if adults are. The animation of the atmosphere is dramatically linked to speech. This does not mean, of course, that children should be bombarded with continuous talk.

Especially from the second year on, in concert with intrinsic maturational processes, the language of the adult is important in facilitating the development of logical thought and the beginning understanding of symbols. Acquiring names of people and of things and the use of speech to communicate needs, feelings, and ideas are almost always delayed in environments in which adults do not talk with children.

Consistency and Repetition; Variety and Contrast

An environment in which consistency and repetition are conspicuous elements is quite important in organizing and supporting a child's development. Consistency in the way a child is cared for and the repetition of experience of being fed, moved, touched, talked to, or having things to look at, feel, and listen to are crucial factors in stimulating and organizing development. Consistency and repetition help to create within the infant physical and mental states that facilitate learning and adaptation. Ideally, such consistency is founded on the presence of one person who provides steady nurturing day after day. The infant who comes into daycare already has at least one such person in his mother, and must adapt to at least two other people in the center who take care of him often for long hours a day, five days a week. That this puts an additional stress on his adaptive capacities seems inevitable, and is a strong argument for limiting the number of caregivers he has in the center. For the older child, too, it is important that the daycare program provide a predictable human environment and a familiar physical setting.

Too often, in an attempt to provide consistent care, a rigid schedule of meals, naps, play periods, and so on, is arranged. The pattern or routine of a day in the center (or at home) is at first organized around fulfilling the child's needs for food and comfort, with playtime and rest time provided in between. The infant's biological rhythms help us to select, for example, the feeding times. Later, when the child is older, he becomes aware of the usual pattern of a day and it seems to be beneficial to his development that certain events be predictable. But while some scheduling is supportive, the consistency of which we speak resides primarily in the adult, not in the clock. We do not mean that any caregiver in a daycare center, nor for that matter any skilled mother at home with the child, is going to be consistent to the point of being automatic and unvarying in her behavior. We are speaking of the personal qualities, of ways of taking care of a child, and of social interactions with him that are consistently affectionate enough that the adult becomes recognizable, predictable, and trustworthy in the child's mind.

Variety and contrast are important, too, when they take place within an atmosphere created by consistency and repetition. Under these conditions, variety and contrast sharpen a young child's perception and awareness, creating those mild tension states that call for adaptive response. As long as the tension state is not so great as to overwhelm and disorganize the child, it serves as a stimulus to development. A monotonous, bland environment fails to meet a child's needs because it does not ask of him that he look, listen, move, feel, or in other ways use his faculties.

Variety and contrast might mean a new food at mealtime, a new picture, mobile, or other object in the visual environment of the infant, a new person who accompanies a familiar one; it might mean a new activity within the room or outside; a ride, a walk, a small trip; a new toy or other play material; a new song or dance, a new dress, coiffure, or glasses on a familiar person. It has been our experience that when the center is well staffed it is not difficult to encourage adults to provide adequate variety in the child's day. On the contrary, especially in relation to playthings and activities, adults get bored much more often than the children do. The child's love of repetition may make him at times an uninteresting companion. When an adult has, at the child's insistence, looked at the same book with him every day for weeks or played with the same toy or gone through the same game of hide-and-seek, she may well be more eager than he is for something new. When a center is understaffed, however, the danger is that the day will become so rigidly routinized that monotony prevails and that what contrast occurs will most often be an eruption of anger or aggression from children and adults that spoil the learning environment and creates a disturbing rather than supportive emotional atmosphere.

Toys and Other Playthings

While a responsive human partner is crucial to the young child's development, he has need also for toys and other playthings that he can use with others and independently. Toys bring even to the young infant a variety of stimuli and challenges because of their color, texture, form, size, and other physical properties. Much has been written in recent years about suitable toys for infants and young children and how these toys stimulate intellectual development. There is indeed a rationale, based upon developmental tendencies, for the selection of toys that are likely to appeal to children of various ages, and there is considerable data on how they use them.

Piaget (1952) has emphasized the indispensable part that the child's attention to and manipulation of toys plays in the early phases of intellectual development. In addition to the usefulness of toys for intellectual growth, they serve an important function in the child's emotional life. One of their advantages is their neutrality: the child can use a toy in many ways to work out his feelings and ideas without evoking an emotional response from it. He can feel himself to be in control of the toy; he gradually learns that he not only controls what happens but is personally responsible for it, that is, that his act has consequences. In the long process the child goes through in learning to know himself and his environment, the opportunity to play with toys and other inanimate objects has an importance place.

Quiet Moments

In a daycare setting and indeed in many families it may be difficult to arrange for the child to have quiet times. Every child needs peaceful waking moments. They help to replenish his mental and physical energies and allow him increasingly to be aware that he has an inner world of thought, fantasy, and feeling. A constantly stimulating, highly charged environment is not conducive to harmonious balance between the child's inner and outer worlds, and it adversely affects various aspects of his development, especially intellectual development and the process of learning to regulate his own behavior.

Planning the daycare setting to provide private, peaceful moments does not mean ignoring or isolating children. A center that is grossly under-staffed is more likely to have a situation in which the child is overstimulated from too much time with other children and too little protection by adults. In the midst of the crowd, if he can turn off the bedlam, he may do so for psychological survival. But his isolation may be bitter loneliness, not replenishment; mental apathy, not enrichment, a diminished rather than heightened awareness of himself and others.

Arranging a program that insures the child these important opportunities to be comfortably alone is not an easy task, for his peace of mind requires adult participation. Someone must decide whether a toddler put down for his nap can feel comfortable and at rest only if he knows that a benevolent adult is nearby; someone must arrange that there are quiet corners, boxes, curtains, barriers into which a child can retire if he chooses, or can be helped to retire to if he is getting too excited. Someone must know each child well enough to decide when he needs to be held, to be taken for a walk alone, or simply to play quietly in the presence of an adult or an-other child. The unobtrusively watchful eye, the ear attuned to the sounds of contentment or distress are universal and essential qualities of those who nurture children well.

Limits, Prohibitions, and Expectations for Conformity

Harshness, coldness, and severe punishment have no place in rearing the young child. But neither can development proceed in a healthy way for a child whose caregivers are overindulgent, excessively permissive, or very inconsistent in what they require of him. He needs to have limits and requirements clearly defined, just as he needs other things to optimize his development, and setting reasonable limits, imposing reasonable require-ments are just as much a part of loving a child as are feeding, cuddling, and speaking to him. By benevolently but clearly regulating the child's be-havior the adult helps him gradually to take over responsibility for self-regulation.

In the long process of teaching and socializing the child, every society sets certain limits and prohibitions, makes certain demands for compliance, communicates its expectations for behavior. Whatever society he is a part of requires that at the very least he develop a certain competence in social interaction and that he be able to control his own body and behavior. In our society it is important for the child's development that he learn to wait for things, to defer immediate gratification of his own needs and wishes, and eventually to acknowledge the needs and rights of others. Such complex knowledge is acquired slowly, and is most effectively conveyed through the kind of child rearing that acknowledges that the process is gradual and uneven at best. Moreover, it appears to be most constructively imparted to the child if the necessary training takes place in an atmosphere of affectionate attention. Harsh behavior, unloving and impersonal attitudes on the part of adults do not facilitate this process for the young child; they interfere with it.

A baby, for example, begins to be able to cope with waiting for something he wants or needs when he has developed a feeling of trust that his parent is going to take care of him. Such trust is based upon repeated experiences in which he has been fed when he was hungry, soothed when he was uncomfortable, and had other needs responded to appropriately. He comes to accept and benefit from the limits set for him if he believes the adults responsible for him are trustworthy and are seeing to his needs. His wish to please his parents, to have their love and approval, is the most powerful influence they have in his training and socialization.

However, it seems to be a very difficult thing for many parents and other adult caregivers to accept the long-term and gradual nature of this process in the face of their own goals and expectations for the child. If they especially value neatness and orderliness, they may begin to impose demands on the child long before he has the capacity to be a neat eater, long before he can acquire sphincter control, be expected to clean his hands and face, or be responsible for picking up his toys. If they value the ability to fight back, they may begin to introduce hitting games at a time when the child is simply overwhelmed or frightened by them. If they strongly disapprove of aggressive activity or language, they may stamp out, to the child's detriment, the expressions of normal, healthy aggressive feelings. Their goals usually are appropriate, but the timing and intensity of their educational measures may be such that they are ineffective or that the child pays too high a price either for conformity or rebellion. It is possible for those who understand children and their development to help parents to be reasonable and supportive to the child while he acquires gradually the capacity to regulate his social behavior. This is one of the ways in which a daycare staff can make a positive contribution to the child's development.

The foregoing, then, were needs we addressed in planning and carrying out our programs for the children. We turn now to a description of these programs, first of that for infants and toddlers, and then of that for older preschool children. A resumé of the specific arrangements for the daily operation of Children's House is given in Appendix 1.

CHAPTER 7

The Day-to-Day Experience for Infants and Toddlers

How does one translate principles and recommendations into practice? How do infants and toddlers behave in a daycare setting and how do adults respond? What specific daily experiences can be planned that follow developmentally based recommendations? What does it look like when an adult is involved as a social partner or is providing physical care or is energizing a child to be interested in an object or an activity? What is involved in adults seeing that a child has an opportunity to practice emerging skills or that a favorable balance is maintained between experiences of pleasure and those of frustration? What are some details of the transactions through which an adult recognizes and responds to a young child's emotional needs?

We hope to show that infant care that is responsive to developmental needs *can* be thoughtfully planned, if based upon solid knowledge of children and carefully individualized. There is no other time in the child's life when there is so much discussion about the caregiver's "doing what comes naturally" or "following her intuition." Possibly the tendency to resort to nonspecific advice or to sentimental statements about maternal instinct has reflected two different factors. First, there is traditional respect for maternal wisdom, based upon the expectation that the biological relationship between mother and infant, which usually facilitates the establishment of a firm bond between them, will also enable her to know how to take good care of her baby. Second, there has been the difficulty of describing in precise language some of the interactions of mother and infant that are crucial for the child's development. But in regard to the first, it now is certain that we have been wrong in our blissful assumption that the biological fact of giving birth says something about a woman's readiness or aptitude for nurturing a child; such aptitude is absorbed or learned both long before and during the child-rearing experience. In regard to the second, many of the complicated communications between mother and infant, as well as many of the details of care can at least be illustrated in a way that should be of use to others.

Millions of children have grown up well without any kind of professional intervention and many will continue to do so. In group daycare, however, one cannot affort to rely entirely on the knowledge and common sense of women who have reared children successfully, valuable as that experience is. The kind of attachment such a successful caregiver offers, while often warm, affectionate, and genuinely interested, does not match the strength of a devoted mother's care for her own child. Furthermore, the daycare staff member must take care of more than one infant at a time. She must therefore learn about development in general, and become skilled in recognizing different infants' readiness for a new experience or the various ways in which fatigue, hunger, or other distress may be reflected in behavior. A woman who has been able to read her own child sensitively and provide him with excellent care may not be able to do this for another woman's child, unless she is helped to observe the infant and herself in the process of caregiving. Moreover, those who would be the teachers of other caregivers need to teach, both by demonstration and by conceptualizing, the art and science of infant care.

While we were carrying out, as best we could, a developmentally supportive program of care and education, we recorded many observations of child and adult behavior. Some of these observations will be used to try to convey a picture of the children and how the caregiver-teachers performed their role. We have organized the observations to reflect either expectable developmental phenomena or familiar situations in the life of the child. It is important that the reader be aware of the age of the child at each observation and tie that in with expectable behavior, skills, feelings, and responses to adults, and adult responses to the child. We hope that descriptions are vivid enough to involve the reader in thinking about children and what their behavior might mean, and what adults were trying to do, with particular reference to the principles described at the beginning of the Introduction.

We have only occasionally used examples of behavior that would be considered unusual or deviant and have said when we have done so. All the rest are descriptions of normal behavior in a particular kind of daycare program.

Young Children at Play

The significance of what is called play for learning in infancy and early childhood has been the subject of many publications. People have referred to play variously as the child's work, as a source of pleasure, as important to general learning, as a means of specifically stimulating intellectual growth, as a way for the child to express and become aware of his own feelings and those of others.

Play, both with and without toys, is important for physical, emotional, and intellectual development. When it is rich and age appropriate, it is both a sign of healthy development and a facilitator of further progress. The physical environment and objects in it should be arranged for children in a way that encourages them to play in accordance with their developmental tendencies and needs. In a setting in which there are children of varying interests and needs, much attention must be given to how to meet both phase-specific and individual needs. Moreover, since needs change, considerable adaptability of staff and program are necessary.

Adults are of enormous significance in making the child's play possible. They are important as arrangers of the environment, as indicated above. They are also partners in play. This partnership ranges widely, even with the very young child, from a playful game of imitating sounds or peek-a-boo to play with a child as he makes sand pies, paints a picture, works a puzzle, manages the rocking horse, feeds his baby doll, and so on. Furthermore, the protective presence and social responsiveness of adults create an atmosphere in which the child is secure enough and stimulated enough to play. Adults are comforters, organizers, and sources of renewed energy. Through being available to comfort the child when he becomes upset and to provide respite when he is tired, adults minimize the disorganization that interferes with playful activity. While such resources are important when one is with a child alone, they are called upon even more often when young children are together in groups. Among the most difficult aspects of the child-care worker's role is supporting play without directing it, shifting between organizing a child's play for him, which is a frequent need, and allowing him to find and pursue his own interests.

Infants and toddlers gathered together in groups, while increasingly aware of one another in various ways, most often play alone or with an adult. A corollary is that they cannot usually play productively if there are many others of the same age competing for toys or for adults, or simply needing help at the same time. The implications for staff and program will be illustrated.

Infants (to 15 months)

Throughout the first year and a bit beyond, as indicated elsewhere, much of the baby's play goes on in relation to the care of his body, i.e., while he is being fed, bathed, changed, cuddled, and put to sleep. Play begins in interaction with an adult and gradually is extended to the child's use of toys and of his own body in spontaneous, self-initiated activity as well as in activities the adult makes attractive to him.

Planning a program for infants' playtimes is more informal, more fluid, and necessarily involves less specific scheduling than is appropriate for older children. While in working with young children of every age good teachers are alert to what captures a child's interest and how to use that to teach him, at no time is this attitude and alertness more important than in the earliest years. Nonetheless, when taking care of several infants in daycare one must thoughtfully plan experiences over and beyond their bodily care. Among these are physical activity, toys to look at and manipulate, social stimulation, and conversation.

Our observations of infants up to fifteen months are grouped together under various categories to illustrate typical developmental events as well as the role of the caregiving adult who is also the baby's teacher.

Looking, Moving, and Grasping

From the time they were admitted to daycare, the young infants at Children's House were provided with variety in their visual environment through the use of mobiles, pictures, and changes of position. Playtime was sometimes in a crib, sometimes in someone's arms or in a supportive chair, sometimes on a rug or mat on the floor, sometimes out of doors on a blanket. The observations begin with two very different infants and illustrate early responses to outside stimuli.

At 3 months Leslie was competent for her age in motor skills. She had good head control, and while lying on her belly could elevate her torso and lean on her forearms as she looked around the room. While lying on her back she could almost, but not quite, turn all the way over. She could not yet reach out to grasp toys, but enjoyed looking at a brightly colored mobile or toys near her on the mat. At 3½ months, after repeated attempts, she was able to grasp the dangling figures of a mobile and bring them to her mouth for additional exploration with her lips and tongue, and bat them around, vocalizing or breathing excitedly.

Leslie was free to look at or away from the mobiles and toys as she chose, and often her visual activity was centered on the adults in the room. This example is given mainly to illustrate the classical and normal interest in looking, and how looking can evoke other reactions, such as excited breathing and rudimentary attempts to grasp or move toward an attractive stimulus. There was no doubt that Leslie's interest and energy were directed toward these objects.

By 4 months Leslie was described as an exceptionally strong, vigorous, active baby. She bounced up and down while sitting or while being supported in a standing position on an adult's lap. She could reach for, grasp, and wave objects, and move her head and body to view things that interested her.

Several playthings were placed near Leslie wherever she was: in her crib, sitting in the infant's seat, or lying on her belly on the floor. She was offered brightly colored rattles, soft squeeze toys that made a squeaking sound, hard rubber teething rings, and fluffy, stuffed, cloth toys. These provided an assortment of shapes, sizes, colors, textures, and densities, which afforded Leslie a variety of stimuli and challenges from which she could learn. By changing the toys from time to time, her caregiver introduced variety and contrast.

Terry, at age 4 months, was a tense, jittery baby who had great visual interest in toys, but needed special help because of his tension.

Terry was excited by looking at toys and would clutch at them but could not grasp them. MB often held him on her lap and played with him with the toys, sponsoring their use through the social contact. She would hold various interesting toys in front of him, talk with him, and help him to handle them. At other times he was placed in the infant seat in his crib so that he could be very close to the mobile attached to the crib, and as it turned he could touch the bright sponge-rubber animals.

In contrast to Leslie, whose development permitted her to reach out and grasp the toys very soon after she manifested interest in them, Terry needed considerable assistance from the adult in order to grasp and feel the toys. We did not press him to manipulate toys for the sake of manipulation but sponsored his use of them because helping him to be active with them would facilitate voluntary muscle activity and alleviate some of the muscular and psychological tension we thought he was feeling at this time. He seemed tense in part because his motor abilities were lagging behind his visual discrimination and his attraction to his environment.

When infants are well-cared for and reasonably comfortable they are attracted not only to people, but to a variety of things in the environment. These outside things, if they appear in the right place at the right time— i.e., when the child is developmentally ready—can encourage certain developmental achievements.

The first time Leslie was observed to turn over from back to front was at at 4 months. She was lying clutching a blanket when she spied a bright green stuffed rabbit in the corner of her crib. She rolled to her side toward it, reached, grunted, wriggled and finally touched it with the back of her hand but because of her position could not grasp it. Continuing to look at the rabbit, she struggled and maneuvered until she was rolled over onto her belly and could grasp the toy. After this she could turn over any time she chose to do so.

Leslie would undoubtedly have learned to turn over without the lure of the toy, but the stimulus provided by the green rabbit probably facilitated the emergence of this skill. This is a valid and simple illustration of one kind of developmental event: the child was maturationally ready to acquire this motor skill, but it was called forth by her interest in grasping the attractive toy. In a barren environment that provides many fewer experiences of this kind, such motor skills are often delayed in their emergence and functional organization.

Mastery

It is difficult to overemphasize the importance of the intelligent, benevolent, and affectionate presence of the adult in optimizing an infant's development. Developmental progress occurs through a process of interaction between the child and his environment, especially with the adults who care for him. Experiences in which he acquires a new skill or masters some developmental task are a part of development. The adult should be able to judge his ability and readiness and decide how to help and support him. Here are two examples of how that can look.

Leslie age 9½ months, had just learned to take a few steps alone and had become interested in exploring outside the children's rooms. This day she spotted the open playroom door and eagerly crawled across the room, through the doorway, and into the front hall. JR followed her but did not interfere with her exploration. Leslie sat on the floor looking up the stairwell listening to the sounds from the typewriters upstairs, then seeming to decide in favor of the street scene in front of the house, crawled to the front door, pulled to stand, and looked through the glass. Much of the time she was saying "ba, ba, ba, ba." Seeming to have satisfied her curiosity she turned and crawled to the stairs, crawled up on the first one, picked up a stray bit of paper from the second, pulled to stand by holding on to the railing and stood there for a moment while she "talked" some more. She then crawled up three more stairs before stopping to look back at JR who was closely following her. Leslie was smiling and jabbering. JR smiled in response, saying, "Yes, you're pretty proud of yourself, aren't you?" As Leslie neared the top she turned around, looked back down the long flight of stairs, then reached toward the adult as if asking for support. JR steadied her while she negotiated the remaining two stairs. Once at the top, Leslie smiled happily and crawled like a streak into the secretaries' office, where she received an enthusiastic greeting.

JR was allowing Leslie in the course of her play to find and pursue her own interest. In so doing, she was supportive of Leslie's activity and interested in what she was doing, but was not directive or inhibiting. Allowing a child the freedom to be mobile, with supervision, was an important part of the program. In addition, by allowing brief sorties beyond the narrow confines of the playroom, variety and contrast could be provided within the stable environment of the daycare setting. We cannot be sure precisely what Leslie was learning from her brief exploration, but there are several possibilities: she was taking something in as she sat at the bottom of the stairs listening to the sounds from the outside; she was responding selectively to numerous stimuli by electing to investigate the front door first. When she "talked" and was responded to by JR she may have been learning something about communication through the use of language, and by reaching toward JR when the climb seemed perilous, she was acknowledging the need for help in coping with the situation by actively turning to an adult. When JR responded by offering support, Leslie may have felt something about trusting other people. Being permitted this kind of freedom probably aided her developing capacity for initiative, spontaneity, and curiosity. The activity probably enhanced her awareness of her body boundaries, contributing to her developing capacity to differentiate herself from others. Her feelings of pleasure in successful completion of the adventure, reinforced by JR, were obvious and probably enhanced her general feelings of well-being and self-confidence. In any case, this was another opportunity for Leslie to make use of her skills to actively master her environment, and it is virtually certain that by being encouraged to take this step toward autonomy and independence, she was learning something about self-management.

Jackie, almost 11 months, was crawling on the playroom floor, vocalizing as if communicating with Susan and Greg. He pulled to a stand on GM's leg, and as she supported him by holding one hand he walked across the room. He smiled and vocalized as he walked as though proud of himself, basking in GM's enthusiastic approval. Later, standing and holding onto the table he pivoted his torso sideways, then squatted slowly until he could reach the floor with his hand. He then quickly and gracefully got to his hands and knees and scooted across the floor to the cupboard underneath the sink where he pulled the door open and looked inside. Later in the morning GM brought a small scooter into the room and Jackie appropriated it immediately. He pushed it while crawling behind it, turned it over, examined it carefully, pulled to a stand on it and pushed it, walking behind. When it tipped over, causing him to fall, he was undaunted in continuing his pursuit. For ten or fifteen minutes he pushed, pulled, tipped over, and uprighted the scooter before discovering how to climb on it. Then, seated on it, he soon discovered how to push it backward. He was delighted with his newfound toy and GM responded to his pleasure with animation and encouraging comments. He smiled and gurgled, making almost continuous "oooh" sounds in a soft, happy voice.

One sees first in this episode Jackie's pleasure in walking with GM's support and the effect of her pleasure and encouragement. His curiosity appears to be expressed in his investigation first of the cupboard and later of the scooter. Jackie must have experienced pleasure in learning while observing the different things that happened to the scooter in relation to his manipulation of it. Freedom to use his initiative and curiosity was important; interference from another might have robbed him of the experience of examination, evaluation, trial, and mastery that are so clearly visible in this sequence. GM protected him from intrusion and encouraged him. There was no doubt about his pleasure in what he was doing or that he had learned something. An astronomer discovering a planet could not have been more eloquent in communicating the excitement and joy of discovery.

Learning about Other Infants

An infant's awareness and interest in adults is normally much greater than his interest in other infants. Adults are more constant and responsive, and become recognized relatively early by the child as those who provide for him. Nonetheless, when infants are together they do take notice of each other. The following examples show how Leslie, over a period of six weeks, went from rather impersonal behavior toward a child to highly personalized reactions. While the timing of such awareness may well be variable from one infant to another, the sequence revealed here is probably quite regular.

Leslie was 8 months old when Shaun, age 4 months, came into daycare. One day she was sitting on the floor in the playroom when KM brought Shaun into the room and placed him on the floor in an infant seat. Leslie watched Shaun intently, seeming to be fascinated by him, reached for him and patted his face and head with both hands, then put her mouth and tongue on his face and then on his head. She was not trying to bite him but was mouthing him in an exploratory manner. Shaun did not protest, nor did he try to avoid her.

Babies may be fascinated by other babies and we can only imagine what goes on in their minds as they look at each other. At this stage Leslie approached other children almost as though they were animated toys. Her way of familiarizing herself was to pat and lick the other children as she would any object that interested her. She probably had only a vague awareness that Shaun was a person like herself. In this example the feelings that later will give rise to aggressive behavior are not yet operative.

Leslie had become rather adept at getting what she wanted and avoiding what she didn't. Sitting on the floor with Terry one day, she watched him playing with an hourglass containing colorful beads. She looked intently, then reached over and took it from him. Terry did not protest and was handed an identical toy by JR. Leslie again observed Terry, dropped her own and again took his. This she did with four identical toys, always wanting the one Terry had. Finally he protested, squealing, but was unable to retain it against her pull. When he cried, JR, with a comment, stepped in to restore his property, separating them a little and seeing that each child had a toy.

Leslie, in taking Terry's toys away, was probably not competing with him at this time; nor did she necessarily want all of the toys for herself. It seems more likely that the toy Terry had was animated by his movement of it and thus was more attractive than her own toy. It was as though at this stage she was not aware of the sameness of the toys and did not realize that she could create the same visual display with her own. Terry's failure to protest for a time permitted her to continue. While one does not imagine that at this age she learned anything definite about the rights of others, in this exchange she did have to adapt to the adult's intervention. Terry was protected when it became clear he began to object to Leslie's acquisitive behavior.

In the following episode the interaction between David and Leslie seems much more personalized—i.e., there is greater awareness on Leslie's part of David as an agent to be contended with.

David and Leslie, both 9 to 10 months old, were sitting on the floor in the playroom, and David had a cup which Leslie wanted. She tried to pull it away from him but he didn't let go. She then grabbed his nose and tried to pinch it, and grabbed him by the shirt and pulled him toward her, making loud, scolding noises. He began to cry and dropped the cup, but she crawled away without it. Later she tried to take a ball from David, but he held on to it, and while she vocalized scoldingly at him, she let him alone. Still another time she took some linked tricolored rings away from David. He did nothing but look at her, but she waved the rings vigorously in front of him yelling crossly at him as though warning him not to try anything.

Unlike the episode in which Leslie took Terry's hourglass simply because it was attractive to her, now she seemed to see David as a threat to what she wanted. This kind of confrontation over the use of toys provides learning experiences for babies of a quality somewhat different from the experience gained through manipulation and exploration. They are interpersonal negotiations, which are important aspects of learning, and adults must act as moderators when needed. Dozens of episodes such as as these take place when little children are together. Many will escape observation, but many others can be handled in such a way that bit by bit children begin to be aware that others have needs and wishes too, and feelings of identification with others and sharing begin to occur. This, of course, is a very gradual process and spontaneous sharing comes only much later.

From early in the second year on, children learn much from imitating one another as well as adults. The following is one example of imitative play that was enjoyed by five toddlers.

Shaun, 14 months, and Greg, Leslie, Terry, and David, all 17 months old, were supposedly napping, but squeals and shrieks were heard coming from the room in which they slept. When JR looked in upon them they were all standing up in their cribs looking at one another. When one would make a particular sound, such as a shriek, a squeal, or a scream, the others imitated it. They played back and forth in this way for several minutes with the greatest pleasure. A little while later they were taken into the back yard, where a small plastic pool had been filled with water. As the first child was helped to get into the pool, he stood stiff-legged, leaned over and gingerly splashed the water which was a bit cool. Each of the other four in turn imitated this stiff-legged action; they also continued the imitation of sounds they had been engaged in earlier. Similarly, when Leslie climbed out by putting first one foot and then the other over the edge while holding onto the pool with both hands, David and Terry followed suit. They used the plastic cups and other small toys, filling and emptying the cups, watching the water trickle down as they poured repeatedly, sometimes in imitation of another, sometimes independently.

The children's pleasure in one another was quite apparent in this scene.

On warm days the pool was a source of great pleasure for the children. It required close supervision both to insure the safety of the children and to help them to enjoy it without infringing too greatly on one another. Children could crawl in and out of the pool at will, first enjoying the splashing or pouring and the sensuous pleasure of the water itself, then getting out to walk around the yard and play with other available toys or with the grass, sticks, leaves, pebbles, and other things they discovered on their tour. Picking up things, looking them over and putting them in a cup or small bucket could occupy several minutes at a stretch. Banging, running, or playing with the garden hose were other pleasurable activities. It was a time when the supervising adults did not expect to remain dry themselves and were there to keep the children safe and to arbitrate disputes.

Social Play and Conversation

Playful interaction with adults is initiated by well-cared-for infants beginning at around four to five months, when spontaneous social smiling and spontaneous vocalization are actively used to attract the adult's attention. From that point on, self-initiated contact by the infant becomes progressively more complicated and varied; it may include reaching out and tugging, handing a toy, performing little tricks that have evoked a positive response from others, and starting games like peek-a-boo or bye-bye that ask for a response. All this occurs before the baby is able to say anything more than mama or dada. Normally endowed infants who are badly cared for or who are not responded to socially by an adult develop few of these playful social responses and initiatives. Mutual imitation is an important element in this kind of development in infancy. Talking and singing to babies, smiling and gesturing to them, imitating and being imitated provide important learning experiences.

Leslie, age 8 months, was sitting on the floor of the nursery playing with colored plastic discs strung on a chain. Terry was being bathed in the nearby sink by MB while KM was folding clothes and putting them away in the closet. Leslie got the discs to her mouth, licked and bit them, rattled and banged them on the floor. Simultaneously she looked around at people in the room, smiling and vocalizing with happy squeals and "da da" sounds. KM, while continuing her task, responded to Leslie's happy vocalization by smiling and talking to her. When she started pat-a-cake and peek-a-boo games, Leslie happily imitated. She was very much involved with people and worked at entertaining them with her little tricks. For thirty or forty minutes before and during Terry's bath, Leslie engaged in all of these activities with a good deal of vigor and pleasure.

Although Leslie enjoyed social play very much, she could also be happy and satisfied through her own activity, as seen in her spontaneous use of toys, looking about, and movement. At this age Leslie seemed to learn about her environment by watching and listening, by touching, licking, moving, pushing, and banging. While the adults' presence in the room was important, they could be busy with other things. There was no need for them to carry on a continuous interaction, and in fact that would not have been desirable. The adults were aware of what Leslie was doing and were available to respond to contacts she initiated. Leslie could use their presence to facilitate her learning through play and occasional direct contacts with them.

While waiting for breakfast, Jackie, age 10½ months, was sitting on the floor playing with a toy telephone. As AN dialed it for him he held the receiver up to his ear and jabbered "da, da, da, da." AN conversed with him and he continued this game for two or three minutes with a mixture of seriousness and lightness, stopping occasionally to watch others in the room and the preparations for breakfast.

AN was clearly a partner in the play. She enabled him to keep it going by dialing the telephone and responding to his lively vocalizing by talking animatedly to him. There was no doubt that he had developed some sense of reciprocal activity: he knew when to speak and when to wait for her response.

Investigating and Experimenting

Long before the end of the first year infants demonstrate exploratory interest in toys and something that can be called curiosity about the environment. They can be seen looking, poking, inspecting, and manipulating things in a reflective, investigatory manner. Timing is important when introducing new activities or materials. A highly structured program that requires an infant or toddler to move from one activity to another by the adults' schedule rather than his own may be very much out of tune with his rhythms and interests. Ideally, adult introductions are made when a child has exhausted his own curiosity and initiative or when he needs an attractive stimulus to get him going.

In the following two examples both the infants' interest and the limits of their understanding are demonstrated.

Leslie and Terry, age 5 months, were sitting in the playpen with several toys. They were intently engaged with the toys while the adults were busy with other children. Leslie seemed oblivious of Terry's presence as she vigorously and repeatedly banged a rubber giraffe on the floor, apparently fascinated by the squeak her activity produced. When her attention was diverted by Terry's moving foot, she stared at it intently, grasped it, and tried unsuccessfully to bring it to her mouth. With a quizzical expression, she repeatedly stared at, grasped, and released it. She was distracted briefly by the sound of the music box, then went back to Terry's foot. She seemed to become frustrated at not being able to pick it up and put it into her mouth, and started to make complaintive sounds, which soon became angry crying. She was picked up and comforted by MB, who asked her what the trouble was, and explained in a comforting voice that it was Terry's foot, not a toy she was reaching for.

Leslie's activity with the giraffe provides an example of one of the ways infants learn: lifting, manipulating, and controlling the toy, she discovered she could bring about a certain result, the noise, with it. She repeated this deliberately, with obvious fascination, perhaps making some connection between her own action and the result. But Terry's foot was equally fascinating and she reacted to it as though it were another toy. Her perplexity, followed by frustration at not being able to control it seemed clear. MB knew, of course, that Leslie did not understand her words, but Leslie was obviously in need of comfort and must have been reassured by MB's manner of picking her up and talking with her.

Joan, 10 months, was sitting on the floor intently fingering her shoestring. After touching and looking at it for quite a long time, she picked it up neatly using her thumb and index finger and tried to bring it to her mouth. This caused her to lose her balance and topple over backwards. Joan did not realize the connection between the string and her foot. Unable to get the shoelace into her mouth, she lost interest, and played with a magazine by opening it and turning the pages. She also turned it upside down and around as she examined it, intently manipulating and investigating it for at least five minutes.

Joan's play with her shoestring revealed several things that are expectable at her age: she was interested in the string, manipulated it adeptly, and tried to mouth it. She was not yet far enough along in her learning about cause and effect to understand why she had toppled over, nor did she seem to realize that the string was firmly fixed to her shoe. She next turned to the magazine which she enjoyed mainly for the pleasure of manipulating it, and her ability to create novel visual effects seemed to have captured her serious interest. The pictures as symbols were not yet of interest for her.

The following episode shows some of Terry's investigatory interest at age 10 months. It is presented to give a picture of how much concentration a 10 month old can show, and to remind the reader that many an educational toy is in no catalogue, and that, when adults are perceptive and supportive, children can learn from almost anything in their environment.

Terry was playing with an aluminum margarine cup and a flat stick that looked like a popsicle stick. He hit the cup with the stick several times, causing it to flip over. He then used the stick to scoot the upside-down cup along the floor. For ten minutes he continued with great concentration, alternately flipping and pushing the cup and observing what happened. Later, while in the kitchen with KM, who was preparing food, he discovered the dishwater and found he could roll the lower rack in and out. He kept pushing it in and pulling it out, smiling with pleasure as he listened to the changing clatter of the dishes. He then poked about in the soap well for several minutes. All of this was done in an engrossed, exploratory manner. KM spoke to him occasionally, commenting upon what he was doing but allowing him to carry through his project in his own way.

The adults made Terry's play possible by providing the margarine cup and stick, and by allowing him the freedom to pursue his own interest. They supported him by being nearby but did not take an active part in his play at that time. It would have interfered with Terry's self-initiated investigations if someone had swooped down on him while he was so busily and happily engaged with the cup and stick, to take him away for a bath, or to introduce, or substitute a "proper" toy. Later, taking Terry into the kitchen and permitting him the freedom, with supervision, to explore the dishwasher, KM provided a wider variety of experiences than would have been available to him in the playroom. He was learning through following his interest of the moment, supported by an adult. At other times of the day he was involved in adult-initiated activities.

David walked alone at around 10 months of age and began active exploration of the rooms, opening and closing doors, pulling things out of cupboards, and being generally more assertive than he had been earlier. One day when he was almost 11 months old he was observed walking about the playroom, pushing the "popcorn" push toy in front of him, laughing with delight as the colorful balls popped up. Later, sitting on the floor, he pushed the same toy back and forth making the balls pop up, then lifted it and peeked underneath as though looking for the source of the popping balls.

David obviously enjoyed the motor activity involved in pushing the toy, and his curiosity about the source of the balls was sparked. His looking under the toy suggested that he had some dawning conception that there might be an explanation for the appearance and disappearance of the balls.

Joan, 13¾ months, and Curtis, 17 months, were playing on the floor near the bookcase. They were climbing in and out of the doll bed, scrambling over each other to do so. At one point Curtis got too close to Joan, wedging her in and and she cried until GM picked her up and gave her a hug. Her good humor restored, Joan climbed on the yellow truck and half sat, half leaned on it, inspecting it as she ate a cracker. She then meandered about the room, climbed into the large rocking chair, where she sat rocking for a minute or two, then got out and toddled around the room again. She approached JR, the observer, once, and as JR talked to her she patted JR's notebook, then toddled off to crawl under the crib where she sat peering out between the bars of the lowered cribside for a minute or two. Next she crawled out without bumping her head, stood, and toddled around the room again, looking closely at what Leslie, Curtis, and Jackie were doing but not involving herself in any of it.

Joan, except for the single episode with Curtis, was involved in going her own way and finding her own entertainment. One can imagine a somewhat experimental attitude in her use of the yellow truck, the adult's rocking chair, the inspection of JR's notebook, her excursion under the crib. She was quiet for the most part, apparently absorbed in her own activities. This is quite different from the apathetic or restless meandering that characterizes troubled or ill-cared-for toddlers.

Toddlers (15–30 Months)

We found it more difficult to provide a program geared to developmental needs of children from 14 or 15 months to about 2½ years than for younger or older children. To live exclusively with a group of toddlers is not easy. They tend to impinge sharply and more or less continuously upon adults and upon each other. Their rapid shifts from helplessness to independent behavior, from negativism to angelic compliance, from adamant holding on to expulsive casting out, from wishing to be as one with the adult to insisting on separateness and standing alone, from tenderness toward others to hostility, from taking initiatives to acting passively—this radically varying behavior is physically and psychologically taxing to adults.

And the developmental tasks toddlers are expected at least to begin mastering—walking, talking, understanding others, following simple directions, self-feeding and other self-help skills, controlling bowels and bladder, controlling feelings of anger, thinking logically, and many others—make for a marvelously expanding and often tempestuous period that seems difficult for adults to enjoy or even to cope with in a way supportive to the child.

The first problem, then, in planning daycare for children of this age is finding caregivers who can live with toddlers for six to eight hours a day. The most helpful responses to children of this age require flexibility and a sense of fun in the adult, along with an ability to remain reasonably mature in his or her own behavior. Adults having such qualities are, in our experience, especially hard to find. Furthermore, at this age toilet training is started; the child's interest in his genitals and those of others is apparent; anger and aggressive behavior become pronounced; and the child can use words that many adults find hard to take. Any or all of these developmentally normal, expectable behaviors may revive old conflicts for adults that interfere with their responding to the child in ways that optimize healthy personality development.

Other phase-specific characteristics of the toddler that may give rise to problems in planning daycare for him are his anxieties around separation from the emotionally significant people in his life, discussed in Chapter 5, and his preferred style of learning. Much of the learning of the toddler normally comes about through imitation and identification with parents and older siblings. He imitates their actions and forms of expression and is attracted to the things he associates with them. He is much more likely to prefer his father's tools, his mother's housekeeping equipment or pocketbook or cosmetics, and his brother's or sister's toys to any toys selected for him. The vacuum cleaner or broom, the washing machine, the cupboard of canned goods, the stove, the toilet, the sink are objects of his curiosity and attention. His increased interest in his parents and siblings involves him as an active participant in their lives and as an accomplished imitator. Real, life-size objects are likely to be preferred as playthings to miniature versions. He wants not a toy leaf rake or snow shovel, or a safe plastic hammer, but the real thing; the food from his father's or mother's plate looks better than the same thing on his plate; the red lollipop his sister is so obviously enjoying is a greater prize than his own.

As the child masters walking there is an enormous expansion in the variety and number of experiences available to him. He can now easily go from one place to another; at the same time, the growth of his intellect, his social skills, and his fund and range of emotions make him and his world different from before in highly significant ways. Considering the toddler's characteristic ways of acting, reacting, and learning, it is not surprising that group care presents special problems requiring a departure from the usual kind of program for infants who do not yet walk alone, or who have only recently begun to, and considerable modification of the program for older children. His developmental characteristics tax the ingenuity of those who wish to create a favorable environment for him outside the home setting.

The toddler's curiosity, which we value, should not lead him into danger but into experiences that contribute positively to one aspect or another of his development. His assertiveness should lead him not into perpetual conflict with other children and adults, but in the direction of a healthy sense of himself and others, of autonomy combined with basic trust, of vigorous and pleasurable exercise of motor skills combined with the budding ability to pause, observe, reflect upon, and speak about his own actions and feelings and those of others.

It was central to our planning a favorable learning environment for the children to provide a sufficient number of adults not only to feed them and protect them from danger but also to create an atmosphere in which each child could be responded to appropriately. While we only imperfectly reached this goal, the commitment to it determined many aspects of the program. We believed that except for brief periods during the day toddlers would learn best with one adult or with an adult and one or two other children. Even so, there were days when all or certain children could not cope with the entire period of planned learning activities and alternative plans were necessary. We might then take some for a walk, a ride in the shuttle bus, or into another room with one adult for a quieter period. On some days most children were tired or slightly ill. Often, then, lunch might be served early and they would be given a longer rest. Sometimes, these conditions applied to only one or two children, and they might be separated from the others. Staff were helped to understand the importance of their responsiveness to the children and the frequent supervisory and planning sessions provided an opportunity to discuss the needs and readines of each child and how these could best be handled. We assumed that, for most children, if adults were available as needed and the setting provided interesting challenges and opportunities commensurate with their developmental needs, learning would occur. We were aware that some children would regularly require more individual help than others to learn and that all children in this age group would need quite a lot of adult help.

The Transitional Period

As the infants became 15 to 16 months of age, we entered a phase in which we modified the structure of their day. At one time we had eight children in the program between the ages of 15 and 18 months. There was a period of three months during which, for about an hour and a half each morning, two children with one adult would stay together and go through a sequence of planned activities in different areas of the playrooms. We did not expect them to remain more than a few minutes at a time at any one activity. We set up four activity areas. In one room we had a housekeeping corner and dress-up materials; there were dishes, pots and pans, a toy stove and refrigerator, dolls, doll beds, and cupboards. The dress-up clothes were mainly scarves, hats, shoes, and purses. Another room was devoted to small toys and simple puzzles. The small toys included stacking and nesting toys, small wheel toys, a jack-in-the-box, and things to put in and take out of receptacles. There was a third room where the children could be introduced to paints, fingerpaints, dough, and clay, and could play in the sink or in pans of water. They might use the water to bathe their dolls, stir up soap bubbles, to pour water from one cup to another, and so on. In the basement we had swings, a sandbox, a small slide, and a rocking boat, which could also be used when turned over as stairs to walk up and down. After using each of these activity areas for about fifteen minutes, the children and adults would come together in the largest of the rooms for music and dancing.

The major purpose of this plan was to give the children an opportunity to use materials and to interact with one other child and with a familiar adult. We judged that they were not yet developmentally ready for the Toddler School program we had planned, and yet they were in need of more space, more opportunities for motor activity, and more varied experiences than we had provided them earlier. We reasoned that the new program would enhance their pleasure in many things and give them a chance to explore varied materials with minimal competition. The adults would be able to spend time talking with the two toddlers in their care without inter-ruptions from other children, showing specific personalized interest in them and enabling them to make use of the possibilities for activity and learning the new situation provided. While a shift from one activity to another was planned about every fifteen minutes, we tried to respect each child's tempo. If a child was in the middle of bathing a baby, not through playing in the sand, or not quite ready to stop his game of hiding and finding things, there was always time and space to allow him to finish, even if another group of two children and their caregiver-teacher had moved into the same room. Both during it and as we reviewed it later, we were impressed with the value of this three-month transitional period for the toddlers. It created much smoother days for them than they had been having immediately prior to the introduction of the plan. The personalized atention, we believe, also helped them not only to cope with but get great pleasure from being a part of a somewhat larger group in the music, dancing, and marching periods, where they could imitate the adults and begin to imitate and relate to each other in enjoyable, carefully sponsored group activity. We maintained this plan for about three months, until we felt the children could tolerate having their school each morning together.

The Toddler School

From about 18 months on, the children had approximately a two-hour planned morning program indoors, outdoors, or both. Indoors the two largest playrooms, which could be combined into one, were set up so that they contained four activity areas, each manned by one adult. By this time all of the adults were familiar to the children. The areas were (1) the housekeeping corner, which contained dolls, dress-up clothing, a full-length mirror, dishes, tables, stoves, and so on; (2) a table area (one large or two small tables) where water, dough, finger paints, and later crayons and paste were used; (3) a rug area for blocks, cars, small animals, a small doll house with furniture, and so on; and (4) a rug or table area for puzzles and other structured materials to be assembled, or where instruments such as drums and xylophones might be used.

Children were allowed to choose where they wanted to be, and to go from one area to another. Single children or small shifting groups could be seen for a few minutes at a time in one area. It was up to the adult in that area to help a child find something of interest and to support his play. It was here that the creativity and ingenuity of the teacher were of special importance. General planning took place each week in which all of the caregiver-teachers participated, with responsibility for leadership in planning being taken by one person. The group might decide, for example, that they would plan to have water play at the tables for one or two days and on another day dough or finger paints. Whether a particular material was used for one, two, or three days on a stretch depended on the response of the children. The teacher in the housekeeping corner might find herself on one day helping most of the children to pretend to cook or set a table, while some children would be more interested in the dress-up clothes. The teachers were quite free to modify and improvise. The ability of the adult, as a facilitator of children's play, to be imaginative, to show children how to pretend, to pick up and extend the children's ideas was impressive.

The descriptions to follow have been grouped by activity. These resemble the way of describing a program that has become familiar for older children, in nursery schools.

MUSIC AND DANCING   At music time, with all of the children and teachers together, Jackie, 18 months and the youngest, walked over to where EO was getting out some sets of bells, and she handed one to him. The other children heard him jingling and promptly came to get their bells, Paul exclaiming, "Hey." All started ringing their bells and KM turned on the phonograph. In response, Curtis, 23 months, smiled with delight and shouted, "Oh." Jackie began to march around to the music, shaking the bell, and all of the children followed. Two of the teachers joined them while another stood by the phonograph clapping rhythmically. The marching, which the children had done before, assumed a roughly circular, if uneven and interrupted, form. Curtis tripped accidentally and lay on the floor, smiling broadly and obstructing the path of others. EO came over and encouraged him to get up, which he did with a smile. Shortly, however, he ran over to Jackie and pulled him down on the floor with a thud. Since Jackie objected, KM came over and spoke firmly to Curtis who looked impassive but, following Jackie, got up and returned to marching. Jackie stepped a bit aside from the line and with his feet planted began to sway in time with the music. Some other children saw him and imitated him happily, while others continued to march. Their pleasure in themselves, in the movement, sound, and rhythm were abundantly clear. When the record was over Jackie began to bang on the radiator with his bell, fussing crossly, apparently unwilling to stop while others were going on to play with other toys. EO turned the record player back on at low volume and Jackie went back to marching and shaking his bells as other children began to play with toys in other parts of the room. Jackie finished marching before the music ended and wandered over to play with a toy on a nearby table. EO then turned off the phonograph.

At music time no other activities were planned and an attempt was made to involve all of the children, which was not difficult since they usually enjoyed it very much. The size of the group usually ranged from six to ten children and the activity lasted ten or fifteen minutes. On the day described the eight children present ranged in age from 18 to 28 months. The fact that two of the teachers were a part of the marching group helped to keep the circle formed for a time. Each child's pleasure in the music, the rhythmic movements, and the freedom to create variations on a theme was combined with some awareness of what others were doing, with obvious pleasure in imitating, and, we believe, some sense of being part of a group.

Two episodes occurred that, if not handled, could have changed the entire tone of the activity. One was Curtis's first accidental and later intentional disruption; the other was Jackie's fussing when the music stopped. In each instance a teacher was able to intervene with a suggestion before tension mounted. Such awareness and capacity to respond comes through knowing the children and through having enough adults around.

Terry, David, Shaun, Peter, and Leslie, ages 2 years 1 month to 2 years 5 months, all were attracted by the xylophone that SM got out to show them. She sat down on the rug with the xylophone and two, three, or four of them at a time joined her sitting around the instrument. With her help they were able to tolerate her deciding about taking turns. For example, she said, "Terry is having a turn now, then Leslie, and then Shaun," making it easier for them to wait. Keeping the turns brief (one or two minutes) and reassuring each child that he could have another chance facilitated the process. They were free to leave when they chose, but most remained interested and involved for some time, each enjoying the sounds he and the others could make. There was a mixture of serious attention to the process and exuberant pleasure.

In this situation SM did not turn the xylophone over to the children but kept the situation under control and helped them play in turn. Note that they were free to join her or not; it was not a required "lesson." Both their interest in the xylophone and their trust that the teacher would indeed see that they had turns were evident. However, she did not overburden their capacity to wait, and reassured them verbally. With her supervision, each enjoyed the instrument and also experienced doing something with the others. Imagine what the scene might have been with one instrument and no teacher!

PAINTING   MB was standing by the easel as Jackie, age 19 months, decided to paint, having watched the older children do so many times. He was very much aware of MB and turned and smiled at her pleasantly while he painted several long, squiggly lines, carefully holding the brush at the end, dipping it in and out of the single paint cup as he had seen others do. She responded to him, commenting, nodding, and smiling in an encouraging manner. He turned to her again and invited her to look at his painting. She then gave him a second color of paint in another cup, and he used this, adding additional lines to his painting. He looked at his painting and the new color, looked back to her and said, "See?" He decided that he had finished and watched MB hang up his picture. He smiled with pleasure and then again said, "See?" to no one in particular. MB stepped back beside him and said with pleasure, "That's your painting." He smiled happily and went away to play. Later he came back and stood looking at his picture and smiling; he pointed carefully to the lines he had painted and said, "See, see," as though very proud of it.

Jackie, who was the youngest child in the group and who had been with us in daycare since he was only a few months of age, was almost always attracted by what the older children were doing and tried to do as they did. He learned from watching them, as this observation illustrates. For his first painting attempt, he had the undivided attention of a teacher who was very familiar to him. She stood nearby, responding and encouraging him, ready to assist him if he needed help. He managed the whole process of holding and dipping the brush and painting on the paper astonishingly well for one so young. Note that he enjoyed both the process and product, and that one aspect of his pleasure was in sharing it with the teacher. She helped him to sustain the interest he showed by being there to encourage and keep the activity going. Her pleasure in the child and his activity undoubtedly contributed to his interest and pleasure.

Joan, age 23 months, and several other children at a table were introduced to finger painting. Getting paint on her fingers, Joan looked at them, shook her hands, and gave KB a quizzical look, appearing partly amused, partly disturbed. KB commented, "Yes, you have paint on your fingers," and Joan smiled in a rather puzzled way. EO, sitting next to Joan, put her own fingers in the paint and messed, demonstrating fingerpainting to Joan and saying with pleasure, "Oooh, messy." Joan, after watching her, put her own hands back into the paint and seemed to enjoy the activity. However, she periodically lifted her hands, shook them, and rubbed them together in a slightly worried way. EO continued fingerpainting with Joan, commenting with pleasure on what she and Joan were doing and how it felt. Joan suddenly laughed delightedly and showed her now very painty hands to EO, as though to say, "Look at my messy hands!" EO laughed with her. Later Joan began to draw in the fingerpaint with one finger and said to EO, "See? See?"

We had decided to introduce fingerpaints, anticipating that some of the children would enjoy them and some would not. As was our custom when entirely new materials were introduced, the teachers were there to demonstrate how they might be used. At the beginning of this not more than five-minute session Joan's reaction was clearly a mixture of tentative pleasure, perplexity, and mild discomfort. With EO's demonstration and encouragement she kept using the paints, within a few minutes decided she liked it after all, and began to draw in the finger paint, asking the teacher to notice her and her production. In this instance the teacher sponsored the material by actively participating, and showed Joan that there would be no disaster if she got her hands messy. Had Joan decided not to participate, her choice would have been respected.

THE HOUSEKEEPING CORNER   Paul, 21 months, became involved in playing with a doll with KM. He picked up the doll and showed it to her, and she talked with him about it and what he and his "baby" might do: "Oh, does your baby need to be fed?" "Are you and your baby going on a trip?" Paul decided they were going on a trip, and KM made suggestions as to what he might need: "A hat?" "A pocketbook?" "A scarf?" Paul became involved in looking at the clothes and accessories in the housekeeping corner, deciding what to wear. Gradually he seemed to become more interested in dressing himself up than in the doll and when he went off on the trip he left the doll behind. KM said, "Good-bye, have a nice time." He walked about the room in a large circle, returning after perhaps two minutes to KM, greeting her with an enthusiastic, "Hi!" She responded to him and reported that she had been taking good care of his baby, and together they began to feed the baby.

Paul had some rudimentary ideas about using the doll but needed the support of the teacher in dressing up in the adult clothing. The teacher did not insist that he maintain his interest in the doll and responded to his pleasure in the dressing process. He obviously had some idea of a trip, responding when KM said, "Good-bye, have a nice time," and greeting her enthusiastically when he had returned from his two-minute tour around the room. What she did, both with the doll and the dressing-up, was to pick up on an interest he had at that moment and help him extend it; he then was able to carry out part of it on his own initiative. She suggested but did not impose an idea and knew that any one play theme was unlikely to be pursued for very long by a child of his age.

Shaun, 24 months, and Terry, 27 months, put on some of the dress-up clothes with KB's help. They went immediately to the gate as if leaving. She said, "Let's go to a pretend restaurant," took their hands, and the three walked to a table in the housekeeping corner. She talked about the restaurant, helped them to sit down, and prepared "something to eat." Terry first watched her, sitting quietly, and then pretended to eat what she fixed for him, obviously entering into this imaginative play. Shaun got up from his chair and walked around, still listening. After about three minutes Terry got up, having finished his meal, said good-bye, and walked into an adjacent room where he climbed up into an adult chair. KB, impressed with his ability for at least short-term imaginative play, followed and suggested a bus ride in the chair. They sat in the chair together as KB talked about the bus ride. After a short time Terry left and crawled into a cabinet, where he opened and closed the doors, making a game of it and saying, "Hi," to KB each time he opened the door to rediscover her.

This observation and the one to follow are examples of the emerging ability of children at this age to play out imaginative games or activities. Granted individual variations, the ability to sustain such play is very limited at this age; the child cannot continue the play for long, nor can he elaborate the game very much. However, when given ideas by the teacher it is possible for him to extend the play. The themes are quite mundane in adult terms, reflecting the experiences that are a part of the child's daily life: eating, drinking, going to town or to bed, cooking, and so on. Imagining in play is, at this age, still rudimentary but nevertheless can be recognized and supported.

Terry elected to leave this kind of play for play in the cabinet, but note he maintained contact with KB through the game of hiding from and finding her.

Larry, age 2½, and MD played for about fifteen minutes in the housekeeping corner, preparing and having dinner, and conversing. Larry, still very caught up in the play, went to get a dress-up pocketbook from the supply across the room. While he was gone Paul, age 2¼, came into the area and began to play with a cash register that had been part of Larry's play. At this moment Larry, having found a pocketbook, ran back, calling to the teacher, "I found it. Look at it!" Then he saw Paul. He stopped, scowled, walked over to Paul and angrily began to pull him away from the cash register, saying, "No, no." As the boys began to fight, MD intervened, trying to get them to take turns with it. Paul broke into angry sobs and flung himself away, at first rejecting the teacher's holding him and telling him he could play with them. He gradually quieted as she held him and explained that she would help him play. Larry accepted this alteration in the play, though grudgingly, and at the teacher's suggestion handed Paul some of the play money from the register. He accepted it scowling, eyes averted. The teacher remained verbally active, showing how they could both play. They played side by side, though not really together.

Two aspects of this observation are noteworthy. First note that Larry, using the teacher as a playmate, was able to sustain a play theme for around fifteen minutes. However, when Paul came in and wanted to play with one of the props, Larry immediately reacted and the play was disrupted. The teacher, responding to Paul's interest and being responsible for helping them both, coaxed and directed their play for a few moments, helping them see that their wishes were not entirely incompatible. They ended up playing side by side reasonably contentedly. Each was enabled to do something that interested him and to play alongside the other in an accepting manner, though not in communicative play. The teacher's presence and skill insured each of the children a chance to play.

UNPLANNED LESSONS   During outdoor play, KM and EO noticed a seedpod in the yard. They called out their discovery and invited the children to come and examine it. The children, ages 18–25 months, passed it around, looking at it while the teacher explained, "It's a seedpod. See, it's fluffy. It floats in the air." The teachers soon turned this science lesson into a game of throwing the pod into the air while the children tried to catch it, running about delightedly, sometimes catching it, sometimes grabbing for it as it floated away. All had a chance to look at it, hold it, and feel it, then to play with it as they wished.

This is precisely the kind of thing one hopes teachers of young children will do. The seedpod had floated in on the autumn air; the teachers had discovered it and spontaneously decided to make use of it. Their enthusiasm for their discovery attracted the children, and a little lesson in the appearance and characteristics of a seedpod developed. Since the children's interest in facts was limited, the teachers soon shifted to a game that permitted the running, jumping, and grabbing that is so much a part of the activity and pleasure of this age.

CONSTRUCTION ACTIVITIES   In the large playroom on a large round table color cones and mailboxes had been set out. SM was seated at the table between Larry, 23 months, and Steven, 20 months, when Paul, 20 months, approached. MB joined the group, seated herself at the table and helped Paul pull his chair in. Larry and Steven, with minimal help from SM, were intently using the color cones. Paul watched, took a similar one and turned to MB, fussing because he could not seem to get it started. She helped him with the color cone by handing him the pieces one at a time, commenting approvingly when he got a piece on and, when he got stuck, verbally supporting him to keep trying. With this assistance he was able to complete the activity with obvious satisfaction in himself.

On this day it had been decided to have structured toys on the table while other things were going on elsewhere. The children in this scene gravitated to the area to which the two teachers had been assigned, while other children had chosen other areas. Larry and Steven needed no assistance beyond the supportive interest of the teacher. Paul, however, could not make use of the toys without the teacher, who helped him control his irritability and frustration by handling him the pieces one at a time and supporting him verbally when he had difficulty. Both teachers were functioning as supporters and enablers, not as formal instructors.

Curtis, 25 months, with EO's help played with a firm plastic ball with openings for forms in several shapes. As EO's attention was diverted momentarily, he tried to find the right hole but had difficulty fitting the form in and began to fuss helplessly. As she was able to help him again, pointing out which hole each shape went in, he completed the ball with pleasure. She estimated that he would need some help for several days or weeks longer before he could do this completely on his own.

This is another example of how an adult can support the child's problem solving. Here, the child was given more specifically focused help as the teacher guided him toward the successful completion of the task. Had he wanted to leave the scene, she would not have insisted that he stay. In this instance he would have had no option but to give up, however, had she not been available to assist him.

The large cardboard blocks were out on the rug. Terry, 28 months, an intelligent, often tense, volatile child, had become overexcited and was having a difficult time, manifested in his throwing the blocks about. A young student who was observing and working as an assistant in the group sat down on the rug with Terry, suggested that they build something together, and helped Terry begin. While the student remained nearby, handing Terry a block or making a suggestion that was needed, Terry built a number of towers, knocking them down and then rebuilding them with considerable pleasure. After a few moments Leslie, 27 months, who was competitive with the other children for the student's interest, came over and called attention to herself by interfering with their play. The student was able to help both children enjoy the building, knocking down, and rebuilding.

The student approached and engaged Terry before he became entirely disorganized, and by leading the way, got Terry involved in constructive play. Terry's pleasure in knocking the tower over was developmentally appropriate and was allowed, since it was his tower. The student's presence helped Terry keep his excitement and energy under control.

The student knew both Terry and Leslie to be easily charged up, so his method was not to heighten the excitement; he helped the children keep control by his calm voice and by helping them build.

Supporting Speech Development

The importance of the speaking social partner has been described earlier. With older children in daycare, who have developed speech but whose speech is delayed or impaired in some way, the fact that the child talks, even if unclearly, is usually enough to stimulate the adults who work with him to talk with him. Younger children, however, especially preverbal infants, may not evoke the speech of the adult; their caregivers, however supportive and competent in other ways, may go about their child-care activities relatively silently. Some adults feel silly and self-conscious talking to infants; others do it naturally and spontaneously. But even naturally talkative adults, taking care of several children not their own in the daycare setting, may find it hard to remember to talk with them. The pressure of work, the long day, and sometimes boredom may diminish the stimulation the staff provide for speech development. Thus, providing an environment that specifically facilitates the speech of infants and toddlers requires deliberate effort on the part of staff.

When the child's cognitive interest in an activity or object has been evoked by the adult or when the child is enjoying a social contact, he is usually quite attentive to the adult's speech. A toddler who has just walked across the yard and picked up a leaf, showing his interest and pleasure, is much more likely to be ready at that moment to learn the word *leaf* and that the leaf is big or little, green or red, than he would be were a leaf presented to him later as part of a "speech lesson." One tries to notice what an infant or young child is doing or attending or feeling, and give him words that designate those states. This applies both to children whose normal speech one wishes to support and extend and to children whose speech is delayed and for whom motivation to listen and learn words is of special importance. One child, Shaun, in his second year, in whom speech and some other aspects of cognitive development were delayed, was interested for a time only in two things: large muscle activity and food. To help him with speech we could use his interest in movement only a little, because he was in such constant motion that he was largely inattentive to what was being said to him. However, his love of eating permitted us to use the eating situation to interest him in names of the foods, the implements he was using, and some of the qualities of the food. At such times, as he sat in his chair, he was willing to listen to the teacher talk with him about what he was doing, what he was eating, how it tasted and so on. While we used mealtimes as a learning experience for all the children, for Shaun it was of particular importance and, for a time, our most effective avenue to encourage learning, including word acquisition.

The most important considerations in stimulating speech development in infants and toddlers in daycare can be summarized as follows.

• Because of the strenuousness of a full day of child care for adults, the importance of their talking with the babies and toddlers during the day will need emphasis.

• The infant and young child's interest in speech as a form of communication is very much dependent upon whether his environment *invests* language for him, that is, whether adults communicate feelings and information and whether they animate and make appealing to him the process of back and forth verbal communication.

• Speech is learned most naturally and effectively in connection with situations and objects that have captured the young child's attention.

• For children whose speech lags behind or is disabled in some special way, extra time may need to be set aside for helping with speech development. Speech is such a highly valued and useful function in our society that the individual who is speech handicapped has a difficult time. When a speaking problem can be recognized early, assistance should be included in the child's day in the center. Here too, however, picking up on the child's interest, and remembering that his emotional reaction and motivation are essential to getting him involved in working on his speech are vital to its success.

• The adult's recognition and responsivity to the child's feelings, including speaking to him about them, are important influences for children in day-care.

Retreat and Replenishment

Among the most important functions of the adult in the child's rearing is as his comforter and source of security. This is most vividly demonstrated when things go wrong, when fatigue or frustration overtake him. For young children in daycare these frustrations are frequent, signs of distress are often visible, and suffering behind a veneer of apathy or dullness is not rare. Adults need to learn to recognize signs of distress and discomfort in young children. Program planners need to insure that there are enough competent adults present to protect, comfort, and replenish the child. Following are several examples that show the need of the child for the understanding adult and how the adult's behavior restores the child's ability to manage himself.

Following breakfast, Joan, 9½ months, was in the playroom with Curtis, Jackie, Shaun, MB, and KB. Joan played on the floor alongside the other babies for a while. Then, after Curtis took several things away from her, and Shaun hit her on the head with a cloth book, she spotted her bottle on the mantel, crawled toward it, pulled to stand, and whined in a coaxing way. KB responded by putting her into the crib in the corner of the room with her bottle. Joan lay on her side, took some of the milk, then stood up and played with the bottle, using it to bang on a large cardboard box on the adjacent table. Then she dropped the bottle and rocked from side to side for two or three minutes, looking about, before getting restless and fretting for attention from adults. When MB, responding to her sounds, put her on the floor, she crawled from one toy to another, and picked up, looked at, and discarded in turn a wooden block, a rubber squeeze toy, a plastic hourglass, and a wooden spool. She stopped playing when MB left the room, whined a little, crawled to the gate, pulled up on it, shook it soundly, and vocalized in a coaxing way, as if asking for attention. MB came back with a basketful of small toys, which she put in the middle of the rug. She sat on the floor next to the basket and offered one to Joan, who crawled to her. Joan played with the toys until she saw Jackie on MB's lap. She watched silently for a few minutes, then crawled over and into MB's lap with Jackie.

Even though there were two adults in the room, within a very few minutes Joan had several trying episodes with other children. Though none was disastrous and all were to be expected, she was understandably upset. KB picked up Joan's cue and allowed her the comfort of bottle and crib without taking her from the group. After a short period of respite she indicated her wish to get out and, again, her cue was responded to and she was put back on the floor with the other children. MB noticed that Joan looked at and discarded several toys, and provided some variety by introducing others that she hadn't played with for several days. Even though she became interested in the new toys after they had been shown her by MB, it was not surprising that she abandoned them for an attempt to share MB's lap with Jackie. In most instances, for a baby of this age, the chance for a social time with a familiar adult is far more attractive than a toy. MB was able to keep both children occupied and comfortable through a combination of play with the toys and providing a lap.

The following reports an observation familiar to people who spend time with little children—that is, that children frequently return to mother or to a special caregiver during the course of their play, touching home base, so to speak.

Joan, 10 months, was relaxed but active as she crawled about the playroom picking, shaking, mouthing, and discarding various objects (a string of rubber beads, a small wooden truck, a plastic banana, and a plastic ring from a ring-toss game). Once, when MB picked up Jackie, Joan crawled across the floor, pulled to a stand at her knee and seemed to be letting MB know that she didn't want her to hold Jackie. MB reached down, patted her head and said, "What's the matter, Joan, don't you have anything to do?" Joan seemed to be satisfied with that bit of attention and again became involved in her investigation of available toys. She frequently returned to MB for brief contacts, receiving a smile, a pat, or a word, after which she would resume her activity in the room. MB later left the playroom to go to the kitchen, and Joan stopped playing. She soon realized that JR, the observer, was the only person in the room with her and though she smiled when JR talked to her, she kept her distance. After looking JR over for a moment she crawled down the hallway to the kitchen after MB.

The presence of MB, a significant person to Joan, enabled her to maintain an interest in playing and exploring her environment. When MB left the room Joan was no longer able to continue to play and went after her, apparently somewhat uneasy about the observer or about MB's absence.

Following is an example of how a quiet and peaceful place can be created in a playroom for children. We assumed that children might need opportunities to detach themselves from play, to be alone for a few moments.

A card table with a sheet draped over it had been set up in a corner as a sort of tent where children could go when they wished to. Shaun, 21 months, Terry, 25 months, and Greg, 25 months, all used it during the course of one morning as a place to play quietly for several minutes. Each child as he emerged hesitated, seeming lost and unready to get back into the play in the room. Seeing this, EO offered her lap and talked briefly to each child. The lap-sitting seemed to provide a transtion from quiet to more active play. Each child seemed replenished by having had his quiet time, enabling him to activate himself again through the transition offered by the teacher's lap and conversation. On the morning this observation was recorded, these three children spontaneously availed themselves of the cozy space under the card table. A less perceptive teacher or a teacher too busy to notice might have missed the opportunity to help each child reorganize himself. This phenomenon, the need for closeness, even when there is no great distress, is familiar to most mothers of young children and is offered almost automatically in the home situation by mothers who understand their young children well. But it takes careful planning to provide this kind of respite and reenergizing in the daycare setting.

Aggressive Behavior

One of the central developmental tasks of early childhood, and one that extends into later childhood and far beyond, is the control and use of aggressive energy. Developmental theory emphasizes that aggresive impulses are a part of the endowment with which the human child is born and are a crucial aspect of the life force. In the course of normal healthy development the aggressive drives express themselves in various forms, go through various modifications, and, with assistance from the outside, are gradually brought under the internal control of the individual.

One expects that children who are developing normally will display aggressive behavior toward adults, other children, and toward objects in the environment. When little children are together in groups, these episodes occur with predictable frequency as a part of their interaction with each other. Adults who take care of them have both immediate and long-term goals in dealing with such aggression. Immediate goals include protecting other children from being hit, bitten, pushed around, and stepped on, as well as helping the child who is the aggressor learn to express his anger in some other way. All healthy children are at some times victims and at other times agents of aggressive behavior. One hopes that a child will learn to defend himself from attack, either by seeking help from an adult or by coping with it directly. Over the long term we work toward the child's eventually being able to talk about what angers him, rather than solving everything by physical force either in attack or retaliation.

While infants in the first year begin to express aggressive feelings, the forms of expression are such that they do not impinge on other children to any appreciable degree. However, as soon as children begin to move about freely there is a rapid increase in aggressive behavior as well as in all other transactions with others. Normally in the second year, along with many other signs of developmental progress, toddlers become more possessive, more vehement about what they want, and express anger or jealousy more strongly. They often arouse counteraggression from adults when they provoke, tease, behave stubbornly, or commit aggressive acts against other children. Adults, as well as children, commonly find that handling aggressive feelings in ways that are not destructive is no easy task.

Adult caregivers need to be at least reasonably mature people who understand their own aggressive feelings and have them under control. In addition, they need to know what to expect of young children at various ages. Constructive caregiving does not deny that hostile, angry feelings exist or try to stamp them out. It does limit children when they are acting out these angry feelings upon other children, protect them from one another, explain, comfort, and negotiate disagreements. It involves helping them gradually to learn, especially through demonstration and example, how to express their anger or hostile feelings verbally or in modulated rather than intense ways. It is impossible to create an environment for young children in which they learn to control and use their aggressive energy constructively unless there are a sufficient number of adults to guide them. This is one reason very young children cannot tolerate large groups or excessive permissiveness. Without sufficient adult guidance some children become tyrants and aggressors; others become victims. Aggressors feel at times triumphant, at other times fearful and miserable. Victims are both terrified and in danger of coming to accept or even ask for the role. When there are not enough adults to guide young children away from physically aggressive encounters with one another and direct their energy into more constructive social and learning activities, the toddler's room becomes a nightmare for all concerned. Adults are harassed and overburdened; children are upset, angry, and unable to use the program productively.

Following are selected examples of normal aggressive behavior.

Curtis, 15 months, was in the playroom with Shaun, Jackie, and Joan, silently pushing the block cart first into Jackie and then into Joan. In spite of being deflected by the adults he persisted in maneuvering it so that it would bump into them. He then abandoned the cart and toddled to Jackie and pushed him over; Jackie protested by whining. Curtis moved on to Joan and tried to push her over also but she squealed loudly and grabbed his overalls, almost pulling him down. A few minutes later he was sitting on the floor when Joan approached him and he reached out, grasped the seat of her pants and pulled her down, all the time ignoring the observant adult's admonitions not to do it. They were separated and he was given a jack-in-the-box, which he manually explored with deliberate movements. He then spent about two minutes toddling about holding a squeaky toy. When he made it squeak he smiled and looked at KB, sharing the experience with her. She smiled and commented on his making the toy squeak. Several other times during the next hour he approached and pushed, bumped, or took toys away from the smaller children. He hit out at Shaun and pulled his hair. About an hour later he began to cry woefully. KB went to him and he quieted briefly, then crawled a few feet away from her and lay on the floor breaking into loud, sorrowful wails. As she soothingly talked to him, rocked him, and patted his cheek he stopped crying and rested his head on her arm, still sobbing occasionally. He cried while she put his coat on, but once outside he was quiet while being pushed in the cart. He was relaxed and solemn with a sorrowful, woebegone expression on his face.

Only at the end of the morning did the several adults who had had to intervene to protect the other children fully realize how many times Curtis had made aggressive contact. This is the kind of situation that might occur with any child of this age on any day. He repeatedly had to be moved away and told not to hit or push the others because it would hurt. At the same time we realized that Curtis was not having an easy time in his adjustment to the daycare center. So his caregiver tried to provide him with support and comfort and to help him play.

Curtis's behavior is a typical illustration of the difficulty little children have in coping with stress. While we did not know what was going on in Curtis's mind, he was clearly unhappy much of the day and needed comfort and reassurance from his special caregiver. A young child who is unhappy and agitated and who feels dissatisfied with adults, may manifest this by being more aggressive to other children. While Curtis's aggressive behavior had to be controlled, he needed consolation and help, not punishment.

With young children things can go from relative peace to turmoil and chaos within a very few moments. Adults must judge how quickly to intercede. The first example below describes what can happen when intercession is too late. When children are older, as in the second example, the chances of effective negotiation between them are better.

Within two minutes after she left to bring something from the kitchen, MB heard an unusual amount of shrill screaming coming from the nursery. She returned to find Terry, Leslie, and Greg, all 17 months, and Shaun, 14 months, who had been playing peacefully on the floor, now shrieking at each other and aggressively taking things away from one another. The atmosphere was tense with contagious excitement. She was told by the other adult who was present that Greg had started to push the small cart but was intercepted by Shaun. They had had a tug of war with the cart, each being determined not to give it up. An adult had interceded but not quickly enough, trying to distract Shaun's attention and provide him with another plaything. It was not easy to distract him in the face of his determination, and by the time Greg had sole possession of the cart he was so upset he could not enjoy it but collapsed on the floor in helpless, frustrated crying.

This was a situation in which adults should have interceded earlier in the interests of the children. It is appropriate, of course, to allow children to try to work things out for themselves up to a certain point, but babies of this age, each wanting the same thing, can rarely settle things amicably. In this instance, everyone lost. Shaun was angry at having to give up the pushcart, which the adult gave to Greg since he had had it first. Greg was too upset to enjoy it. It is to be expected that children of this age will often want the same thing at the same time, and they do not have the capacity for settling such things in a way that is constructive to everyone. While some such episodes are inevitable and not harmful, when they are frequent, they are disorganizing and interfere with the child's ability to play and to learn.

Greg and Terry, both 23 months, were in the staff lounge with an adult, and Greg was sitting on the floor looking at a book. Terry approached him and tried to take the book away, whereupon a battle ensued in which Greg hit out at Terry several times. Terry held fast to Greg's shirt and persisted in trying to take the book. The two boys seemed to be rather evenly matched; both were shrieking and each was holding his own. The adult allowed the contest to go on for about a minute, since neither appeared to be victimized by the other; finally Terry managed to drag Greg to the floor. They were then good-naturedly separated by the adult; Greg's book was given to him and Terry was given another. Greg moved to the middle of the floor where he sat leaning against the large cushion while he resumed looking at his book. Terry, with his book, joined Greg on the floor sharing his cushion. At this point the boys were in a good mood and friendly to each other as they sat close together, each looking at his own book.

How soon to intervene in a squabble between two young children is a matter of judgment. Had one of these children really been victimizing the other, the adult would have stepped in earlier, but in this instance it appeared appropriate to allow them to try to work it out. When it began to get rougher and they could not settle it amicably, the adult moved in to restore equilibrium. By this time both boys knew the staff well enough to expect reasonable and supportive behavior. This could be thought of as a supervised contest rather than a free-for-all. Had there been three or four children struggling and only one adult, such an outcome satisfactory to all would probably not have been possible.

Eating

One does not have to be persuaded that what and how adults feed children and how the child experiences eating and being fed are of central importance for his physical and mental health. Much emphasis has been correctly placed on providing nutritionally adequate meals for children in daycare. In addition, mealtime should be viewed as an important social and emotional experience around which many kinds of communications between adults and children take place and much learning goes on. Most caregivers feel good when they have fed a child well or helped him to eat his meal with enjoyment. Most children feel loved when given food in a benevolent manner by adults who are interested in them.

Here we list important points concerning meals in daycare.

• Young children need to eat in the company of interested adults who take responsibility for creating an environment favorable for eating and who help the children when needed. The mealtime experience is very much improved for the children when adults eat with them. Nor should a child's having learned to feed himself cost him the company of adults at mealtime.

• Children should be allowed and encouraged to become active participants in the feeding situation when they are able and willing to do so. Among other things, adults should expect and encourage the child's finger feeding as a transition between being fed and self-feeding with spoon or fork.

• Adults must tolerate a certain amount of messiness in the child's eating behavior. Getting hands in the food and smearing are developmentally expectable behaviors for an infant or toddler. If not made a battleground, they are pleasures he can forgo within a few months as he becomes competent with a spoon and more interested in a broad range of activities.

• Children should be allowed to dislike and refuse food without being penalized. Reasonable substitutes for the day's menu should be available. Dessert should not be looked upon as a prize for good behavior or as something to be withheld as punishment, since, when carefully chosen, it has high nutiritional value and is as important as other parts of the meal.

• The adult's reactions to specific foods will often influence the child's reactions of pleasure or distaste.

• It is not unreasonable to urge and coax a child to try a new food or to take a bit more of something, as long as the adult refrains from forcing or fighting.

• Infants may be able to eat happily in the company of two or three others as long as there are enough adults for all and the atmosphere is conducive to eating, i.e., not fraught with high tension or distraction.

• Individualized methods of handling the feeding situation will often be needed, and such possibilities should be built into the program.

Leslie, 4 months, was sitting in the infant seat smiling, looking around, and waving a rattle. She indicated that she was getting hungry by fretting with little coaxing squeals, which quickly became insistent crying. She quieted somewhat as she was placed on the counter where she could see MB prepare her food, but continued to make little sounds until the food was offered. She took the solids eagerly, protesting a little between spoonfuls as if she couldn't get it fast enough. She quieted as MB gave her the bottle, and sitting on MB's lap, she looked at her intently as she sucked. She also looked around the room at the other adults, frowning a little as she did so.

When Leslie was placed where she could observe the preparation of her food the intensity of her crying diminished. The quieting probably meant that she recognized and anticipated the feeding to come, which enabled her to wait a short time. Being visually active and involved in her environment did not seem to interfere with her eating.

Leslie, 5½ months, was sitting in the high chair crying loudly and impatiently as MB prepared her food. Because of her urgency MB decided to give her part of the bottle, after which she would give her the solids. Leslie gave one shrill cry of protest at the transition from bottle to fruit but quieted with the first spoonful. She complained each time MB stopped to refill the spoon, as though she couldn't get the food fast enough. At each mouthful she made a little sound of pleasure. When she had eaten enough to satisfy her hunger, she leaned forward and peered into the dish, inspecting its contents, then picked up the edge of the dish, and let it drop back down on the tray with a bang. She picked up the jar lid, mouthed it and banged it several times on the tray. It was then that she smiled for the first time.

It was clear that on this occasion Leslie was beyond being able to wait quietly. This episode is included because it is such a common one: at any given mealtime a young child fatigued or hungry beyond his tolerance needs his food as quickly as he can get it and adults learn to recognize such urgency. Note MB's willingness to adapt her feeding practice to Leslie's need on that occasion.

As the following example illustrates, an infant's recognition of the feeding situation and his expectation of being fed are usually very clear by 6–7 months. Short-term waiting, with some trust in the adult, can be clearly seen. The meal as a social experience has also become more complex.

When the observer arrived, Jackie, 6½ months, was seated in the high chair with his bib on, watching GM dish up his lunch. He had an eager, expectant expression on his face, made a few sounds, and kicked his legs as if to say, "Hurry up, I'm hungry." GM said lightly, "It's coming Jackie; here's your lunch," sat near him and offered him a few spoonfuls of fruit, which he liked. She offered him a new mixture of meat and vegetables saying, "OK, Jackie, let's try this"; he grimaced, turned his head away, and spit it out. Coaxed to take another bite or two he did so, but he refused the third. GM went back to the fruit and he ate it eagerly, leaning forward for each spoonful until the edge was off his hunger. Then he ate more slowly, looking more often at GM's face and around the room as she talked with him. He made pleasant, happy sounds as he smacked his lips and smiled. Following this, she took him on her lap, where he sucked a few ounces of milk from the bottle, and then refused it by pushing the nipple out and turning his head away. After his lunch he was in a happy, expansive mood, gurgling, cooing, and smiling spontaneously at those around him.

Jackie obviously recognized the feeding situation and eagerly anticipated the meal to come. His eagerness and possibly some feeling of urgency were revealed in his facial expression and body movement, but he was able to wait without crying. Note that his participation in the meal as a social situation increased as the acuteness of his hunger diminished. He gave clear cues about his likes and dislikes. GM did not persist in offering him food that he disliked, nor did she urge him to take more milk after he seemed satisfied.

In the next example the infant's ability to feed himself part of his meal is illustrated. Just as significant, however, is the presence and support of the adult that made it possible for the children to have a successful and pleasant mealtime.

When put in his highchair for lunch Jackie, 10 months, was quiet and remained so while Joan, who was very hungry and irritable, was put in her chair; but Jackie began to fuss and kick impatiently when he saw her plate of food. GM put some bits of corned beef hash and string beans on the highchair tray in front of him, and he quieted for about five minutes as he picked up and ate small pieces with his thumb and index finger. Intermittently, he stopped eating to look at Joan. He listened as GM talked with Joan about what she was eating and about how well Joan used her spoon. As GM began to feed Jackie he reached toward her mouth with a string bean, offering it to her, and smiling with pleasure when she ate it and said, "Oh, that's good Jackie; thank you." A bit later, when being fed pudding, he insisted on holding the spoon and GM took another. Joan by now was beginning to smear her food on the high chair tray with her hand. GM did not interfere. With help from GM Jackie held a small glass of milk and took a sip or two but managed to spill much of it. He slid down in his chair, rubbed his eyes, appearing sleepy and tired, and pulled at his bib. GM took him out of the chair and held him on her lap as she helped Joan finish her meal. Joan then played on the floor as GM washed Jackie's hands and face and got him ready for nap.

GM knew from previous observations that Jackie was able to pick up small bits of things and feed them to himself, and she set things up to allow him to do so. Joan, three months older, had more capacity for self-feeding than Jackie. GM's ability to keep contact with both children was noteworthy. She was there to facilitate their eating through giving help as needed to each child, to encourage some self-feeding, and to keep the mealtime pleasant. It is very hard for most little children, even after they are capable of self-feeding, to do without adult support.

The art of being available to help a child eat while also allowing him to work at self-feeding is not easy for some adults. There is a tendency either to do it all for him or expect him to do it alone. Time, patience, and the capacity to be pleased with gradual change are required. The adult must also be able to accept some messiness as the child handles and smears the food.

A casual observer watching any of the previously described episodes might be unaware of the thought, care, and knowledge of the individual children that determined how the feeding went. A child varies from month to month, while retaining a solid core of recognizable traits and temperamental characteristics. If his caregivers do not know him and he them, if they are not in reasonably good communication, the feeding experience will range from sterile to disastrous. For the very young child, most of the adjustments must be made by the adults. Mealtime deserves the same respect that other aspects of the curriculum are given.

Special needs can often be fulfilled at mealtime. For Shaun, as we have said, mealtime was a good time to help him to learn names of food, to talk with him about what he had been doing, and to get him to use his hands more skillfully, since he was most receptive and was highly motivated when eating was involved. For another child, a tense and often uncomfortable toddler, it was important that mealtime be low-keyed and peaceful, not stimulating. These two children were very different in the amount and kind of help they needed at mealtime.

By the time the youngest children in our program were 18–20 months old and were quite familiar with the center, the staff, and each other, they were able to eat lunch at small tables with adult help and participation. Two or three children and one or two adults were usually together. Mealtime always went better when adults ate with the children. Young children need adult help and interest at mealtime for many reasons. The practice we have seen in many centers, and occasionally in our own, of putting young children at their tables to eat while adults stand above them to supervise and arbitrate, makes mealtime a routine that ignores many opportunities for learning and for feeling valued and well cared for.

In the examples to follow, most of what adults said to children has been omitted to keep the descriptions as brief as possible.

This observation did not follow any one child for very long, and is an attempt to capture some of the more conspicuous occurrences during a mealtime and preparation for nap that lasted perhaps thirty minutes. At one of the small tables, good-humored Steven, solemn Larry, and pouting Joan were being helped by MD and KM. At the second table Curtis, Jackie, and Paul ate with MB and KB. The age range of the group was 17–24 months. The observations and comments are mainly on Larry and Steven. Their behavior during and after mealtime was, of course, continuous with what had happened during the morning and related to what was going on in their lives outside the center as well. The support needed by the children is apparent.

Steven was sitting at the table on one side of KM, still and quiet. Larry, sitting on her other side, was looking very solemn and sucking his thumb. Joan, who was being comforted by MD, was crying, looking somewhat angry, and pouting. Jackie and Curtis entered the room and Jackie pranced around the room vocalizing loud growls. He and Curtis were corraled and seated at a second table with Paul, MB, and KB. When Steven saw the food cart he became excited, smiled, and reached toward the food, waving his hands and kicking his feet. Larry continued to suck his thumb until his food was placed before him. He used his right hand, managing the spoon skillfully and occasionally using his fingers for the meat. He spent rather a long time looking about the room and watching the children at the next table before he began to eat, but once started ate well, continuing to look around the room quietly as he chewed.

Note that Larry was little involved with the adults as he accepted and ate his food, and looked about the room. He was during this period very wrapped up in his recurrent concern about being away from his mother during the day and had seemed quite sad that morning when he said good-bye to her. He had been busy part of the morning with water play, riding a scooter, and playing with the farm animals, mostly by handling and naming them. He went about his activities in desultory fashion, as if preoccupied with other thoughts.

Steven seemed very hungry and ate competently, using the fingers of his left hand for feeding himself while holding the spoon in his right, occasionally using the spoon to take a mouthful. He intermittently looked in a coy and flirtatious manner at KM, who was responsive to his socializing and helped him occasionally by offering him a spoonful. When he had had enough he closed his lips and when offered another bite did not take it. At dessert time he watched KM eagerly while she spooned sliced peaches into his dish. He was silent and businesslike for the most part while he ate the peaches with a spoon, occasionally holding the spoon in mid-air above his dish observing the juice drip off, one drop at a time. When through, he remained at the table, quiet and unmoving, sucking on his pacifier. Finally MD invited him to get up and he went over to the observer's chair and gave her a friendly glance. He did not resist when KM told him it was time for his nap, carried him to his bed, and tucked him in.

Steven had needed much adult support during the morning in order to be able to play. He whined a good deal and for the last half hour before lunch had seemed tired and had used his pacifier. Note that lunchtime seems to have been mainly a pleasure for him as he ate and socialized with KM and that he contentedly, perhaps gratefully, accepted his nap.

After they had finished and while the plates were being removed, Larry got up and pranced to the window, pointing outside and saying something that sounded like, "Big truck, big truck." When KM came for him, telling him it was naptime, he began to cry. He quieted when KM tucked him in bed. Joan, too, began to fuss and cried quite hard as MD put her to bed. It took several minutes for MD to comfort her. Larry, hearing her, had a distressed expression on his face and for a minute it appeared he would cry too, but he did not.

Note that the children behaved differently during the transition from lunch to nap, Steven with ready acceptance, Joan and Larry with some degree of protest and distress.

Terry and Greg, both 21½ months, were seated at a little table while breakfast was being served by KM and GM. Greg looked at the food cart, laughed a little artificial laugh and kicked the underside of the table. Terry imitated him and they both laughed, kicked the table, and vocalized. When breakfast, consisting of juice, eggs, bacon, and toast, was set before them, GM and KM sat down at the table with them. Both children ate bacon with their fingers, Greg offering KM a bite of his bacon. Neither child was particularly interested in eating, but with encouragement from KM and GM they ate their bacon and a small amount of the eggs and toast. They seemed to be more interested in their playful imitation of each other. They pounded on the table, laughed, and vocalized. After a few minutes, when it became clear the boys were not interested in eating more, their faces were washed and their bibs removed. They began to play then with the toys in the playroom. Both children were active and happy and enjoying each other.

This little scene is an example of breakfast time as a social hour for the two little boys, who enjoyed each other very much. Note that the playful interaction was allowed by the adults, whose pleasure in the children's enjoyment of each other must have been apparent to the children. The fact that for forty-five minutes there were no other children in the room with them permitted their enjoyment of each other to be continued in their play with toys.

Naptime

The physical and psychological fatigue engendered by participation in a daycare program demand that the child have a period of physical and mental rest, whether he seeks it or not. He needs a respite from other children and activities, from the stimuli that impinge upon him both from the outside and from his own internal state. Those who cannot sleep must have quiet time away from other children.

Naptime is among the most difficult times to plan well in a daycare center, because planners are presented with a dilemma: if the children fall asleep at about the same time, say in the early afternoon, not all staff will be needed to attend to them. This then becomes a logical time for adults to have a much-needed rest, and a time for the conferences and staff meetings necessary to conducting a good program. However, for children in their second and third years in particular, it may be an extremely difficult time. They may need considerable help in the transition from waking to sleeping states. They may be unable to rest if a familiar adult is not nearby. Naptime may revive feelings about separation and longing for home and mother so that children may be more actively upset at this time. In their quieter moments, as their increasing knowledge makes them more aware of their own thoughts and feelings, they may experience not only feelings of longing but also anger toward parents and fear of losing them, which may make resting very difficult. Then, too, episodes during the day in the center—perhaps an altercation with another child or a feeling of being aggrieved at an adult—may upset the child and affect the naptime on any particular day. When one knows a child reasonably well, it is often possible to figure out why he is having difficulty sleeping. Sometimes one is aware of the specific factors that cause difficulty at a particular time; at other times one cannot be certain what is behind the upset; but there is always the need for someone to be available to deal with it.

It is, of course, up to the adults to arrange the program and the rooms in a way that invites rest and sleep. Cutting down the noise and reducing the number of other stimuli are familiar ways of preparing the setting. There are distinct advantages to regularity and routine for most young children. Providing a routine or ritual in preparation for nap such as rocking the child, reading him a story, or letting him look at a book; providing as much as possible the same place to sleep and a familiar adult; providing a comforting toy or bottle are all appropriate ways of helping children rest. Once the children are settled and the staff not assigned to naptime duty are having their own respite or attending a conference, it is important that at least some staff be available to be called for children who cannot be helped to rest by the person supervising naps on that particular day. This "on call" duty can usually be done on a rotation basis once the children are comfortable with all the staff.

The number of children in any one room should be small, or temporary partitions should be used to provide children with a cozy place. This is of particular importance with children under 2½ or so, although, for all preschool children there are distinct disadvantages to having large numbers of children sleeping in the same room. One child who is having a difficult time or refuses to sleep can disturb an entire room. In our first years of operation, when we had twenty-five children at a time in the program, we had to use all our playrooms for naps and thus had cots and cribs all over the place. Some children simply could never sleep in a room with others; most could share a room. A few of the children were good nappers most of the time, and some frequently had difficulty. Most children, however, were variable, with periods—from days to weeks—when they needed a great deal of help to go to sleep, and other periods when they went to sleep without difficulty.

Children are probably not more variable in their naptime behavior than they are, for example, in their eating behavior. What can make naptime difficult for adults is that the adults need to have the children rest as much as the children need to rest. A disrupted naptime can render both child and adult much less able to negotiate the rest of the day with one another. Both, because of fatigue, irritability, and exasperation, may find themselves in more frequent trouble. At the very time when the child needs the most patience and forbearance from his adult caregiver, she may feel the least able to give it.

On the following pages are some typical descriptions and comments about naptime. The descriptions begin with children in the second year. In the first year most babies had at least two naps a day, of varying length, and were put in for naps whenever they seemed tired and sleepy, quite independent of whether anyone else was having a nap. When the children were around 18 months and concomitant with toddler school, their naptimes were scheduled for right after lunch. Even then, however, if a child needed extra sleep or rest, he might be taken out of the group for a morning nap, or have a second late afternoon rest period.

Joan, 20 months, at this time slept in a room with Larry, 23 months, and Steven, 20 months. When she saw the cots being brought out she started to cry. MD picked her up and held her on her lap as she undressed her and talked with her about taking a nap, mentioning that she would stay with her while she went to sleep. She then put her on the cot, staying nearby.

Joan stopped crying and fell asleep in about ten minutes. She had not for several weeks asked for a bottle at naptime and when she awoke she was usually able to rest quietly on her cot with a book or toy. When Larry or Steven was awake at the same time she would talk and laugh with them.

Joan was known to the staff as a competent and reasonably comfortable child who nonetheless had difficulty in letting her mother go in the mornings. Our assumption was that she would need help in going to sleep, which is another kind of separation, now from the mother substitute. MD's presence and reassurance were enough at this time to help Joan make the transition and she seemed replenished and comfortable when she awoke.

Jackie, 18 months, became quite upset when put down for a nap on a cot on the first day back after a month's vacation. He cried and got up, rejecting his usually beloved bottle as an aid to going to sleep. He quieted as KB rocked and sang to him, but began to fuss again when put down. He finally dropped off to sleep as she patted and talked softly to him. On the next three days he settled down more easily with his bottle and the adult nearby. When he woke he would get up and go into the room where Curtis was or into the kitchen to find an adult.

That it was Jackie's first day back and that sleeping on a cot was a new experience were probably responsible for his distress. It was relatively easy to comfort him and help him get to sleep, since there was an adult available to acknowledge his distress and take appropriate action. Failure to respond to a child's distress in a supportive way, that is, ignoring or punishing, would not only heighten the distress but would prolong it. Having staff available at the right time who can be supportive of the child in the long run saves much wear and tear on the child, staff, and parent.

Steven, 22 months, was almost always ready to take a nap and went to sleep promptly. He liked to have a blanket to put his head and face on besides the one with which he was covered and would not lie down until he had it. He usually also asked for his "binkie" (a pacifier tied onto a diaper), though he often wanted not to suck it but just to have it near him.

Steven's binkie had been a particularly important source of comfort to him since his first year, when he had spent many weeks in the hospital. He asked for it at various times during the day at the center, seeming to need it on some days far more than others. Our attitude, with which Steven's mother concurred, was that he could have his binkie whenever he seemed to need it. By this time he could ask for it if it had been put away.

Several children over the years of the program took unusually long naps. In some we came to recognize the long sleep as a reaction to stress. One specific example follows.

Curtis, 24 months, was usually quite ready for his nap, lay down on his cot, dropped off quickly, and slept at least two hours. He usually roused slowly after a long nap and lay quietly awake on his cot. On his first day back after a month's vacation, he took a very long nap—almost 3 hours—then lay for a long time, seeming reluctant to get up. After two or three days of very long naps he went back to his more usual pattern of waking after about two hours.

The staff was grateful for Curtis' behavior because he always seemed ready and eager to sleep. While one can argue with some validity that the long rest was probably good for him, since he felt under stress, we also viewed it as an indicator of his reaction to the daycare experience. We knew that he slept well at night and did not take long naps at home during vacation, and realized that the long sleeping might be from physical fatigue or psychological fatigue: he could be coping with the long day by sleeping it away. Perhaps it was a bit of all these things. Curtis had reacted to coming into daycare at age 12 months with several months of being often apathetic and passive. While by this time, 24 months, he was much more lively and used the program well, it was plausible that, for this child, the long sleep was an indicator that he still felt some stress in our setting.

Toilet Training

Control over bowel and bladder function is, in our society, expected of most children in the second or third year. There are, however, great variations in the expectations and attitudes of individual parents regarding timing and methods of helping the child master this developmental task. If a daycare center accepts infants and toddlers, it is inescapable that staff will be involved in the child's mastery of bowel and bladder function. Coordination of the efforts of parents and daycare staff is important if the child is to master this developmental task without undue stress.

The middle to the end of the second years is a favorable time for most children to begin in terms of developmental readiness, for the following reasons.

• Walking will have been mastered for a long enough time that the child, with benevolent help, should be able to sit with reasonable contentment for ten to fifteen minutes. The child who has just begun to walk may be so preoccupied with activity that he is not satisfied to sit for such a long time.

• The child will have enough understanding of the communications of the adult that he can associate specific words or gestures with the act. Speech is a helpful though not an essential part of this awareness.

• His motivation to please the adult, in spite of a tendency toward negativism and oppositional behavior, has usually progressed to the point that the child and adult can work together.

• Voluntary control over the sphincters is fully possible as far as maturation of the neuromuscular apparatus is concerned.

The adult's role is

• To make a judgment about the child's developmental readiness for toilet training.

• To provide a physical and social atmosphere conducive to the mastery of the task. This includes providing a comfortable and secure seat, since any feeling of uneasiness can interfere, and a time and place free of major distractions.

• To give clear cues to the child about what is expected of him.

• To show approval without excitement; to show disapproval without great intensity or punishment. Fighting with the child may make him behave with stubbornness or excitement and thus greatly prolong his achieving control. Harsh punishment may cause him to submit only out of fear of the adult, robbing him of self-respect and pleasure in mastery of his own body, which are important aspects of his healthy personality development. Such harsh measures are highly likely to make the child more vulnerable to psychological disorders.

• To be patient with the process, i.e., to be aware that a span of time is required, that mastery is gradual, that ups and downs are a part of the picture, that immediate and continuous compliance from the child is not to be expected.

It is important that the child be trained by someone with whom he has enough of a relationship that there is some motivation to please, for the wish to please the adult is one of the most important reasons toddlers accept and cooperate in the toilet-training process.

In the beginning the child should not be required to sit more than five or ten minutes and the adult should stay with him. The seat should be comfortable and steady. Some children accept a small seat placed over the large toilet. Others are more comfortable and feel more secure in a "potty chair" that permits their feet to touch the floor. It is usually most effective if both adult and child keep to the business at hand; therefore, reading stories or providing toys or food may be a distraction rather than a help. When the toddler has urinated or has had his bowel movement, the adult should let him know that she is pleased, but should not show exaggerated excitement. Giving clear cues to the toddler about training also includes the adult's letting him know that she is displeased when he wets or has his bowel movement in his pants or diapers. He should not be punished, but it does no harm to show him that she does not enjoy the smell or the incessant cleaning up. He should be allowed to see the product, if he wishes, and most children in the second year are likely to be interested. Some children may be frightened by the sound of the flushing toilet and disappearance of the stool; others may want to participate in the flushing away. The child's reaction will guide the adult in this respect. If he wishes to smear or play with the stool or urine this should be prevented with a clear "no," but not punished.

As indicated earlier, it is important that he have enough words, or enough understanding of them, to associate a simple word or phrase with toileting. These words vary in different families and ethnic groups. It does not matter what word or phrase is chosen, as long as there is some consistency in its use. The words help the child to have a more specific knowledge of this function of his body; they also help him to understand that he is being asked for something specific. Later he will use the same words to communicate his request to go to the bathroom or to comment on his performance.

There will be ups and downs in the process of establishing control. Fatigue, illness, or involvement in play are common causes of toilet accidents. In many children, there are also periods of resistance to training, which reflect their feelings at those times. If these are not met with anger and anxiety by the adult, they are usually of short duration. It may be necessary to suspend training for a time if stress or conflict seems severe. For some children, regularity and control are fairly well organized by age 2; for others they come somewhat later. There can also be a loss of already achieved control (regression) in response to stress of various kinds, such as illness, separation from an important person, or other disruption in his life situation.

Training for urinary control does require that the adult take the child to the toilet often during the day. This means that in the daycare center there have to be enough staff available to carry out the plan. Timing will depend upon how frequently the child urinates. It is advisable, at this time, to put him in training pants during the day, because this helps to clarify what is being asked. As long as he is in diapers, he will be tempted to use them as he always has, and can be confused if he is asked to use the toilet and then put back in diapers. One exception to this is that having diapers at naptime may be advisable as a transitional practice because of the child's natural tendency to regress during sleep.

It should not be expected that toddlers in groups will be ready or able to control their sphincters on a group schedule. It is important to adopt an individual approach. But children do learn partly by imitation of others, and sometimes the example of another child is a help. In the group day-care setting it is probably somewhat more difficult to be aware of the child's readiness and to take advantage of the auspicious moment than in the home situation. On the other hand, the fact that there are other children who have either already achieved control or who are also in the process sometimes make it easier for other children to do so. While the normal oppositional behavior of the child of this age may occur around toileting in the center as at home, it is often not as intense if the adult at the center does not become embattled with the child. On the other hand, the motivation of the child to please the daycare staff member may be less than for the parent.

In Children's House there was one bathroom with four small toilets and four wash basins such as those found in many nursery schools. In addition, there were several potty chairs, which could either be used in the bathroom or be taken to another area. The fact that our pediatricians were seeing parents regularly made it simple to discuss the timing and method of the parents' toilet training their children and to stress the importance of co-ordinating parental efforts with those of the center's staff. In the exchanges of information that took place when children arrived in the morning and were picked up in the afternoon, it was not always appropriate or con-structive for the child to hear discussions about his progress or the lack of it. In such instances other opportunities to talk with the mother had to be arranged.

In the following pages descriptions are given of several children in the process of achieving bowel and bladder control. They have been selected not because they are startling in any way, but because they are ordinary.

Leslie Nichols   Leslie was 19 months of age when the daycare staff, coordinating their efforts with those of her mother, began toilet training. At 26 months of age she had mastered bowel and urinary control. The staff and her parents considered that the process had been relatively easy for everyone.

A note from her record at 19¾ months was typical of the early period. One morning after she had breakfast she was asked if she would like to go to the potty. The first mention brought a big frown but after a little thought she smiled and ran to the gate and, when it was opened for her, into the bathroom and over to the seat. Her diaper was taken off and she sat down without needing any help. She seemed to want to let MB know that she was trying and grunted expressively to show it but produced nothing. The next day she was put in training pants when she arrived and was taken to the pot several times. During the next three months the procedure was to take her several times during the day, when the staff felt she might use it. Their cue about an impending bowel movement was that she would get very quiet, go over into a corner and get a strained look on her face. She seemed not to mind being taken to urinate and at such times usually did so, but she gave no clear clues about her need, and if the adult did not catch her in time she would wet her pants. If taken, she would sit down without protest, urinate, smile and say to herself, "Good girl," and then try to play with the urine. She did not protest when not allowed to do so. The staff noted that when she did wet her pants during that period, if nothing was said to her, she would wet them again soon; but if reminded about what was expected she was able to keep dry. For about a month, when she was 23–24 months, she protested if anyone except KM, her principal caregiver, took her to the pot. There was no doubt that she had an investment in pleasing KM and liked being commended by her. It was also noted at this time that from another room she would recognize the sound of the toilet flushing and comment on the other children. For instance, one day she looked up at KM and asked, "Terry go pee pee?" When this was answered affirmatively she repeated it to herself a few more times and then went back to her play. At almost 26 months she was staying dry all day except during naptime and seemed quite pleased with her ability to control. By 26 months and 10 days she had things well in hand and would ask whatever familiar person might be available to take her when she had to go to the pot.

At around this time there was an interesting but not unusual observation recorded when Leslie went into the bathroom and tried to urinate standing up as Terry did. Unable to do so, she got to her knees and tried again. When she discovered it wouldn't work out very well this way she said nothing and simply walked out of the bathroom.

Three weeks later she showed her knowledge and her identification with the adult caregiver by helping David with toileting. Leslie and David woke from their naps and David said to Leslie, "I want to go pee pee." Leslie took him by the hand, led him to the bathroom, helped him pull his pants down and get up on the toilet seat. After he urinated, he got off the toilet and smiled and Leslie clapped and cheered. Then she helped him pull his pants up, he flushed the toilet, and they both went back to the playroom quite satisfied with themselves. By 27 months she was able to manage the toileting independently except for needing some assistance in pulling up her pants. Within a very few days after this she was taking full responsibility for her toileting needs, and thereafter there were no lapses in her control. Her parents reported the same success at home.

David Ferris   With David the course of training was somewhat less smooth, though not really difficult. The staff began suggesting, as they had with Leslie at about the same time, that he might like to go to the potty, and removing his diaper and putting him on the potty chair. On the first day he usually wet himself as his diaper was being removed. However, he seemed to get the idea somewhat; on the second day he had a bowel movement on the pot and seemed very pleased with himself. For the next few days he would occasionally urinate or defecate in the pot with some pleasure. Then he entered a period when he wasn't sure the whole thing was a good idea at all. At 20½ months, when asked to go to the pot he answered vehemently, "No pot, no pot!" He was taken anyway but did nothing, though a few minutes after he was off the pot and back in his training pants he wet himself. Then for a time David's attendance was irregular, making it more difficult for him and the staff to pursue the training in the center. At 26 months he was adamantly refusing the pot and efforts were simply suspended for a time. A note was made that he did not mind being wet and did not indicate any wish to be changed when wet. However, he was not protesting the change of diapers and was very lively and active, interacting in a playful way with KM, his major caregiver. That his oppositional behavior had something specific to do with KM as well as with his mother was suggested by an observation made at around 26½ months that, while he would not go to the potty for KM, he would allow any one of three other staff members to take him and seemed very happy and pleased with himself at such times. This is a good example of a typical kind of struggle often seen around toilet training: the child wishes both to be and not to be trained and may express one side of his feeling with one person and the other side with others. Responding to this cue from David, we arranged that for a time he be taken to the pot by someone other than KM. He then began to ask to be taken and to be pleased with his own mastery. At 27 months he was using the toilet willingly, was standing to urinate, and was wearing a diaper only at naptime. A week later the note was made that the only time he was wetting himself was while napping, but he rejected any attempt to put a diaper on him for his nap. By the time another week had passed he either took himself to the bathroom or asked to be taken, having gained full control and assumed responsibility for self-regulation in this sphere.

The following examples of behavior of three other children were selected because each represents a type encountered frequently.

When Curtis was 24 months old, his grandmother began to put him on the potty at home, so we began also. When taken he would sit relaxed and without resistance, but he did not use the potty and did not get up from it until invited to do so. He would wet his diapers without giving any indication that he would like to go or that he was wet. He lay passively during the diaper changing. He reacted very little to the sensations of his body and seemed less aware than most 2 year olds when he urinated.

Obviously Curtis at this point was not showing any interest in using the pot, but there was no evidence of active resistance either. Had it not been for our wish to cooperate with his grandmother's efforts, so as to not confuse Curtis, we would have deferred these efforts on the basis of lack of readiness.

One morning Steven, 22 months, was in the yard, and said something in turn to KB, MB, and MF. No one was certain of what he had said but soon he had a bowel movement in his pants and then announced to everyone, "Poo pee." Two days later he went up to MF and said, "Poo pee," grabbed at his penis and was taken to the bathroom. He urinated in the potty and seemed proud and happy.

This is an example of how Steven began to call attention to his interest, though, because he was dealing with three people and not his regular caregiver, who was ill, he had difficulty making himself understood. We are not sure why Steven had such an investment in achieving control and so little ambivalence about the process. However, he showed less oppositional behavior in general throughout this period of his life than did most of the other children. This may well have been due to the fact that his mother was accepting of his babyhood, and made attempts to understand his behavior and to deal with it without letting any issue become an intense problem.

A note at 23–24 months documents his progress: "Steven uses the potty when taken to it and occasionally asks to go. He uses the words *potty, poo poo,* and *pee pee.* He seems relatively at peace with the training process, enjoys the approval it gets him, and seems to have no particular need to rebel. He also seems pleased with his own achievement." At this same time, one day playing in the water at toddler school he held up a baby doll. As he saw the water drip off he said, "Pee pee pee pee pee pee," and then wanted to take the baby to the pot in the bathroom.

That this play was a reflection of Steven's interest and involvement in toileting is apparent. On the same day Curtis, playing in the water, was noted to pour water from one cup to another saying, "Water," and then to pour water on the baby doll. He held the cup under baby like a potty.

Larry's mother began toilet training him at around 16 months, shortly before he entered daycare. At home, at this time, he was characterized as a sociable, friendly toddler obviously strongly attached to his mother and very sensitive to her moods and behavior. She reported that at first he seemed agreeable to sitting on the potty but after a few weeks began to protest, so she dropped it for a while. She resumed at 18–19 months, but we did not attempt to train him at school because his attendance was quite irregular and he was having a difficult time adjusting to the separation from his mother. Much of the period between 18 and 26 months was difficult for Larry and his mother. She found it hard to go to work and leave him and alternately behaved sympathetically or angrily when he cried for her. In the center it appeared she was never far from his mind. He was apparently cooperating with her on toileting at home but was resistant to using the pot in the center when we began to suggest it at around 25 months, holding his urine as long as he could.

Larry, 25 months, was sitting in the wooden carriage next to the sandbox. He began to look very sad and started crying. When MB asked what was wrong, he couldn't answer. She went over and picked him up, discovering that he was wet. He had been asked several times during the morning whether he wanted to go to the potty and had refused each time. She took him to change him and he cried the entire time, until she reminded him that she was not going to spank him. With that reassurance he stopped crying while she finished dressing him, and went back to play until lunchtime.

This episode occurred at a time when Larry was showing symptoms of acute generalized anxiety. He had, for example, been set off on prolonged crying the day before at the sound of the doorbell. We were able eventually to connect this acute anxiety state with certain things that were going on at home. In addition, we learned that his mother had threatened him with severe punishment if he did not use the pot at the center. This episode reveals how difficult this was for Larry, and how very much he needed reassurance that the adult was not going to scold or punish him.

Up until a few days before he was 26 months old, Larry had continued to have a very hard time and would start to cry and scream at the mention of going to the pot even though he had a full bladder. He would also try to hold the urine rather than let it come out. At this time, however, he began to use the potty and to talk about what a big boy he was for not fussing.

At this point Larry seemed to resolve—we do not know quite how—his conflicted feelings, and he achieved sphincter control. We had been aware that his mother, quite close and loving to him in many way, was often harsh and punitive around the issue of toileting. We tried to help her be both more reasonable and more consistent. In the center, realizing his distress, which had elements of stubbornness but also of anxiety, we tried to alleviate his anxiety as well as to help him use the toilet.

The Bath and Dressing

When one has infants and toddlers in daycare, giving baths, changing diapers, and dressing them are frequent experiences during the day. Being bathed or dressed is for the infant as much a part of the curriculum as working a puzzle, looking at a book, building a house, or counting is for an older child. Once this notion is accepted, adults are ready to think about what these experiences bring to an infant that promote his development. He cares little about the adult's preference for a clean, sweet-smelling baby, but he relishes and learns from the social contact and from varied sensations as he experiences changes in temperature, texture, position, sight, sound, and smell. The fact that the bath calls for close adult attention makes it a marvelous opportunity to talk to an infant about himself, what is going on, what he is doing, and how he is feeling. A person who enjoys infant care can easily see how the bath experience can be used to stimulate the child's learning in a perfectly natural and informal manner.

At Children's House, each of the two infant and toddler rooms contained a built-in sink and counter unit used for washing and changing babies. Cabinets above and below the counter and a closet nearby made the supplies of soap, towels, diapers, clothing, and so on conveniently available. Although the children were bathed at about the same time each morning, it was far from a routine experience. It was usually a time when one or two children could be with a favorite caregiver, away from the interruptions and demands of the group, and was usually a pleasant time for both adult and child. Indeed, we were especially impressed with how much the adults enjoyed bathing the children and the important role of their pleasure in making the experience a positive one for the child.

Leslie, 4 mos., being bathed by MB, was happy, smiling, and relaxed as MB talked with her. She reached for a container of nipples nearby. These were moved out of reach and a small, red plastic fish was put into the water to attract her. She looked at it intently, activated her arms, and tried to reach and grasp it, splashing the water. This activity seemed to fascinate her and she continued to splash more and more actively, squealing with delight. A little later she was fascinated by seeing water being squeezed out of the sponge by MB for her entertainment. Before her bath was over she had succeeded, after several attempts, in grasping the floating fish with both hands.

Here, in addition to the physical and social stimulation of the situation, Leslie was stimulated by the objects provided for her to grasp and manipulate. In this instance the nipples had just as much stimulus value for learning as did the floating toy, but since they had been made ready for the day's use, they were removed and the fish substituted. Had she reached for the soap, the sponge, or the plastic tube of shampoo, she would have been allowed to keep it.

Jackie, 8½ mos., was sitting quietly in the sink while GM washed his hair, playing with a plastic shampoo bottle she had given him. He soon became active, reaching for the soap dish and the plastic cup on the counter until he managed to get both of them into the water and enjoyed manipulating them as they floated about. He twice pulled to stand by holding the edge of the sink, smiling broadly. At one point he smilingly held the cup out toward the observer as if showing it to her. When Joan, age 11 months, approached the sink to put her hand on the counter, Jackie touched her hand, smiled, and gurgled at her. Removed from the water and placed on the counter to be dried, he seemed to enjoy being rubbed with the towel, smiled at GM, and made happy squeals and a "da da" sound. He remained inactive lying on his back while his diaper and shirt were put on. GM communicated with him frequently during the bathing and dressing, and Jackie responded by making soft, pleasant sounds. When placed in a sitting position to have the rest of his clothes put on, he did not try to move away, nor did he actively enter into the dressing process. When he was dressed GM helped him stand up and invited him to look at himself in the mirror. He smiled, vocalized, and waved his hand at the observer whose reflection he could also see. He then looked at his own reflection, smiled broadly, and bounced up and down as though charmed with what he saw.

Although GM could have left Joan in the larger playroom with the other children while she bathed Jackie, she knew Joan would prefer to be with her. While Jackie was being bathed, Joan played with toys GM provided, and toddled about the room, often watching the bath activity and sometimes protesting the attention Jackie was being given. GM, while bathing and talking to Jackie, also managed to keep in contact with Joan, who remained reasonably well satisfied.

Jackie obviously enjoyed having his body washed and dried by GM, and her pleasure in bathing him and dressing him in attractive clothes no doubt communicated the message that he was valued and appreciated.

Motor Activity

Most of a young child's play involves motor activity and the child's motor skills emerge in a variety of situations. Almost all of the descriptions of children illustrating various aspects of development and learning serve to illustrate motor development. They reveal that motility is not only a means to an end but often provides great pleasure in itself. Moreover, movement is often used by the child to express his feelings.

Opportunities to move about, to use emerging motor skills were offered at all ages. Healthy, well-cared-for infants are usually stimulated toward self-initiated activity by being provided toys, by having people to move toward, by being placed on the floor where a firm surface, space, and the lure of an interesting situation ask for a response. Toddlers, fascinated with walking, move out toward new things and new experiences. Balls, scooters, climbing equipment, swings, rocking toys, tricycles, and walking boards are familiar to everyone as objects that invite large muscle activity. Similarly, the development of small muscle skills and eye–hand coordination through the manipulation of small objects is well understood. Involvement in motor activity is so much in the nature of the young child that it does not seem necessary to detail the many ways it can be supported.

Perhaps it is worth emphasizing, however, that children may need encouragement at times to use their motor skills, and at other times to tone down activity. Adults need to plan space and activities in the child's day that both encourage activity and help to channel it. An overemphasis on large muscle activity can interfere with developing skill in the use of small muscles and may discourage thought and reflection. A balance between experiences that promote body skills and experiences that promote the activities of the mind is, of course, necessary. What varies with age, and often with individual temperament, is the amount and kind of experience that forms a harmonious balance.

Of special relevance in the daycare setting is the realization that time for motor play has to be more consciously scheduled for children than is true when they are at home. Indoor play rooms have to serve as spaces in which the child plays, eats, and sleeps, and it takes planning to work out areas in which climbing equipment, slides, rocking boats, scooters, and so on can be used. Obviously, too, those things that were a part of conventional space and furnishings in our remodeled residence—stairs to climb, a long hall to run or crawl in, doorsills to step over, cabinets to hide in—

were well utilized. Outdoor play space and equipment that supported both large and small muscle activity included scooters, tricycles, swings, slides, climbing equiment, and sandbox toys specifically furnished and leaves, twigs, pebbles, and blades of grass provided by nature. Here as elsewhere the young child achieved most skill and pleasure when the adult was near enough to protect and keep an eye on him, and when needed, to directly encourage and support his activity.

CHAPTER 8

The Day-to-Day Experience for Older Preschool Children

The description of the program for 2½ to 5 year olds stands in a somewhat different context from that of the program for infants and toddlers. Because of the accumulation of knowledge about children in nursery school, and the vast amount of experience, thought, and conceptualization from the early childhood education movement, this section is organized and written from the perspective of the educator of young children. There are many more explicit descriptions of teaching methods and references to curriculum than are found in the material on infants and toddlers. Nonetheless, these ideas fall within the framework of the guiding principles described earlier. Our belief in the importance of human relationships in the child's development, the need to base programs for children on knowledge of developmental tendencies and needs, and the need to establish a partnership with parents in the interests of their children underlies all that is said here.

All of the children who entered the pilot group were chosen because in some way their development had already been adversely affected in varying degrees, as illustrated in the vignettes in Chapter 2. Because of this, the task of the teachers was much more complex and strenuous than it would have been in work with children whose life experiences had more effectively supported their development. Our experience is not unique. The growing enthusiasm for early education for children at risk, which received a great thrust from the extending Head Start programs to younger children, the emphasis on early recognition of developmental problems, and the increased demand for daycare, have made all of us aware that thousands of the nation's young children have significant developmental lags and disabilities that could be alleviated by good, timely programs. Most of the daycare centers with which we are familiar contain many young children whose educational and developmental needs simply cannot be met by current staffing practices and programs.

In most of the children in our first group of 2½–5 year olds there was less harmony among the cognitive, emotional, social, and physical aspects of development than there is in well-functioning children. There was often great competence in one area combined with substantial delay or distortion in others. Some of the special attitudes and techniques required to temper these disharmonies are emphasized in the material to follow. Even so, the role of the teacher as it is conceptualized here applies to the education of young children in general, for it is based on knowledge of the developmental process and on those characteristics of the teacher that stimulate and enable the child to learn.

Aims and Approach

Our educational goal was to help the child develop competencies and attitudes that, based upon research and experience of skilled educators, appear to be essential for any young child who is to function well in a school setting and, it is inferred, who will be able to continue to progress in his development. His strengths, capabilities, and competencies are viewed as assets to be supported by education; his limitations are viewed as deficits with which he needs help. Built into this approach are explicit and implicit assumptions about what, in general, children are like, the nature and processes of growth and development and how learning is supported and facilitated. We believe that the goals are sound regardless of the child's socioeconomic, ethnic, and individual situation. What must be varied by educators are the types of experiences that relate to these goals and the routes by which they can be reached. The kind of nurturance of body and mind considered sound for children in general must be adapted for each individual child, according to his particular need or readiness. One of the responsibilities we accepted was to enhance each child's learning, to help prepare him for the next step in his education. These educational goals were formulated primarily in terms of developmental processes, that is, the sequential and orderly emergence of functions and abilities and their integration into the whole. We see this focus on process as being more helpful, both to teacher and child, than emphasizing discrete performance or achievements at any one point in time.

At the risk of being repetitious we will emphasize another conviction that guided planning and practice: that one cannot educate a young child adequately without paying attention to his emotional and social development as well as his cognitive development. A program that attends to both aspects is vitally important for the young child in daycare because his healthy development is much more dependent on the program, especially his social and emotional development, then is that of the child who spends two to three hours a day in nursery school and is otherwise with his family. These aspects of development have a complex interdependence that demands careful consideration if any child's learning is to be facilitated. The development of self-esteem, a sense of identity, self-regulation of behavior, and interpersonal relationships cannot be separated from the growth of cognitive functions such as acquiring and ordering information, reasoning, problem solving, and the use of symbols.

Organization of Space and Equipment

The playrooms and playground at Children's House were organized as centers for the child's life at school. The teachers, through their selection, preparation, and arrangement of physical space and materials, determined the nature of this environment. The wall colors, the draperies and other decorations, the quality and kind of materials provided and their appropriateness and accessibility taken together formed a statement about how the rooms were to be used. They also formed a statement of the kinds of relationships that were to be encouraged among children and between teachers and children, and the way in which teachers expected children to be engaged in learning.

The program centered around the children's need to play in order to learn. We wanted children to be able to use their experience in the day-care center in ways productive and useful to them. This was no easy task to accomplish, since the house was a large, old three-story structure planned for a single family. However, it was on a corner lot and there was adequate play space behind and beside the house. A side door and a back door opened out onto these areas, and a part of a three-car garage could be included in the fenced-off yards and used for outdoor storage. The play yard was adjacent to the playrooms and the outdoor storage was adjacent to play areas where materials and equipment were most likely to be used. A sturdy fence around the yard provided protection from the two busy streets that bordered this space.

Space was arranged so that children could move from one room to another and to the toilet without having to ask for adult help. The plan of the house was so simple and compact that a child could quickly gain a sense of orientation. We wanted to provide a balance between a child's being able to do things for himself and having adult help when he needed it. Teachers could give unobtrusive supervision to all rooms from any one room when folding doors in the wide doorways between rooms were open, and could intervene quickly if needed. These doors could also be closed, for we realized that the children needed opportunities for semiprivacy and freedom from the stimulation of being with others. A large glass window gave teachers a view into the toilet, yet provided quiet and relative privacy for the children. Because the children worked, ate, and slept in the same rooms, the space arrangements had to allow for quick and relatively easy changes. With each change the room and its arrangements again made a statement to the children regarding what was to take place.

All arrangements took into account the premise that in order to be free to play a young child needs protection from danger; he needs judicious help as well as freedom from unnecessary interference. The total environment was planned for exploration, understanding, and use. Teachers encouraged children to be self-directed, to use their changing abilities and skills, and to make choices. There were opportunities to make mistakes without being "wrong" or "bad" and without endangering themselves and others. Children were given many opportunities to do things for themselves and to ask for help, so the burden of being small, weak, or powerless could be relieved by the realization of realistic competencies.

The objects in the rooms, in the play yard, and in storage space were ordered in terms of functional relations. Materials and equipment were stored where they could be used. For example, easel, finger paint, construction and drawing paper were stored in a long cabinet under the sink. This area was where art activities usually took place. In the block area, which was a part of a room not in the main line of traffic, blocks were stored on shelves, with like kinds together. Block accessories such as small trucks, cars, airplanes, animals, people, and color cubes were in baskets that fit on adjacent shelves. The order of the space was viewed as a way of teaching and learning; it was logical, relatively stable, and communicated to the children. At first teachers made statements like, "You need a paintbrush. They are in the cupboard under the sink." Language was then supported by action as the child and teacher went together and found the paintbrush in the expected place. After the paintbrush was used it was washed and returned to the cupboard with a comment like, "You can put this paintbrush back in the cupboard so we will know where it is when we need it." It did not take children long to learn where materials were stored, how an area was organized, which were teachers' cupboards and which were children's cupboards. As one would expect, they first learned the location of things that were most important to them. That is, their learning was at first self-centered and highly personal. It very gradually became more general and intellectually organized. By the end of eight weeks, almost all of the children knew the location of materials and equipment that they had used.

We assumed that children have various preferred modes of learning and expression, and that repetition with the same and with different materials facilitates learning and understanding. For these reasons, there were many and varied materials offering opportunities for work and play with different media and a variety within media. Furthermore, the classroom was not equipped at the beginning of the year and then lived with. Matching the materials to the children proved to be difficult. We gauged the children's tolerance for stimulation poorly the first few days of school. The new place and new people presented them with a very big demand for adjustment that was undoubtedly stressful. Some reacted by becoming immobilized, while others were overactive and obviously disorganized. We found it was necessary to remove all but the simplest, most basic kinds of material for several weeks. New items were added as the children required and could tolerate the stimulation of variety, as their skills and abilities developed, and when such items were needed to facilitate transfer of learning to new situations. Objects and materials that could not be used without teacher support or supervision were placed in "teachers' cupboards." As children gained skills and control these materials were placed on shelves where they were available for them to use at various times during the day. At first we always had available three or four of each item, since it was extremely difficult for children to wait for turns. Gradually, as they could tolerate the frustration of waiting, one-of-a-kind items were introduced.

More detail is given elsewhere about the children's use of the setting and the program. Here we wish to emphasize only that space, equipment, and materials can be set up so that they facilitate the child's learning or interfere with it, and it is the responsibility of the leaders to take this into account.

Four Children

The following brief descriptions of four of the children in the older group were formulated from a teacher's observations of the children during the first ten days of school. Some of the children at risk were introduced in Chapter 2; here we want to convey a more specific understanding of the functioning of typical members of this group of children as it confronted the teachers.

Stuart   Stuart, 4 years and 5 months old, was a tall, slender boy with brown, tousled, curly hair, dark eyes, and long eyelashes. He had fair, pale skin, frequently with small bruises and scratches on arms and legs. He walked with a quick clumsy gait, shoulders hunched forward. He was accurate and effective when handling materials, even small ones, though he looked awkward. He spoke in a hoarse voice, his articulation of beginning consonants was very poor, and his syntax was awkward. However, he had a good working vocabulary and used language well to convey ideas. His mouth was often open and he licked his lips so much that a large area around his mouth was sore and chafed. At snack- and lunch-time he ate with his hands, cramming his mouth full of food and attempting to talk at the same time. Stuart's behavior ranged from uncontrolled to well controlled and was characterized by intense concentration. When out of control he could hurt himself and others, and adult help was required for Stuart to get into control or organize himself again. When in control he built complicated three-dimensional, functional buildings with blocks and was skilled in the use of construction games. A steady stream of obscenities often accompanied his block building, but seemed entirely unrelated to the task. He worked alone and watched others as if ever alert to protect himself. He was aggressive toward people and objects, as if they were there to "do him in." At what looked like the smallest dissatisfaction or what he perceived as a threat, he would push, hit, and spit. However, in one-to-one relationships with adults he was affectionate and sensitive. He would wiggle up close to a teacher to hear a story. Often he could listen to the content and respond thoughtfully, but a detail of a picture could set him off talking about food, things being broken, things stinking or being rotten. He often smelled materials and small cuts and bruises on himself, asking if he were rotten inside. Such questioning was usually accompanied by his jerking his head to one side, blinking rapidly, and licking his lips.

Sandra Sandra, a lively, alert girl 4 years and 9 months old, was the oldest child in the group. She was of medium height for her age, long boned, and slender. Her dark hair was parted in the middle and two thick braids extended below her shoulders. Her ebony skin was somewhat mottled on her face and arms from eczema. She had an engaging smile. Sandra's first days in the center were spent in demonstrating what she could do and she seemed quite independent and competent in personal tasks, spontaneous play, and the use of several materials. She was ready to associate her past experiences with this situation and she played imaginatively in the doll corner with Jennifer. In her relations with adults and children she seemed to be desperately seeking attention. In situations of conflict with children it was difficult for her to seek or accept help directly. She tired easily at these times, her attention lagged, she was easily distracted from work and play, and she seemed depressed. She then became whiney, and her usually good language was reduced to infantile speech. Her response to disappointment was to cry inconsolably; she found it almost impossible to wait for anything, as though waiting meant she would not get to enjoy whatever she wanted.

Callie Callie, introduced in Chapter 2, was a large, well-developed 2½ year old with prominent brow and eyes. She sucked her thumb almost constantly. She had a minimum of hair in tiny braids and very smooth, warm brown skin. Her beautifully shaped hands and body were used in purposeful, well-coordinated ways to get quickly something she wanted. Under stress she became awkward, clumsy, or immobilized, standing with legs wide apart, head forward and down. She cried soundlessly in this position and great tears fell from her eyes and splattered on the floor. When others behaved aggressively or cried her face reflected concern, as if their feelings were her own, and all visible movement stopped. She seemed not to recognize herself in the mirror and repeatedly tried to get behind it as if to find the other child. She was distracted by noise and was highly aware of people, but did not seem to expect interaction. Although aware of others and of objects, she could not get involved unless a teacher worked directly with her. She often looked at the teacher's face to see what to be pleased about or to enjoy and then her expression mirrored what she saw there. She made guttural sounds of protest, but did not speak spontaneously except when a teacher encouraged her and then said only, "What dat?" or repeated the names of the toys and other objects. She followed simple directions and seemed to find genuine pleasure in helping with cleanup. Her mother had reported that she was toilet trained at home; at school, however, she was not able to maintain bowel or bladder control at this time. Callie would eat bits of food from the floor, grass, leaves, and sand from the sandbox. She was distractable at mealtime, smearing her food on the table and attempting to walk around the room eating, and either ate with her hands or did not eat at all.

Cindy   Cindy, whose situation is also described in Chapter 2, was 3 years and 9 months of age, unusually small and very thin. She had pale, almost transparent white skin, which mottled when she cried. Her fine, thin, pale blond hair was waist length with bangs that extended over her eyebrows and almost hid her light blue, watchful eyes. She usually appeared either very happy or very miserable. When happy she was charming and her face lit up with a bright smile. When miserable she sucked her thumb and twisted her hair, whined, scolded in high-pitched jargon, screamed piercingly, "No! no! no!" and stamped her feet. Her moods were reminiscent of those of a toddler, but more difficult to predict. She wanted an adult near but found physical contact intolerable. She tolerated the presence of other children quite poorly, as if their very physical presence represented the complete loss of the adult or a real threat to her materials. On the other hand, she was eager to please adults and often could play and seem quite comfortable with the full attention of one person. Cindy was quite competent as she imitated household tasks such as washing and setting the table, dressing and putting the dolls to bed, or sweeping the floor. Her vocabulary consisted mainly of commands and greetings, and her articulation was very poor. She had much less everyday knowledge than others of her age. She found it almost impossible to listen to anyone except in a one-to-one situation. Cindy would not urinate until she was extremely uncomfortable and then screamed and objected to going to the toilet. Every time she toileted, one adult had to help her through a tantrum. She was distracted by others at mealtime, would drink only milk, allowed only mashed potatoes or noodles on her plate, and ate only plain jello or pudding for dessert. She scolded and screamed, and each mealtime she seemed to try everything she knew to involve the adult in a battle over eating. At naptime she repeated the same behavior and she finally went to bed with a blanket, sucking her thumb, tickling her nose with her hair and making a high-pitched singsong sound that increased in volume as she almost fell asleep. She rarely slept more than ten minutes at a time and then with her eyes open. The slightest noise would arouse her and she would repeat the same behavior. Cindy was one of the more difficult and disturbed children.

There were fourteen other members of this group of 2½–5 year olds with which we began the program of daycare and education, some of whom functioned better and some even less well than those described above.

The Teacher and Her Role

The young child's teacher is a very significant adult who in part substitutes for his parent, but who has other important functions as well. She develops a relationship with the child in which she transmits and interprets to him what it is important to learn and to do in the daycare setting. Personal warmth and interest in children are undeniably important but are not alone sufficient to enable her to be a good teacher. She should be able to recognize a child's thought and feeling, that is, to understand and identify with him while remaining in the adult role. She should be able to invest a great deal of her energy, skill, and feeling, and at the same time be aware that she and the center cannot be all-important to a child; she must realize that the child's relationship to his parents is central to him and deserves her support. She should develop an ability to observe her own behavior as she interacts with a child so that she can be more aware of what affects him. She must learn to help children find pleasure in their work and excitement in learning, and to assist the child in developing an awareness of his own feelings and those of others. She should learn to share her observations with her coteachers and other colleagues and be open to continued learning about the development of children and the educational process.

But there is no single right way to perform the teaching role. Teachers vary in style, temperament, cultural background, and individual experience. Variations in a group of teachers are not disadvantages but can be utilized as strengths.

The person who is responsible for the program for children as a whole must have other knowledge and competencies in addition to the skills and qualities described. She must have detailed knowledge of child growth and development and must be able to particularize the approach to each child through her ability to perceive his uniqueness. She must understand learning as a process and be able to identify and to implement its essential conditions. She must be able to communicate the purposes of the educational and child-care program to her colleagues, to parents, and to the community. She must be a leader who can build staff relationships in such a way that the teachers' energies are directed toward their central task.

It is important that the person in the program who has the above qualifications spend time in an active teaching role in the classroom. The value of this approach was repeatedly confirmed in our program. Working alongside the teaching staff, our educational director gained an intimate knowledge of what happened. Her participation had a positive effect on staff morale, as teachers realized from firsthand observation that the director understood the reality in the classroom and was aware of what they individually were doing. When specific situations were discussed in staff meetings and everyone knew what had happened before, during, and after a particular situation, problem solving was effective and learning was rapid.

As teachers at Children's House began to know the children and to define where the children were in relation to the educational and developmental goals set for them, the immediate task of the teacher could be formulated and expectations modified in accordance with each child's status. This process is described in the material that follows, derived from specific observations recorded during the first few weeks of the children's attendance in the center. The discussion has been organized by the various areas in which children needed help.

Building Relationships with Adults

Teachers accepted the major responsibility for helping children build relationships that were meaningful and supportive of their learning and development. The teacher's relationship with children was considered crucial since it was seen as mediating the children's learning. We assumed that building relationships would take time and involve a great deal of learning to be sensitive to each other on the part of adults and children. This learning would involve both verbal and nonverbal communication and would take place not in activities specifically aimed at fostering such learning but in all the events of the child's day at the center. Such abilities as attending, reflecting, persisting in a task, solving problems, making choices, resolving conflicts, taking turns and sharing, and relating to other children and adults would be supported through and demonstrated by teacher action as well as language.

Success in building relationships requires that teachers retain a learning attitude themselves and be able to risk making errors. Such attitudes are contagious and help to create a sound environment for the child's learning, a place where it is natural to try, to wonder, to succeed, to make mistakes, to feel, and to express feelings. With this kind of openness to experience, teachers allow themselves the opportunity to assist children in feeling, in thinking, in doing, in reflecting on actions and feelings, in building confidence and competence and in evaluating their own learning.

An inherent difficulty with the teacher's role was providing adequate physical care and affection without interfering with the mother's role. To overcome this difficulty it was necessary continually to assess teacher behavior in regard to what was known about the child and his family. Before school began, the social worker assigned to each family got family and developmental histories from the parents, which helped the teachers gain a great deal of specific information quickly. Medical histories yielded further information for the teacher's task. Information from these two sources was continually enlarged during the children's years at the center. Case conferences held with the research staff were very valuable to teachers in clarifying and defining their role in such a way as to support rather than compete with parents.

For example, one naptime Sandra wet her bed and when she woke was upset and cried. As the teacher helped her wash, put on dry clothing and tried to reassure her that children wet their beds sometimes, Sandra said, "Don't tell Mommy I peed in my bed!" Her teacher could not fail to support Sandra's mother by falling into a conspiracy with Sandra. The teacher told Sandra that her mother cared about her, cared what happened to her, and would understand. In addition, the teacher explained to Sandra that her mother needed and wanted to know what happened at school. At the end of the day, the teacher helped the child tell her mother what had happened and the mother was sympathetic. The next day Sandra said, "My mommy wasn't mad about my peeing in the bed. She wants me to be dry, but she's not mad. No, not one little bit!" It is important to realize that this approach was possible with Sandra because the staff knew the mother well enough to know that although she carried a heavy burden of responsibilities, she did have a great deal of feeling for her children.

As indicated earlier, many children were wary of adults and our feelings and behavior toward them and others. Though their overwhelming need for care, contact, and attention seemed most of the time to override their distrust of teachers, one incident in the early spring of the first year illustrates that anxiety was often just below the surface and that teachers had to be responsive, at a moment's notice, to the needs, doubts, and fears of the entire group of children. One day at naptime, Cindy had a ripped toenail and it caught on her sheet and blanket, keeping her awake. Other children were already settled in for naps and some were almost asleep. MD took Cindy into the toilet room where the first aid supplies were kept to get some scissors to cut the nail. In spite of MD's explanation, when Cindy saw the scissors she began to scream and cry. JE went into the nap room to be with the other children and found vigilant looks and frightened faces. Annette framed their question, "Why is Mrs. D beating Cindy?" JE said, "Wait while I get Mrs. D and Cindy and we will see what made Cindy cry." When Cindy and the two teachers returned to the room all the children got off their cots and came to Cindy. JE said, "Cindy, show the children why you were crying." Cindy showed her nail proudly, basking in the attention of all. JE asked, "Why did you cry, Cindy?" Cindy looked perplexed. MD said, "I think Cindy was afraid of the scissors." Whereupon Cindy covered her toe and began to whimper, although the scissors were not in sight. MD suggested covering the nail with a Band-Aid rather than cutting it. By this time all but a few children had lost interest and had headed back to bed. The teachers used this incident, which at first appeared to be a simple first aid situation, to teach something about cause and effect, to clarify the reality, and allow the expression of what was a natural feeling for the children. That is, they allowed the children to express their fear, and they made explicit the cause of Cindy's crying, so that the children would understand the reality of the situation. Variations on the same theme occurred many times during our years at Children's House. Increasingly, some of the explanations and demonstrations came from the children themselves.

Many of our children had a great need for adult help, but seemed unable to risk asking for or accepting it. This became evident in the initial separation from their mothers, when teachers took initiative in asking them to say good-bye as their mothers left. The children, with the exception of three, seemed puzzled, surprised, or did not acknowledge that this was the day they were to stay alone at school. Two children, Tim and Jennifer, were overtly anxious and could accept their teacher's help. Tim had a favorite Matchbox car and Jennifer had a blanket, which supported their transitions from home to school. Bill cried bitterly, finally bade his mother good-bye, stood silently for a time, and went into a flurry of action, only to have his feelings break through and to cry again, and repeat the process.

Several children demanded astounding quantities of food, dawdled over eating and dressing, and had complex rituals for going to sleep. It was difficult to determine what was a compelling need from what was a momentary desire. Giving and loving and grasping and hurting seemed all mixed up in their minds. The teacher a child liked best became the target of merciless testing. Such demands on a teacher required all the emotional maturity she could muster, and a great deal of support from her peers and the leaders of the program—including relief from the child, "permission" to express her feelings in staff meetings, and suggestions of specific approaches to working out a realistic relationship with a particular child.

Obviously, we hoped that teachers could acknowledge and deal with their feelings, though not at the expense of the children. Those aspects of the teacher's role in which her own feelings are of primary importance to her effectiveness cannot be contrived. What kind of human being she is, how she feels about children, parents, and herself, how well she is able to use her own emotions to enhance her effectiveness as a teacher are enormously important factors in her ability to function in this role.

Learning Self-Observation

One of our goals throughout all types of activities was to create an atmosphere in which it was natural to express feelings. We wanted to help each child to recognize his own response, relate his response to a possible cause or causes, express his feelings increasingly in socially acceptable ways, and connect feelings that were not relevant to the immediate situation to the real cause or causes.

As models for such behavior we needed to be honest, spontaneous, feeling people ourselves, who usually could do what we wanted children eventually to be able to do. Starting with the weeks before school began and continuing through the years of the program, the teacher-director attempted to become a model and to make clear through her behavior and language that it was natural and desirable for adults to express their feelings relevant to the task at hand and to each other, as well as to children. The time the teaching staff had together during the preschool planning and later as we worked together with children, during rest or lunch periods, and in regular teachers' meetings, offered many opportunities for us to express our feelings in honest, direct, and natural ways. Of course, there were times when we lacked sensitivity, when feelings or pressures overwhelmed us, and such communications broke down. We gradually developed a method, applicable to the entire staff, of solving problems based on an honest, direct approach. This method was described in Chapter 3.

In the beginning we found that many of our children were unaccustomed to self-observation and simply did not know how they felt. Half of the children did not know when they were hungry, cold, or hurt. Others did not know when they were tired, lonely, or even pleased. One large task for us, therefore, was to learn the meaning of their behavior, respond to minimal cues, and make them explicit to the child by our own affect and language. A teacher might say, "You look cold, Callie, let's get your sweater," or after lunch, might smile while patting her own and Callie's stomachs and say, "I feel full. Feel your tummy, Callie; how does it feel?" It was a long, laborious task to help Callie to feel, to reflect, to evaluate, and to look into herself, and to express even the immediate physical sensation of being full. We were delighted when, in her last year at Children's House, she began to be able to say with a fierce look on her face, "I hit her 'cause I'm mad at her!" or "That's a dumb rule," or, with a warm smile, "Read it again—I like that story," or, with a sad look, "My mommy, she cried cause, well, I think she was feeling sad. Would you cry, Miss G?"

Most of the teachers had seen and taught children before who did not know how to protect themselves or found themselves repeatedly in dangerous situations. In our group at least half of the children had little idea about what was safe or unsafe. It was not an uncommon experience for children to fall or get hurt and act as if nothing had happened. Teachers had to find many ways to let children know they were cared about, valued, and would be protected. For example, one teacher might say to another, "Help me make these boards steady so children won't get hurt," as she set about placing a cleat over a rung and testing it for safety. Actions were often accompanied by the teacher's sharing the process of her thinking in this manner—"I want to keep you safe," "I'd rather you'd get angry with me than get hurt," or "I want to take care of you so you will learn to take care of yourself," or "I know that was a bad bump; sometimes children cry when it hurts," as a teacher rubbed a shin that had been bruised. While it took some children only a short time to grasp the idea, others did not learn to feel cared for until well into their second year at Children's House. They questioned us, "You like me, you don't want me to get hurt?" One child might say to another, "Stop that, you know that ain't safe," or to a teacher, "You be the policeman. You stop me and you help me when I get in trouble." This to our minds was not overindulgence nor infantalization, but served to enhance the child's sense of autonomy and self-esteem through genuine interest expressed clearly.

Learning Self-Regulation

The teacher was also a supporter of the child's regulation of his own behavior. In practice this aspect of the teacher's role was not independent of helping the child learn self-evaluation. The two are discussed separately in order to make clear and to emphasize the importance of each aspect.

Over time the preschool child must take on the task of mastering his feelings and impulses; but regression occurs frequently and easily. We anticipated that, with regard to self-regulation, there would occur both active efforts toward self-control and resistance to progressive steps in its mastery. We expected regression under stress and were prepared to give children support at these times. We also expected evidences of autonomy and were prepared to allow and encourage children to take active independent roles. We wanted children to get direct satisfaction from their successes in self-regulation and we wanted to help each child recall his successes and gain awareness of his maturing behavior.

As the teacher supports the child's regulation of his own behavior, she defines and maintains limits for the child's actions that are appropriate for his developmental level: limits that provide protection of the child's health, safety, and individual rights; limits within which children have freedom to act with increasing self-reliance and initiative; limits that are imposed in such a way as to support self-regulation without the loss of self-esteem and to recognize the child's right to dignity. Such limits had to be predictable and defined in such a way that they could be understood, honored, and protected by both children and adults.

Helping the children learn self-regulation was complex and often difficult because many of our children appeared at the mercy of feelings and impulses that they did not even recognize. Most had very limited capacity to delay gratification, did not differentiate between small and large disappointments and deprivations, and lacked the ability to anticipate or plan the immediate future. Over half had direct, primitive, impulsive ways of coping with what would be minor stress to most children. Screaming, throwing, hitting, grabbing, and tantrums were common occurrences, particularly at lunchtime, naptime, and when toileting. We had constantly to demonstrate by our language and actions that we could see situations from the child's point of view, while remaining enough in authority that the child could rely on us for protection and security.

Dressing and Undressing

We anticipated that all of the children would need help learning skills related to dressing such as buttoning, lacing, tying, and front and back positioning of clothes. But when school began, children in the older group with four exceptions could almost completely undress and dress themselves. At least half could complete this task with help only with difficult fasteners, and placing the right and left shoes in proper position. Several children could tie their shoes and many could fasten buckles. Only two children were totally dependent on adults dressing and undressing them. Teachers found themselves grateful that so many children were competent in these tasks, and focused their main support and attention on the children who needed help, at the same time talking with the other children about the next event in order to keep in contact with them.

However, we soon discovered we were starting beyond where the children were. Many found it impossible to tolerate a teacher's helping another child with a sock or shoe without getting the same treatment. Children became competitive, whined, and dawdled, creating an unhappy time for children and adults. They lacked pride and pleasure in their own competence in dressing and undressing and in their excellent memories for detail in recalling what shirt, sweater, or hat belonged to whom.

We decided we must respond to the deeper need for attention and care if we were to help the children take initiative for themselves with pleasure, not from coercion. We acknowledged that all childhood is a period when physical competence or skill is not always paralleled by the emotional maturity to use the skill at all times. We therefore made two changes in these situations: we carefully planned transition and routine times so that only one teacher with her group of four children was involved in dressing or undressing at a time, and we planned a longer block of time so that what had been thought of merely as a routine became a significant part of our curriculum. We answered the children's need for adult attention by being available for a great deal of help.

It was striking to see the sheer pleasure of the children in having their teachers care for them in this manner. "Let me fix your shoulder strap; I think it will be more comfortable for you," "Let's find some dry socks for you so your feet won't get cold," became typical comments; a teacher would carefully tuck a shirt into pants, saying "so you will look neat," or smooth hair or tie a ribbon "so you will look pretty." There was little if any regression in the children's skill. By spring, the children were dressing themselves not only competently but with pride and with pleasure. However, from time to time through the years the children were with us they needed an unusual amount of adult attention during dressing and undressing, not because they were incapable but because help was a tangible evidence of adult interest, which children needed and thrived upon. Teachers remained willing to give such help when it seemed beneficial to the child.

Mealtimes

We served breakfast to children who needed it, midmorning and afternoon snacks, and a hot lunch comparable to dinner. Fresh fruit, milk, juice, bread, butter, and peanut butter were always available.

Breakfast, which was served to only two or three of the older children and at different times from seven-thirty to about eight-thirty, was handled on an individual basis. Usually several options were given the children—

for example, an egg or hot cereal, and milk or hot chocolate. Often, with the adult nearby, the child made his own toast and helped to prepare the rest of his meal. Breakfast presented specific individual problems common to many children and families. Strangely, however, complaints about the way an egg was cooked or that the cereal had too much milk, and so on, so familiar to all of us, did not arise. So the teacher set about to give the children permission to be discriminating; she would say, "Is that the way you like your egg?" "Is that enough milk?" or "Is your chocolate warm enough?" To our satisfaction, by Christmas the children were beginning to be quite discriminating about their breakfast requests, expressing both approval and complaints.

Snack had been planned for the time of transition from outdoors to indoors in the morning, in the small "family groups." The teacher's role was to facilitate the children's having a relatively quiet time to rest and recover from active outdoor play, and eventually to help the children organize what had happened earlier and anticipate coming activities through conversation.

One morning during the second week of school, Tim objected to going inside for snack. A teacher, accustomed to taking cues from children and responding spontaneously, said, "It's a nice day; let's have our juice in the sandbox." This change bewildered and disorganized many of the children. From this incident it was brought home to us what reliable, predictable, structured routine situations meant to the group. The teachers did not cease to be spontaneous people, but from then on we considered whether any change in routine would bewilder the children and make them apprehensive or whether it would be a pleasurable, satisfying experience. By the first spring, it was possible for teachers and children to plan a variety of places to have snacktime. By summer, snack and even lunch could be a picnic in the play yard or at the beach, which most children looked forward to as a treat. Thus, more flexibility was possible as children became more secure with us and as they no longer needed completely predictable routines.

Lunch was served family style at eleven-fifteen. A cart was placed in a central place and children, as they were able, returned their plates, glasses, and sliver to the cart after eating. Because we knew this routine would involve a great deal of learning, one adult did not eat at a table but was a floating helper. She would help children and teachers as needed—to take care of spills, to replenish food, to help children learn to scrape their plates, place dishes on the cart, and return to their tables.

At the beginning of the year, after initial visits by the children, we attempted to use what we knew about the children and ourselves as a basis for making decisions about family groups for lunch. Some of the considerations were which children had beginning relationships with each other and with a teacher, which children needed a great deal of help because they were young, which were disorganized and disruptive, whose impact on the group could be diluted if they were at different tables, and how many staff were available. We started out with four children and an adult eating together in family groups formed on the basis of the above considerations.

At this time the teacher's role at mealtime was considered primarily that of a model and supporter of children's learning. That is, she would sit at the table throughout the meal, serve the children, and eat some of all the foods offered. She would take cues from the children regarding their readiness to serve themselves, clean up their own spills, and converse with other children as they were able to cope with these opportunities.

Although we knew this was going to be a new and complex experience for the children and had tried to simplify the situation in many ways and provide support for children's learning, we were not prepared for the disorganizing impact of the children on each other. Their need for adult attention was increased in a total group situation and when food was offered. They became competitive and disorganized in response to even a minor disappointment, such as another being served first or having what seemed a larger portion. They were highly sensitive to stimuli from other tables or outside the room in the street—for example, a child crying or angry at another table or a truck going down the street. They showed sudden outbursts of anger by striking others, screaming, throwing food, or crying. Some children panicked when the serving bowls looked as if all the food were gone.

Furthermore, the number of foods many children were familiar with, had eaten before, or would tolerate on their plate was limited; several children seemed unable to feed themselves; others could not keep their food on their plates or use tools for eating; several children did not know when they were hungry or when they were full; and some ate scraps from the floor and from the scrap pan.

After the first few days we knew that two adults were needed for each table. The research staff was informed of the situation and began to join the group at lunchtime. Special arrangements were made for three children who could not manage in the lunchroom, with its many opportunities for stimulation and distraction. The decrease in the number of children present and the additional adults allowed the staff to focus on children in a one-to-one or one-to-two relationship. Thus we began to be able to meet the children's need for attention. Because of such attention, children's disappointments were not as frequent. Sudden outbursts of anger and the vigilance and responsiveness to stimuli from other tables were not so intense. Reassurance and evidence that plenty of food was available could be given in response to minimal cues from children. The children could be helped to use tools, to learn a routine, to try a new food, and to be discriminating about what they ate. Gradually, they developed the capacity to control themselves in this situation and to enjoy it, not from coercion, but from steady, consistent adult behavior.

Among the children for whom special arrangements were made was Callie, a large, well-nourished two and a half year old. By eleven-fifteen she seemed too tired, hungry and overstimulated to eat in a group situation, so she was given lunch early, in the kitchen. A highchair was used to establish a boundary, which facilitated organization. At the beginning she held a spoon in her hand much like a young toddler. For a time she needed and was content to be fed, but within several weeks she began to feed herself while a teacher sat beside her to help her as needed. At the end of about eight weeks she joined her group at the table for lunch at her own request. During her three years at Children's House, Callie learned to use her spoon, fork, and even a knife skillfully. She would eat very large servings of food and then still pick out morsels of food from pan scrapings at the cart or from the floor. But by her last year with us this behavior occurred only when she was under particular stress, and we understood it as regression.

Cindy and Jane, the other two for whom we made special arrangements, ate lunch at a table we set up for them in the kitchen, where there was much less stimulation, with one teacher. Cindy, almost 4 years old, had been disruptive in the group, for she spent all her energy trying to involve her teacher in a battle over minute details regarding food. She screamed and flung food from her plate, disorganizing herself and others. In the less complicated situation of the kitchen a teacher could, without the pressure of the needs of other children, help Cindy gradually to understand that this adult had no wish to fight with her, but would become involved with her in other, appropriate ways. This idea was expressed directly to Cindy by talking quietly with her about the food, inviting her to think about what she wanted, and giving her time to do so. The teacher's wish to be supportive was expressed indirectly by waiting for Cindy to take the initiative in deciding what she wanted to eat. By talking with her about what the teacher had seen her do in the morning that she had obviously enjoyed, the teacher conveyed an interest in Cindy that did not involve fighting over food. Cindy began to serve herself, then to ask the teacher to do it. She began to eat enormous amounts of food. Gradually she was able to listen as the teacher talked about a whole variety of subjects, including how children needed attention and the pleasant ways to get it, her food likes and dislikes, and why she was so hungry. Her need to battle at mealtime diminished, and she returned to eat with her group after six weeks. However, throughout her two years at Children's House she continued trying to fight at mealtime, though with less intensity. The behavior recurred after a prolonged illness, when she was teased or threatened by other children, and to some extent on every Monday. (For a possible explanation of Cindy's disturbance, see Chapter 2.)

Jane, just over 3 years old, desperately wanted and needed the attention of adults but nevertheless could rarely tolerate a direct look, physical contact, or being given anything by an adult. She was totally disorganized by her own great needs and the needs and behavior of others. At mealtime, the sight of Jane with food smeared over her face, hands, and hair was repellent to children and adults. Her behavior and appearance required an adult who was not squeamish to work with her.

Jane ate in the kitchen. The teacher sat near both children but took care not to make Jane feel watched. Jane seemed vigilant about the teacher's behavior with Cindy. She would stuff food into her mouth with her hands and wash it down with milk. This was often accomplished in a flurry of activity which ended up with milk spilled on the table, floor, and down her sweatshirt. From her knowledge that Jane could not accept a direct approach, at first the teacher wiped up the table and floor, then Jane, often saying something like, "Let me wipe your shirt, you will be cold." Later, when Jane could tolerate it, she said, "You need a little taking care of, let me wipe your shirt [or face]." Often Jane fell onto the floor and crawled around barking like a dog. When she spilled something or seemed to want or need attention, she might first accept help and then shout abuses. Sometimes she simply burst into tears and wailed mournfully, and rarely could she accept direct comfort.

One day while crawling around barking, she crawled up into a high chair and then allowed her teacher to feed her a few bites. Another time, while crying, she allowed the teacher to take her on her lap and hold her close. Abruptly, as she had started to cry, she stopped and huddled there. After a few minutes the teacher picked up a spoon and began to spoon food into Jane's mouth. Jane pulled her feet up into the teacher's lap, burrowed close to the teacher's breast, and was fed a complete meal in this position. It was like feeding an infant.

While this was dramatic, it was no permanent breakthrough for this child who so mistrusted adults. Her teacher had to respond to what Jane could tolerate at any one time. Sometimes in a high chair, sometimes in the lap, and sometimes at the table, Jane could be fed. She gradually began to use a spoon and partly feed herself. She began accepting food from the adult, and often care and physical contact in relation to food. When Jane joined her group at the table after four months, she had learned to drink from a glass and to eat most food with a spoon. She could usually accept adult attention and help. For example, a reminder to keep her eye on the spoon could help organize her. A teacher ate beside her for the first year and often after that. She was an unusually vulnerable child who regressed under what seemed to us minimal stress.

In summary, the anticipated teacher's role as a model for and supporter of children's learning at mealtime had to be adapted to take into account the severe deprivation of a large number of children within this group. Several children were repeating intense battles from long-established home relations. Special arrangements had to be made to allow for far more individual attention than is usual in many daycare centers and nursery schools.

Naptime

After lunch the playrooms had to be rearranged as a nap room. Food had to be swept from the floors, tables and chairs wiped, the food and dish cart returned to the kitchen. Cots, which were stacked in a nearby closet, had to be rolled in the room ready to be placed according to a chart we had posted on the bulletin board. JA, our all-around helper, would come in to sweep the floor and put out the cots. This quick change required careful planning and extra help, for we anticipated this could be a difficult time for children unless adults were very clear about just what was to be done and who would be responsible for each part of the transition.

In addition to planning for the mechanics of the transition of the room, we planned a routine for the children. Six children went home after lunch; two adults took these children into the locker room and helped them get ready to go home. If the weather was nice they went outside with a teacher as soon as they were ready and waited for their mothers. This part of the plan worked very well because these parents were unfailingly prompt and the children left by ten of twelve.

As other children finished lunch their teachers took them in small family groups to the toilet room to wash faces, brush teeth, pull off shoes, socks, and tight clothing, and toilet if needed. The first lunch group to finish went first to the toilet room. As the other groups finished their lunch they went to a rug in one of the playrooms while others used the toilet. Their teacher selected ahead of time some material for them to use until it was their time to go to the toilet room and get ready for nap. We anticipated that children would begin to make their own choices about materials they would use at this time when they became familiar with the options and had preferences.

Cots were put out after the floor was swept and children coming from the toilet room went directly to their cots. Each family group had its cots placed in a cluster so their teacher could help them settle down for rest. There were toys for them to use on their cots until all children were ready and in bed. We wanted to use this time as an opportunity for children to learn and thus gain independence in personal tasks. We structured the transition so as to free teachers to help each child learn at his own pace and developmental level.

It was a good plan on paper, but again, it did not work easily. The children were so disorganized that the simplest activities required much more adult help than we anticipated. The research staff who had come for lunch stayed and helped with our original plan. They stayed at the tables with children who took a long time to eat, cleaned tables and chairs, helped children get to the toilet, helped children who had finished toileting get to their cots, read stories or played with toys with children, and generally became teachers for this time. One teacher coordinated all aspects of the physical change of the room and the flow of children as space became available for the various groups.

When lunch, cleanup, and preparations for naptime were completed at about twelve-fifteen, and all children were on their cots, two teachers stayed with the children. When children went to sleep, only one teacher remained in the room with them. We anticipated that children would wake at different times and as they awoke their teachers would be called to help them get dressed and start them in their afternoon activity. This part of our plan worked well and by Christmastime of the first year the adult who stayed with the children after they were asleep was the cook-housekeeper, a person well known to the children. In the late spring of the first year only one teacher stayed with children as they settled in for nap. However, there was always an adult immediately on call to help when needed.

We had set up small groups so that each child would have one adult who got to know him well, help him at lunch, naptime, and as he woke up. Because we were impressed with its effectiveness, the family group idea was extended after the first week to all transitions for the first year. As children got to know teachers and each other, changes in these groups were made on the basis of special relationships and attachments.

When teachers left children at naptime they made a special point of telling children where they were going and when they would come back. On return, they talked about where they had been and what they had done. At first, any adult would do and what teachers said was often not acknowledged by the children. Teachers continued these monologues and soon children began to express anger and disappointment when teachers left and surprise and pleasure on their return. Many children learned their teachers' schedules and kept track of who would stay for nap and who went upstairs to rest.

All but two of the children who stayed for the afternoon had been taking naps at home. We expected all children of this age to rest but not necessarily to sleep. We anticipated that going to sleep in a strange bed and in a group would be anxiety producing for the children. On the first day, after some tucking in and moving around to be comfortable, some thumb sucking and masturbation, all but two children fell into an exhausted, deep sleep, as if it were a welcome release from the overstimulation of newness. Cindy folded and unfolded her blanket, sucked her thumb, twisted her hair, rubbed her nose, masturbated by rubbing her thighs together, made high singsong noises, and fell asleep with her eyes open. She slept for about ten minutes, woke and repeated this process over and over until two o'clock. Bill sobbed quietly and bitterly. He could not tolerate a teacher touching or comforting him, although she was able to sit nearby. He cried himself to sleep in about half an hour.

At two o'clock only Cindy was awake and her teacher came to help her get dressed, wash her face, brush her hair, and get some milk to drink. Cindy talked loudly, scolding the teacher, but others continued to sleep. Finally, at quarter to three, we decided to wake children who showed signs of waking. As children awakened during these first weeks we were not surprised to find that most had wet their beds. Several children were openly distressed and fearful about their wet beds and clothing. We tried to reassure them matter-of-factly that this often happened when children slept in a new place, that they had dry underpants to put on, that their wet underpants could be washed and put in their cubbies for them, and that their beds could be changed.

The sleep pattern during the first weeks continued to be about the same except we began to wake children between two and two-thirty if they were still asleep after a two to two and a half hour nap. A teacher would wake a child slowly, talk with him about afternoon plans, remind him that his mother would return, acknowledge that children missed their mothers, and give him some juice, milk, or fruit. There continued to be many wet beds each day, but this gradually diminished to only three or four during the first weeks.

Gradually during the first month, the pattern of going to sleep and waking changed. As children felt more secure they began to behave as young children are likely to do at home, wanting to go to the toilet, or needing help to rearrange their blankets. When all of these needs were satisfied and all the children looked as though they were about to go to sleep, a child would slip out of bed, come to a teacher and charmingly seek to talk or sit on her lap. Soon another would join the first. We knew if this continued there would not be enough laps to go around. So, hard as it was, teachers, after a brief response, sent children back to bed in a firm, friendly way: "Now it is time for rest; I can't talk with you now, but I will later."

At other times, as one would expect, a child had difficulty going to sleep because he was worried about whether his mother would come, worried because his mother or special teacher had been angry with him, concerned about wetting the bed, or preoccupied with jealousy or rivalry and other concerns that beset young children. At such times teachers tried to learn the reasons for restlessness and help children cope with them. It should be remembered that times of fatigue and the transitional periods between wakefulness and sleep are accompanied by heightened feelings of helplessness and vulnerability. It is therefore important for teachers to be available to children at these times.

By the end of about the sixth month, the length of naps became more regular, about one and a half to two hours. If a child was particularly tired he might sleep longer; several children whenever they were under great stress would sleep for a long time, and we learned that for some children this was not so much a sign of fatigue but of a need for respite from feelings of distress. We gradually learned how each child was likely to react to stress and tried to find ways to help him deal with it.

Throughout the years at Children's House, any new staff person at naptime was tested mercilessly. It really took a teacher who knew each child's way of settling down to sleep to help them rest. By the second year, however, the cook-housekeeper could come in and sit in a rocking chair when the children were almost asleep and not unsettle the group, relieving the teacher for a meeting or rest period. Sometimes the teacher and children sang together, listened to a favorite record, or the teacher told a story before the children went to sleep. Although there was considerable variation among individuals, the children as a group continued to take somewhat longer naps than most children of comparable ages at home.

The waking-up time was one of the most pleasant in the day for teachers and children. It was a time to talk over concerns, plan for and anticipate the afternoon, and to have a cozy time with a few people.

Over time most children learned to put out their cots, help change their beds, and put the laundry in the washer. This came only very gradually, was not forced, and thus led to pleasure and pride in the acceptance of appropriately limited responsibility.

Using Materials

Since learning takes place over time, materials for instruction need to be provided in a temporal sequence. For example, at first one primary-color paint with one brush was available for use. After a child had several opportunities to use them, had developed some skills with the materials, and had learned to look at his painting, we provided two brushes and two primary colors, which the child could mix on the paper into a third color. The teacher made decisions about the order in which materials would be used. Two considerations relevant to making such decisions were the psychological factors in learning, such as the particular child's experience, interests, and abilities, and the logical order in which skills in various areas could be learned.

We wanted the children to learn to take pleasure in the process of using materials as well as in the products they might make, to explore and exploit the qualities of a variety of materials in a variety of ways, to learn the functional and formal properties of the objects and materials. More specifically, we wanted them to learn to know the names of objects and materials, to discriminate likeness and difference among objects in a variety of dimensions, to understand the regularity of objects and materials, and to order and reorder them in different ways. We wanted them to understand the causal relationships between their actions and the materials, to predict the reactions of the materials, and to be able to correct their own thinking. In general, we wanted them to learn to find answers for themselves, to be active in their own learning. But we selected activities and ways of doing things that would specifically encourage learning in these areas; we did not simply wait for such learning to occur incidentally.

Some materials and activities had to be invested with value by the teachers themselves. That is, teachers used materials themselves and by their behavior showed the children that the materials were interesting and worthy of use. The teacher actively explored ways of using material, demonstrating, that the process rather than the product was important. Her statements and questions as she talked about the material and demonstrated its use were designed to help each child start to explore materials and find answers for himself. She might say; "Do you know what this is called? It is clay. What is it for? Let me see what I can do with it." The teacher could begin to work with it, squeezing, rolling, and bending it. "Here is some for you. What can you do with it? What happens if you pull it?" Over time, with repeated use of clay, the children would explore the properties of clay. Playdough and cookie dough were also used and eventually provided a basis for children to compare similar looking media that are in some ways the same and in some different. "How does clay taste?" "How does cookie dough taste?" "How does Playdough taste?" "How does it smell?" "Is it rough, smooth?" "Can you make it rough?" "How can you make it smooth?" "How do you know?" "Why do you think that?" "What would happen if you put water on it?" "Baked it?" Cookie dough could be used to help children understand time and a sequence of events: "First, you put the butter and sugar together, then the eggs, and last the flour." "What is going to happen when you put the eggs in?" "Do you remember what we do next?" "Soon they will be ready to bake." "Yesterday we had egg custard that Susan made." "Next time we will put raisins in the cookies."

"Let's put the cookies in the oven and then we will read a story. After the story the cookies will be baked."

We anticipated that a primary source for language learning would be the language and thought accompanying work with materials. What particular materials we used would be related to children's interests. We would introduce and make interesting materials that were developmentally appropriate and would lend themselves to helping children learn useful ways of thinking. The children would learn concepts and language for causation, seriation, number, space, time, and functional and formal properties of objects as teachers provided appropriate opportunities, labels, comments, and questions.

In our group, in many daycare centers, there was a wide range of individual differences in the use of materials. For the purpose of a general description, the children can be roughly divided into two groups. The first comprised four children for whom life was markedly unpredictable. They were so angry and behaviorly disorganized that, from their point of view, materials were things to be acquired, fiercely defended or hoarded, and then cast aside. Our first task with them was to be predictable and provide a structure for their days at school that was organizing and over time became predictable to them. Within the overall structure of predictability we planned opportunities for teachers to work with these children to help them as a first step find pleasure in using materials, explore some of the qualities of material, learn where materials were located in the room, and learn the names of objects and materials.

Within the second, better organized group there was still a wide variation in the children's freedom to become involved in using materials for learning. This range of difference may be best understood by the following examples of five children's approach to materials during the first few weeks of school.

Rusty   Rusty, age 3 years 10 months, seemed mildly curious about a variety of materials, but used only construction toys such as floor blocks and plastic brick. His buildings were all very much the same. With blocks he built an enclosure and put himself in it. With plastic bricks he built an enclosure and put a car in it. This was a repetitive, persistent pattern in which he became very involved, but in which he showed no pleasure. He was more skillful than one would expect considering his awkward and hesistant movements, and he persisted in structuring careful buildings. With coaxing from his teacher he used puzzles (he firmly refused other materials), and he seemed to use size and shapes as cues for putting them together. He did not seem to see individual pieces as part of a whole. He showed mild pleasure on completion of puzzles, then made direct appeals for affection and approval in which he seemed to beg us not to push him further.

Carla   Carla, age 4 years 7 months, could be interested and enthusiastic with a number of materials. Yet left on her own she would wander from place to place and make comments like, "I can do that," but not become involved. Sometimes she joined a group to demonstrate a particular skill, such as printing her own name, and then said, "I'm smart," or "That's easy." When her attention was sustained by the presence of an adult, she became interested in, even enthusiastic about the qualities of the material and explored and exploited the materials well.

Sandra   Sandra, age 4 years 9 months, used and was interested in many materials, which she handled with assurance. She preferred using them to make products rather than freely exploring their potential. She often protested that she did not know or could not do something, but as long as an adult was nearby, she continued working in a skillful manner. She was painfully aware of the teachers' responses to her and relied heavily on their taking pleasure in what she was doing in order to find pleasure herself.

Stanley   Stanley seemed mildly interested in a variety of materials. At age 3 years 7 months, he lacked pleasure in using the materials and was not responsive to children or adults' pleasure in his skill and success. He showed a marked lack of interest in exploring toys and materials for their potential. He often destroyed what he had made or worked with a shrug of his shoulders and a half smile that seemed to convey, "Well, what could I expect?"

Tim   Tim, age 3, used a limited range of materials with skill and imagination. He could often sustain interest on his own with cars and trucks used with sand or blocks. He tolerated the nearness of other children very poorly, but he asked questions of teachers as he explored and exploited the potential of these materials. When he encountered the slightest problem with materials, however, he became impulsive and destructive.

We expected the teachers to be sensitive to these levels of skill and interest in the individual children. They were to provide an assortment of opportunities at those levels, giving the children a choice of activities, and remaining physically near to support the children's interest in them. By remaining in close contact with the children, a teacher could ask the questions and make the comments that would be most useful to the child with whom she was working, and she could recognize a child's pleasure in the use of a material and make this explicit to the child along with her own pleasure in the child's increasing skill and persistence. Thus, the teachers did not simply present an example and wait for the children to follow it, but actively supported each child's efforts in a personal way.

Gross Motor Skills

The play yard (or a large room during inclement weather) was planned for active play with materials and equipment that would enable children to gain confidence in themselves through control and mastery of their own bodies. Most materials and equipment were portable and could be arranged in many ways. We wanted children to derive pleasure from the mastery of their own bodies—the use a wide range of joint motion, and adequate strength to bend, stretch, twist, crawl, squat, sit, and hang by arms and legs. We wanted them to be free and easy in tasks that required different kinds of movement: pushing, pulling, twisting, dodging, spinning, falling, lifting, carrying, riding, digging, pounding, throwing, walking, running, jumping, climbing, balancing, hopping, galloping, and skipping. We wanted them to become as agile as possible in their use of speed, force, space, and to be able to vary their base of support readily.

The differences among the children were striking. The wide age range of the group did not account for the wide range of skill, confidence, poise, carefulness in movement. The children differed grossly on six dimensions:

• Level of skill attained. One child was barely walking, some children could jump in various speeds and directions.

• Use of different bases of support. Two children needed a hard surface on which to walk, other children could hop on the unstable surface of a springboard.

• Tolerance for new positions in space. Some children could only manage or toleration upright and lying-down positions, others could hang by their knees upside down and turn somersaults.

• Use of space. Some restricted their movement to a limited amount of space, others freely used large areas of space.

• Affective content of moving. Some children were immobilized in new situations; some enjoyed the challenge of increasing their skills and derived great satisfaction from mastery.

• Variety of apparent purposes. The children's movement was motivated by different urges: for self-protection, for self-destruction, for competition, for mastery, for recognition, for challenge, for locomotion, for exploration.

Annette and Lynn   Annette, 2 years, 5 months, and Lynn, 2 years, 8 months, were free and easy in most tasks that required moving. They used a wide range of joint motion and had adequate strength to bend, stretch, twist, swing, crawl, squat, and sit. They were able to push, pull, twist, dodge, spin, fall. They were also agile in their use of speed, force, and space, and could vary their bases of support readily. Running, jumping, climbing, hopping, galloping, and a rudimentary skip pattern were all accomplished by these girls as a part of their play activity. In our experience, this kind of skill, poise, and freedom of movement was unusual for children under three years. Annette had a natural grace and these skills seemed to be acquired with little effort on her part. She watched others and after a few tries, sometimes with verbal cues from an adult, mastered pumping in a swing and rotating a hula hoop and became competent with right and left foot in a game called "footsie." Lynn practiced with a great deal of persistence and was often the first one to accomplish a new or more complex activity using one or more skills. She was less able to use verbal cues, and relied heavily on imitation or an adult's placing her body in particular positions in order for her to learn. Throughout the three years these two girls were at Children's House they derived pleasure from the use of their bodies, increased the complexity of their skills, using them in play and dance.

Six Children   Stanley, 3 years, 7 months; Jennifer, 4 years, 5 months; Sandra, 4 years, 9 months; Carla, 4 years, 7 months; Susan, 4 years; and Jane, 2 years, 8 months, had acquired almost as many movement skills as Annette and Lynn but were characteristically awkward looking. They lacked poise and freedom in movement, became fearful and were quite cautious in some positions and in new situations. These children often needed a supportive situation, with increments in complexity of the tasks carefully planned, for them to feel comfortable enough to use their bodies fully and with pleasure. For example, when learning to hand walk a horizontal ladder, these children functioned best when an adult was with them. Jane and Sandra needed active physical support while the others needed only verbal assurance. At first they needed to be able to touch the ground with their feet, and the ladder was placed at a height so this was possible. A day or two later the bar could be raised six inches to a foot with a mat underneath. What would have been frightening a day or two before then provided an acceptable challenge. After this intial learning, all but Jane devised ways of making the task challenging and asked for help to lift their legs and hang by their knees. An adult helped them learn to hook their toes under the adjacent bar, giving them a way to feel secure and steady. Several needed verbal assurance that they were all right or that the teacher would not let them fall. Stanley and Sandra needed to be held when in an upside down position several times, until they were sure they could manage it alone. Sandra, Susan, and Jennifer could jump "hot pepper" and run into a moving jump rope by the spring of the first year.

Tim   Tim, 3 years, also used a wide range of joint motion and could vary his base of support readily. He could hop on either foot; his gallop was rudimentary with a simple hop-step rhythm. He was unusually skillful at catching and throwing a football. The striking thing about Tim's movement was his unusual lack of caution and self-protectiveness. He usually needed an adult nearby to keep him from using his good skills in ways that were dangerous to himself.

Stuart   Stuart, 4 years, 5 months, was quite skilled, but his movement was jerky and looked uncoordinated, with a great deal of random and extraneous movement such as arms and legs flailing, head jerking, and eyes blinking. He was in almost constant motion and was fiercely competitive. He seemed driven to move, deriving little pleasure from his accomplishments. His movement in a group situation was usually aggressive, difficult for the teacher to manage and for other children to tolerate. Stuart and his movement were better organized and more tractable when he was with one child and a teacher away from the group.

Rusty   Rusty, 3 years, 10 months, had a narrow range of joint motion and moved in a jerky, awkward manner when walking and climbing. His legs and hips seemed particularly restricted: he walked bent forward from the hips with his knees flexed. His well-worn shoes had no creases on the top and he did not use his ankles, arches, and toes in a springy manner to facilitate running. He used a small amount of space, usually close to the ground, and often crawled from place to place. He toppled over often and one got the impression he did not know where his feet were or that he could not adjust his center of gravity quickly enough to maintain balance. Yet Rusty participated in most activities and had a surprising degree of skill in walking a two-inch balance beam, using the ladder bars, and pumping himself in the swing. He seemed totally unaware of his jerky, awkward movement and participated with many signs of real pleasure.

Peter   Peter, 4 years, 7 months, was as skillful and agile as a deer. Much of this skill was directed against others and for what he must have perceived as self-protection. One adult was required at all times to protect others from his fierce aggression and his intractable behavior.

The teachers actively supported the children's developing motor skills and enjoying movement. Children could choose from several possible activities on the playground, but outdoor play was not a loosely supervised "free-play" time. Teachers were responsible for planning a variety of movement activities in the same way they planned the use of materials. They arranged equipment to suit the children's gain in competencies and changing interests over time; they actively helped children to learn new skills on an individual basis by providing physical support, encouragement, and verbal cues as appropriate for each child; they made explicit to each child his increments in learning; and they showed honest pleasure in the children's skills. As with other activities, children became increasingly independent and skillful over time, requiring less direct teacher assistance. Teachers continued to communicate their interest in the children's safety, however, and to encourage them to feel competent and aware of their own skills, in order to promote movement activities in a manner coordinated with other aspects of their learning.

Language and Thinking

Throughout the discussion of the teacher's role, many references have been made to the importance of the children's language and thought in their learning. The purpose of this section is to make explicit that many relationships and activities offer opportunities to help children learn to speak and to think.

Since the most intensive language learning occurs between two and four years of age, we assumed that the children could and would learn to speak the language they heard. We further assumed that all of the children had heard a great deal of language at home and that they had learned many nonverbal as well as verbal ways of communicating. As is always true with two and three year olds, teachers would have to be skillful at understanding the children's nonverbal communications and use them as a base from which the children could extend their use of relevant language. In addition, the teacher's role would be to provide a good model and a dependable and consistent source of corrective feedback for listening and speaking. Teachers were to speak with clear articulation, whatever their regional accents.

Language was to be taught casually and spontaneously in a setting mutually pleasurable to the children and adults. Adults would consistently express appropriate affect for the verbal and nonverbal messages received from the child or given to the child, through intonation, timing, gesture, and facial expression (this is of special importance for children whose language skills are not well developed). They would match words, phrases, and sentences closely with those of the child, and then expand them with functional words while maintaining the order of the child's speech. One way of doing this was to use precise language when the child's language was nonspecific—Child: "I put it over there, Miss E." Teacher: "Thank you, Tim, for putting the puzzle in the puzzle rack." Teachers could also elaborate the child's speech and ideas in conversation—Child: "What's that?" Teacher: "It is an egg beater. Would you like to beat the eggs with it? See how the beater makes the eggs look yellow and frothy." But we assumed all such techniques would be most effective in the context of experiences meaningful to the child—while beating eggs or cleaning up. Often a teacher simply thought out loud as she went through activities with the children: "I'll put the cookie cutters in the center of the table so everyone can reach them." Snacktimes and lunchtime were especially potent times for social interaction, and we used them not only for conversation about food and eating, but as occasions for recalling and sharing experiences. Eventually, true social conversation took place among children and teachers.

We realized that coming to Children's House would present children with a new situation, many new people, and familiar and unfamiliar events and materials in a new context. We assumed that children would listen and respond to language that was responsive to their needs and interests, and that was directed toward them, knowing that a young child is most interested in himself. This meant that there had to be many opportunities for teachers to listen to and talk with children on a one-to-one basis.

We also thought that much of the language and thinking would center around children building relationships with others. As relationships and interests emerged, teachers would provide opportunities for individuals and opportunities in common for small groups as a basis for learning language, thinking, and organizing ideas.

A teacher did not directly correct a child's grammar or speech pattern. Rather, in conversation, she used acceptable forms herself, supplied correct names, and added words the child left out as she understood his intent while keeping the child's structural pattern. We did not want children to feel rebuffed when they spoke. Improvement in speaking skills would not be carried out at the expense of other equally important aspects of their development.

Looking at books and hearing stories told and read aloud to them were important to the children's language development. We provided opportunities for children to think and talk about the pictures in books, think and talk about their experiences as compared with those of the characters in the stories, to take part in simple dramatization recalling sequences and lines of the parts being taken and expressing feelings appropriate to the characters, to take turns being actors and being a part of the audience. Also important was encouraging children to make up stories about their own experiences and to retell stories told them. Teachers wrote down children's stories, which could be read back to them. The children made their own books, some with pictures only, and some with pictures and words the teacher wrote for them. We helped the children to discover rhyming words, to talk about words that sound alike, and to act out and talk about differences in word meanings. Poetry, story records, tapes of the children's own speaking and singing, spontaneous singing, and singing groups were used as opportunities for attending, responding, learning new words, and putting words together in structurally different ways.

Learning language is intimately tied to learning to think clearly. We made sure that there was ample time for children to talk with adults about what they observed in the center, on the playground, on trips in and around the Children's House, and on trips in the neighborhood. These opportunities were used to help children learn to be careful observers, to help them mentally organize their environment and experience, and to use language to convey their thinking. This required that teachers be interested in observation as a way of learning, be able to verbalize their own observations, understand the young child's way of thinking and raise questions with children in such a way as to heighten their interest and curiosity. In all activities, we wanted to help children develop ideas about causation, seriation, number, space, time, descriptions and classification of the functional and formal properties of objects, and measurement. Teachers had to be alert to these ideas themselves and understand young children's thinking in order to raise questions in such a way as to help children express their own ideas and discover relationships for themselves.

There was more variability within the group in the area of language and thought than in any other, as will be clear in the following descriptions.

Callie   Callie, at 2 years, 5 months, was the youngest child in the group. She was just beginning to say words but she rarely vocalized spontaneously except for commands like "Look!" and "See!" The only two words she used together were "na won" (another one). She had learned to point to an object, listen to its name and attempt to repeat it, but these words did not become part of her spontaneous speech. She seemed to understand more than she spoke, for she was able to follow simple directions like "Come sit by me, Callie." But it was difficult for teachers to know whether she followed the verbal directions or relied on nonverbal cues, since it took her a long time to respond.

Rusty   Rusty, 3 years, 10 months, communicated mainly with gesture and the sound "Aaaeee." The intonation, timing, and gestures accompanying this sound communicated both strong negative and positive feelings. His pantomime was so well developed that adults often felt and spoke as if they had had a conversation with him. His speaking vocabulary consisted of seven words: "me," "hi," "bye," "no," "es" (for yes), "Mommie," and "top" (for stop). "Me Mommie" were the only words he put together. "Stop" was a word he had learned during the first week of school and it was a potent word for him to use to protect himself from the intrusion of others as he built a wall of blocks around himself. His total vocabulary was articulated quite clearly when he whispered. In a normal speaking voice he softened, substituted, or omitted consonant sounds.

Teachers found it difficult to know the extent of Rusty's displeasure or pleasure and to distinguish between his fear and his anger. There was also a marked discrepancy between his understanding and his output. His receptive language seemed age-appropriate and he responded to statements such as "After you brush your teeth, you may get some cars to play with on your bed" by following through on this sequence. He could follow two directions in a variety of situations.

Stuart Stuart, 4 years, 5 months, omitted beginning consonant sounds, saying, for example, "at" for "that." Familiarity with his speech pattern and the context of his language were necessary to understand what he was saying. He rarely used gesture, except pointing, to support communication. Sometimes he opened his mouth to speak, but was able to produce words only after several seconds of intense effort. At other times he might say the first word or two of a sentence then repeat these two or three times, as if he were gaining momentum to say the rest. When using sentences, the order of words was awkward and the referents nonspecific—"Why that boy do that?" He used words as if they had no specific meanings. For example, he might say "Shut up" in a friendly tone as if the actual words did not matter. He asked questions but did not seem to anticipate answers. At other times he asked questions when a request seemed to be intended: "Wots that" in context seemed to mean "I want that truck." His response to a question like "Do you want another block?" might be "It tinks," while he took the block as if it were indeed just what he needed. His language was liberally sprinkled with four-letter and derogatory words like "knucklehead." These words were articulated clearly but were said more or less at random, rather than in an expectably expressive way.

Carla and Jennifer Carla, 4 years, 7 months, and Jennifer, 4 years, 5 months, were quite competent in their use of language. They spoke clearly; only their articulation of uncommon consonants such as *z* was still immature. They used simple sentences with modifiers and series of sentences to convey sequences of well-organized ideas. Their vocabularies included precise names of objects, people, animals, actions, and classes. They used many precise descriptive words, pronouns, prepositions, and some conjunctions and conditional words correctly. They had good memories for detail and learned new words in context quickly. They responded easily to "who" and "what" questions within their experience, but "how" questions usually required the presence of visual props or actions to support their language. For example, when asked, "How do you think the cow looked to the upstairs mouse?" Jennifer had to find the page in the book before she could describe the cow. Answers to "why" questions were often highly personal. When asked, "Why do you think the children waited for William?" Carla, who was competitive and not the fastest runner in the group, answered, "Because he couldn't run so fast."

One striking characteristic of our group that was evident even in the first weeks of school was the tremendous amount of language regression even under what seemed to us very minor disappointment or stress. We expected the language of children within this age group to be vulnerable to stress, but we were not prepared for the magnitude and pervasiveness of language regression even with the oldest, most able children.

The Teacher as Observer and Curriculum Builder

Because ours was a research project, teachers were called upon to observe and document many aspects of the children's behavior and their own experience. We used the Criterion Model for Preschool Curriculum developed by June Patterson, who was the educational director of Children's House, as a tool for making systematic recorded observations of the 2½–5 year olds. Information about each child was contributed by all the teachers, and one teacher was responsible for the recording on each child. While this method imposed a great work load, it also produced material that included the teacher's own thoughts and feelings, in contrast to the usual records of child and teacher behavior made by uninvolved observers. Without in any way questioning the usefulness of the latter, we chose to rely strongly on teachers' records for a very large part of the data on the children's day.

The model we used is based upon the behavior of well-functioning children who have been able to use the school situation to learn and to grow. It is meant to serve as a basis for determining a child's competencies and as a basis for planning opportunities for each child that use his strengths and alleviate his limitations. The model was developed over a period of five years, starting in a laboratory nursery school for privileged children which was quite different from Children's House in many ways.

The development of the model was approached from the descriptive phenomenological point of view that has proved useful in other areas of child development. After many teachers and other colleagues were interviewed, many written records of children in both elementary school and nursery school were analyzed, a composite of observable behaviors of children who function well in the school setting was formulated. Since the composite was developed, it has been examined for its validity for children of privileged homes, children living in an urban slum, and children in a small town. It has proved to be applicable in all three settings; that is, one finds these characteristics developing in children from all these socioeconomic and ethnic backgrounds who function well in school. The attributes listed and defined below will be recognized as characteristics that in adults as well as children are required or at least valued and rewarded by our society at this time. They are developed only gradually over many years, some more slowly than others, but are clearly recognizable in preschool children. They imply the central responsibility of daycare programs: to help the child deal effectively with himself and his environment.

A healthy child, we believe, has the following attributes.

• HE TRUSTS HIMSELF AND CAN TRUST OTHERS. He is a self-respecting person who is aware that he can be guided to some degree by how he feels about people and things. He believes in the trustworthiness of important people, i.e., that he can rely upon them and what they say, and ask for and accept help from them.

• HE IS GAINING A REALISTIC CONCEPT OF HIS PERSONAL STRENGTHS, LIMITATIONS, AND VULNERABILITIES. He is learning to recognize the difference between what he can really do and what is wishful thinking. He recognizes his personal strengths, but can also judge when something is far beyond his capabilities. He can look forward to the time when he will learn to do more complex tasks. While his judgments are not totally realistic, since he is still a young child, one can nonetheless see that his perception of reality is growing gradually closer to that of a more mature person.

• HE IS LEARNING SELF-DISCIPLINE. The responsibility for regulating his own behavior, for holding himself to certain standards, develops very gradually, but these qualities are increasingly visible in the young child. Both his emotional and his cognitive development enable him to become more self-disciplined, particularly in areas requiring delay in fulfilling immediate needs and pleasures.

• HE IS GAINING AWARENESS OF OTHERS AND ABILITY TO FEEL WITH THEM. The egocentricity of the very young child gradually diminishes. He begins not only to react to others but to observe how they look, what they can do, and how they feel. He learns to see them not exclusively in relation to himself, but as individuals and in relation to others. He comes to recognize that other people have thoughts and feelings unrelated to him. Implied here is an integration of his observations of others as they express a feeling and his increasing ability to recognize his own feelings. Eventually he becomes able to empathize with another without deep involvement. This is a more complex psychological process than the developmentally earlier response of feeling emotions evoked by contagion.

• HE IS SPONTANEOUS IN EXPRESSING FEELINGS. A child who is emotionally constricted is unable to respond in a manner expected in a given situation and can express neither pleasure nor displeasure spontaneously. In this context spontaneity does not mean a lack of control but free, natural expression. It implies considerable personal and situational security.

• HE IS BECOMING SELF-RELIANT AND SELF-STARTING. He knows that he can depend upon himself in certain ways and is increasingly willing to use his competencies in his own behalf. He can also take considerable initiative in choosing, planning, and carrying out an activity, in tackling a project, and in negotiating relationships with others.

• HE IS BECOMING INCREASINGLY RESPONSIBLE FOR HIS OWN BEHAVIOR AND SAFETY. He is learning that his behavior has consequences that he increasingly expects to regulate, that how he behaves is determined to a great extent by himself, that this responsibility includes how he works, plays, and conducts himself with others, and also how he uses his judgment to keep himself from physical harm.

• HE IS DEVELOPING A SENSE OF HUMOR. The well-functioning child shows progressively more signs of a sense of humor. The capacity for humor is complex and multifaceted. What one sees as humorous is related to developmental phases and characteristics, as well as to individual experience. The young child's sense of humor often manifests itself as he reenacts his mastery over what earlier made him uneasy. This kind of humor suggests that he has enough emotional security to laugh at, to get pleasure from what earlier might have upset him or made him anxious. It is also based on sufficient integration of intellectual and emotional development to enable him to enjoy incongruity and novelty in what he perceives.

• HE IS CREATIVE IN IDEAS. Inventiveness and originality can be seen in many aspects of the behavior of the well-functioning child. The development of creativity with respect to ideas is observed in the child's ability to extend a game, or song, or other activity he has been taught, to introduce variations, to play with how it can be elaborated.

• HE IS EXTENDING BASIC SKILLS OF MOVING, MANIPULATING, AND SPEAKING. Consolidation and progressive development of competencies in gross and fine motor skills and in speech follow a familiar and easily documented course. Speech, too, progresses from simple to more elaborate structures and is increasingly used to communicate information, ideas, and feelings.

• HE IS ABLE TO LISTEN WITH INCREASED AND MORE PROLONGED ATTEN-

TIVENESS. He is learning to take in a series of communications and to consider and reflect upon them without being disrupted by them or having to go into action. Such ability implies considerable capacity for control of impulses and a resistance to distraction.

• HE IS GAINING FACTUAL INFORMATION AND DEVELOPING THE CAPACITY TO CONCEPTUALIZE. The well-functioning child learns facts at a rate that is often astonishing. In addition, ideas and concepts such as similarity and difference, space, size, number, and time, to mention only a few, develop and are integrated with previous learning.

• HE HAS A VARIETY OF INTERESTS AND RESOURCES. The well-functioning child is able to enjoy both the familiar and the novel. He usually does not need to be entertained or sustained in an activity by other children or adults and is resourceful with materials. He has several approaches to problem solving, several styles of adapting to situations, and several possibilities for coping with stress.

• HE FINDS PLEASURE IN PROCESS AS WELL AS IN PRODUCTS. The child takes pleasure in functioning, in experiencing his efforts to master something new or to repeat and elaborate an already learned activity. Such pleasure extends to thinking and imagining. While he may very much enjoy or value the product of his doing or thinking, the process carries a pleasure of its own.

• HE HAS THE URGE TO TRY, THE COURAGE TO FAIL, AND THE PERSISTENCE TO CONTINUE AN EFFORT. This urge is related to being self-starting and to the drive toward mastery. The same urge to try that is seen as the infant struggles to walk characterizes the child who is willing to enter new situations, to try new materials, and to make new relationships, as well as to work hard to dress a doll, complete a complicated block structure, or to write a name. If he has the courage to fail and basic confidence in the possibilities of his own efforts, he will not be utterly undone if he does not succeed; he may be disappointed, or angry, or upset, but not to the extent that he permanently retires from the activity.

A detailed description of the Criterion Model for Preschool Curriculum and a case illustration are given in Appendixes 2 and 3. A condensed version is presented here to make clear what behavior was observed, what the program for the older children was, and how the teachers went about their daily work.

The statement of attributes was translated into sixty-nine specific items of behavior that could be observed by teachers, grouped under five main categories that define relevant areas of observation and provide a means of ordering the data. (The table below shows the five main categories and the subcategories of each.) The five categories are Relationships to Self,

Summary of the Criterion Model for Preschool Curriculum *

1 Relationship to Self (Skill and Personal Style)	2 Relationships to Adults (Ability to use adults)	3 Relationships to Children	4 Relationships to Groups (Group membership)	5 Relationship to Objects and Ideas
1.1 *Personal Tasks* Shoes & socks off Clothing off Socks & shoes on Clothing on Toileting Washing Caring for personal property	2.1 *Adults as Supporters of Self-regulation*	3.1 *General Interaction (Cross-Situational)* Quantity of interaction Quality of interaction	4.1 *Basic Responsibilities* Care of school property Respect for property of others Observation of space boundaries	5.1 *Objects Manipulated as Body Extensions* Riding a tricycle Throwing a ball Catching a ball Using a pencil Cutting with scissors
1.2 *Speaking Capacity* Articulation Structure Usage	2.2 *Adults as a Resource for Assistance and Self-evaluation*	3.2 *Situationally Specific Interaction* Conflict resolution Taking turns and sharing	4.2 *Participation in Group Activities* Story groups Music groups Movement activity groups Trips Snack or meal groups	5.2 *Objects Shaped or Reformed* Work with clay Work with finger paint
1.3 *Moving Capacity* Control of basic movement Walk Run Jump Balance Hop Gallop Skip			4.3 *Conduct During Transitions* Arrival Organized change in activity Dismassal	5.3 *Objects Used for Construction* Block building Structure sets Woodworking Pasting and gluing Puzzle working

1.4 *Patterning of Affective Expression*

1.5 *Situational Responses*
Making choices
Approach to problem solving
Persistence in a task

5.4 *Drawing and Painting Activity*
Drawing with pastels, felt-tip pens, soft pencil
Easel painting

5.5 *Language Activity*
Attending, observing
Writing symbols
Reading

5.6 *Dramatic Play Activity*
Player interaction
Properties and place
Role structuring

5.7 *Concept Usage*
Causation
Seriation
Number
Space (map)
Time (calendar)
Description and classification of objects
Measurement

* The numbers identify the items in the model. They are *not* scores. See Appendix 2 the complete Criterion Model.

Relationships to Children, Relationships to Adults, Relationships to Group, and Relationships to Objects and Ideas. Each of these categories contains several subcategories, which describe behaviors along a developmental continuum of increasing complexity, flexibility, or sophistication. In each subcategory are two statements: one that defines the usual skills of the two to two and a half year old, and another that defines the skills of the well-functioning five year old. The top level of each continuum is an institutional (long-term) goal: a child who achieves that level is ready and able to use successfully the next, more complex school situation. For example, in category 1, Relationships to Self, the teacher observes the child's performance in common personal tasks such as dressing and toileting, his capacity in speaking, moving, and affective expression, and his behavior in selected common situations. If one looks at the items under "articulation of speech," a part of subcategory 2, the items range on a continuum from using speech comprehensible only to one familiar with his speech pattern to speaking clearly enough to be understood by any listener; articulation of uncommon consonants or consonant blends may still be immature.

The defining statements had to be specific enough to allow the characterization of an individual child, but general enough to avoid the necessity for an infinite number of items. They provided the form for the teachers to follow in giving specific, behavioral descriptions for individual children. In helping teachers to learn to use this model in a comprehensive way it was necessary to illustrate for them ways of looking and thinking that would enrich the descriptions by individualizing them. Each subgroup of items includes also a series of questions designed to assist the teacher in describing the outstanding characteristics of a particular child. For example, it is relevant for a particular child not only that he usually "speaks clearly enough to be understood by one familiar with his speech pattern," but also that his predominant pattern changes to clearer speech when saying to another child, "Did you see Mod Squad? Did you see Linc hit that guy?" or to less clear speech in a story group when a teacher asks him directly, "Why do you think Frances was afraid?" or that the pitch and tone changes when he says in response to a loud sound in the street, "What's that, a fire engine?" or that he uses less clear speech than he is capable of—"I wanna dink of wawa"—on Monday morning or after a prolonged absence from school. These changes in pattern should be noted.

In the second category, Relationships to Adults, observation of the child's interaction with adults is focused on his relationship with the teacher. Our society and individual parents seem to expect that teachers are to assist the child in developing his capacities for self-regulation, control, initiative, and social adaptation, and that the child is there to incorporate and master a body of knowledge. This category, then, includes the way in which and the extent to which the child uses the teacher as a regulator of behavior and a resource for assistance. In the third category, Relationships to Children, observations of the child's relationship with other children are gathered by looking at interaction in terms of both quality and quantity, and by noting action taken in situations where conflict arises and where sharing or taking turns is called for, in situations with one other child or a small group of children. The fourth category, Relationships to Group, focuses upon the traits basic to group membership. Behavior is observed with reference to the exercise of privilege and the assumption of responsibility in the general school situation (care of school property, respect for property owned or being used by others, and observation of space boundaries), as associated with participation in specific group activities, and as appropriate during periods of transition from one activity or situation to another. In the fifth category, Relationships to Objects and Ideas, observations are schematized in three ways: first, by looking at his actions in the use of objects that are (a) manipulated as extensions of the body, (b) shaped from plastic materials, and (c) used as elements in constructing or assembling given and created structures; second, by looking at the child's behavior in activities such as play, music, and dance, in which ideas can be both formulated and expressed; and third, by assessing his capacity to use basic ordering concepts by which the attributes that identify and classify events and objects can be distinguished. Time, number, and description of the formal properties of objects are examples of such concepts.

With such a structure the teacher is ready to collect quite specific information about the child's knowledge—his values, attitudes, skills, abilities, and feelings. To gather material for a complete workup on each child is the next step. The terms *educational diagnosis* and *educational prescription* are used to stress the importance of both assessing each child and planning his experience. The decision to prescribe should be the result of a conscious evaluation. *Not* to prescribe should be the result of an equally conscious process and not inaction by default.

The availability of colleagues from other disciplines who can supplement the observations of teachers and who can offer formulations about data from their own fields makes for fuller and richer observations of children. This method makes it possible for such colleagues not only to understand the teachers' goals and rationale but also to understand and to react to each child in an individualized way. It also provides a systematic description of the child by those closest to him in a way that does not interfere with their work but rather stimulates consideration of his individuality.

This method of systematic observation involves a great deal of time, both in record making and in the many hours of discussion and thought that are needed to use it in a comprehensive form. Because ours was a research project we were able to staff our center to allow for this kind of extensive educational diagnosis and prescription. We are entirely aware that the method can be fully used only when there is ample time and supporting staff. But it may also be useful, if in a more limited way, in other settings.

CHAPTER 9

Staffing for Quality Daycare

The subject of this chapter has been dealt with only briefly as it related to our particular setting. In what follows we propose to discuss in more detail aspects of staffing in relation to the quality of daycare in any setting. Throughout the discussion, however, the limitations of such generalizations should be kept in mind. Not only is each situation unique but many factors relevant to staffing for high quality daycare are too intangible to reduce to a set of recommendations. The atmosphere in which an enterprise exists, the general staff morale, the skills of each staff member, the teamwork among the staff members, the kind and amount of administrative support available to the staff when it is needed, the effect of the physical plant on facilitating or impeding the work to be done—all these factors help to determine the quality of a program.

Staff Qualifications

Much has been published by various government agencies, standard-setting organizations, and practitioners concerning staff qualifications for the various roles involved in operating a daycare center. Recommendations and requirements vary little with respect to desirable personality characteristics but greatly with respect to the amount and kind of education and the amount of experience considered necessary for various roles. One survey of state daycare licensing requirements (Social and Administrative Services and Systems Association and Consulting Services Corporation 1971) found that twenty-seven states require "some" college or equivalent education for directors, eight require only high school graduation, and sixteen specify no educational requirement. While some publications specifically recommend the requirement of a master's or bachelor's degree in one of several fields of study for the daycare director, others omit mention of any formal educational qualifications and describe only necessary knowledge and skills. But the standards at best are not high, and the requirements allow latitude for each category of staff that does not serve well the needs of children and their parents.

The reason for this latitude is undoubtedly related to such realities as the small number of well-trained people available, the great pressure for more and more daycare, the wish to supply jobs to unfortunate people with few marketable skills, and, of course, to the high cost of excellence in daycare. Because of these realities most parents in this country who must have daycare for young children will probably have to settle for less than good daycare in the foreseeable future. The center that is able to offer really good services will continue to be the exception. We are aware of many reasons for this situation and feel only compassion for those who are struggling—sometimes under appallingly difficult circumstances—to do the best they can for the children in their care. However, daycare standards must be raised dramatically if children are to be helped rather than harmed. If enough people in the country become aware of the need, standards that seem idealistic and unreal today could become common practice. While well-trained staff in sufficient numbers are not the only ingredient of good daycare, they are the most important one. Therefore, in what follows we present our ideas about staffing for high-quality care and education of infants and young children in a community daycare center.

The Director

We shall not cite here the many and varied tasks a director must be capable of doing herself, supervising, or assigning to someone who is responsible to her. Formidable but realistic lists of such responsibilities and of desirable personal qualities are given in handbooks and guides listed in the bibliography. We are aware of no formal course of training that alone provides all of the various kinds of knowledge and skill necessary to direct a center providing good services to infants, young children, and parents. Nor do we know of any one discipline that encompasses within its body of knowledge and practice, even at the most advanced level, all that a director needs to know and be able to do. Perhaps if there is sufficient commitment to good daycare at the national level, there will one day be training programs to prepare people specifically for this important role.

Meanwhile, how are board members to find a well-qualified person? To what field of study are they to look and for what academic degree, if any, within that field? Our answers to these questions may be disappointing because no simple prescription can be given and easily followed. Perhaps the most basic guiding principle we can suggest is simply that there is no one exactly right field of preparation, and therefore, with rare exceptions, the director's areas of knowledge and skill will need to be supplemented by those of other staff members and/or consultants. Furthermore, the ability to work cooperatively with the board of directors, to weld a staff into an effective, task-oriented team, to relate warmly and respectfully to parents and children, to represent the center in the community, to use good judgment in decision making, to use authority constructively, to be continuously seeking ways to improve the quality of the program involves skills and personal qualities that no training guarantees and that must be assessed in any candidate regardless of his or her educational background, though if reliable reports of previous work experience can be obtained, they may be of help. Candidates also may or may not be skilled in the business management of the operation or in fund raising, including grantsmanship. However, these are skills that the willing person of good intelligence can usually learn fairly quickly.

Let us examine a few possible choices and see what the strengths and shortcomings of each might be, in light of the fact that developmental disturbances are very common in children in daycare centers. The center may be used as a resource for solving children's problems, but the use of daycare may also create or exaggerate problems in young children.

• THE EARLY CHILDHOOD EDUCATOR   Of those who have had some relevant training for daycare, early childhood educators are probably most frequently chosen as directors, and, indeed, the well-trained and experienced person in this field brings a great deal of knowledge to the task—knowledge of child development, of theories of how young children learn, and of ways to implement learning goals. In our opinion not all learning theories are equally effective as bases for program building and working with young children, and a board of directors might want to seek consultation on this important subject before interviewing candidates about their particular theoretical approaches. Another asset of the early childhood educator is the ability to help teachers plan and carry out the daily program for the older children and to provide some of the in-service training not only through supervision but through active participation in the staff training program.

A common deficit in the early childhood educator's training is that it has been focused on the child from three to five or six, and knowledge of infant care and even of the educational components of good infant care have not traditionally been an important part of training, though there is now some tendency to extend the curriculum to include more orientation to the infancy period. Without some supplementary study or help from other staff or consultants, a person whose training and experience is only with three to five or six year olds would not be properly prepared to direct a center serving children much under age three. Furthermore, many early childhood educators have had experience only in nursery-school settings, which differ markedly from daycare in several important respects (See Pizzo 1972).

Another deficit in the early childhood educator's preparation—again, with rare exceptions—is specific training in work with parents. Here we do not have in mind parent–teacher conferences about children: all teachers are, or should be, prepared for that kind of contact with parents. We are thinking rather of the role described in the Child Welfare League's guide (Boguslawski 1966), which assigns this role only to an experienced social worker with a master's degree. This role is fully described in Chapter 4 of this book, in which some reasons were given for separating this role from that of the educator. We know of nothing in even the best training of educators that qualifies them for the kind of work with parents we believe is a necessity in good daycare. Therefore, the educator-director who is expected to carry the main responsibility of working with parents needs additional training with appropriate consultation, or the services of someone whose special area of competence is work with parents.

Obviously the early childhood educator as director would also need the help of at least a part-time nurse, of a physician on call, possibly initial consultation with a nutritionist or access to good literature on nutrition, and occasionally the services of a clinical psychologist and/or child psychiatrist as consultant.

• THE CHILD PSYCHOLOGIST   Psychologists from at least three special branches—developmental, clinical, and educational psychology at the master's level or above—have skills relevant to directing a daycare program. Training in child psychology in any of these three areas includes familiarization with theories of psychological development and human behavior, characteristics of the child's intellectual and social development, and the personality development of adults. Some child psychologists will have had training in group dynamics. All should have the knowledge and ability to conceptualize that makes them valuable in training staff, and all are likely to have some expertise in organizing and writing proposals and program descriptions.

In addition, they will have special qualifications in the specialized areas mentioned. Developmental psychologists, for example, are often strong in research design, including program evaluation, and are familiar with several developmental theories. For some the training has included direct supervised experience in working with young children; others may have had little experience translating theory into practice. The clinical psychologist who has worked closely with young children will be trained in recognizing problems of development and behavior, in administering diagnostic tests and in helping teachers and other staff make plans to alleviate the problems. Depending upon previous work experiences he may or may not be familiar with behavior of young children in groups and with planning an educational program. Interviewing skills are likely to be stronger than those of the other two specialists. The educational psychologist will have had considerable training that bears upon learning and learning environments, which is valuable. If this has included preschool education it is especially relevant as a qualification for the daycare directorship. The educational psychologist is not necessarily attuned to the recognition of developmental problems, however, especially in the very young child.

Experience with infants is not a regular part of the training of child psychologists, though it is becoming more common. Nor are child psychologists necessarily prepared to give parents guidance.

• THE CLINICAL SOCIAL WORKER   The knowledge and skills that a clinical social worker might bring to directing a daycare center are probably much less obvious to the average person than are those of several other disciplines. This is partly because the stereotype of the social worker in this country is that of the welfare worker, who often has no specific education for social work except on-the-job training and who may deal only in matters of welfare eligibility and budget determination. But professional social work is a broad field encompassing a number of specialties within it, and while some educational content is common to all, areas of specialization even during training result in quite dissimilar kinds of skills. For example, a social worker trained in what is called community organization has a different kind of competence from one trained for clinical social work. It is the clinical social worker whose potential as a competent director of daycare we will examine.

Among the expectable assets of an experienced clinical social worker are sound theoretical as well as working knowledge of development in both children and adults, and knowledge of normal and abnormal behavior and of environmental, cultural, and psychological factors in determining behavior, including parent–child interaction. Formal training plus work experience should also equip the clinical social worker with the knowledge and skills necessary to help parents with problems affecting their relationship to their children and with environmental problems. Some clinical social workers will have had specific experience in work with young children, but even without direct work experience they can be expected to have sufficient knowledge of child behavior of all kinds to be helpful to the teaching staff in working out some of the problems individual children may present. Knowledge of common human needs and emotional reactions should be an asset in developing good working relationships with board, staff, and community.

The main deficit of the clinical social worker is that while he may have knowledge of early developmental stages and of the needs and developmental tasks of young children, including infants, he does not ordinarily have the educator's knowledge of how to plan and carry out a program of education. The social worker's knowledge of how to provide good psychological care should, however, be adequate with respect to any age group, including infants. The social worker as director, then, might be a wise choice in a situation that permitted the hiring of a competent early childhood educator to supervise and train teachers and assistant teachers, an educator who could also, with help from the director or a consultant, formulate an infancy program. The clinical social worker and early childhood educator together should be able to set up a program providing both good care and good education, which are so inextricably intertwined in infancy and the early years of childhood. The social worker, like the educator, would need to have the supplementary help of some nursing, medical, nutritional, and psychological or psychiatric consultation.

• THE NURSE   Just as early childhood education is a specialization within the general field of education and clinical social work within the general field of social work, so various areas of specialization exist within nursing. All baccalaureate nursing training now includes some child development content. It is increasingly common for basic training programs to include experience not just in hospitals but in such settings as community health and rehabilitation centers and well-baby clinics. In the latter, the nurse-trainee is expected to take developmental as well as health histories and to give some child-care advice to parents. If the nurse who completes the baccalaureate program is interested mainly in the care of sick people, she probably elects to work in a hospital or clinic that serves sick people. However, if her concern is less with specific pathology and more with general health care, she may work in a visiting nurse association or maternal and child health clinic under the supervision of a nurse who has an advanced degree in public health nursing. In addition to public health, graduate programs available in some schools of nursing lead to master's degrees in maternal and child health, in pediatric care, and in mental health nursing. Each of these programs gives the trainee considerable experience in working directly with children and families.

The pediatric nurse specialist would obviously bring most to a daycare center serving the very young, especially children in the first twelve to fifteen months of life. She would not generally have training in how to translate what she knew about early development into a daily program that would foster learning as well as give good care. However, it would probably be easier to add to her knowledge of infant care the necessary educational component than to add the infant-care knowledge and skills to other kinds of training. If the center serves children beyond the first twelve to fifteen months of life, at least one staff member needs to be an experienced teacher of young children capable of planning the educational program and supervising other teachers. This deficit exists for nurses with other areas of specialization as well. The mental health nursing specialist might bring less knowledge of early development and infant-care skills than the pedi-

atric nurse—though her knowledge in these areas would probably be sufficient—but more knowledge of human behavior, especially abnormal behavior. All nurse specialists, including public health and maternal and
child health specialists, have as assets their ability to be responsible for the
health supervision of all the children, not just the infants.

Nurses also bring skills related to advising parents about some aspects
of child care and development. This area is somewhat problematic, however. The traditional way nurses, physicians, and other health service personnel have been trained to work emphasizes advice or prescriptions. Probably the parent most willing to use direct advice about child care, especially
advice about tangible matters such as how to cope with a diaper rash or
when to introduce solid foods, is the inexperienced mother of a young
baby. Even then the advice is often not followed, especially, of course, if
it is unsolicited. If it is not followed, reasons may be difficult to identify.
No matter how scientific and valid advice may be, the parent's ability and
willingness to follow it depend on a great many complicated cultural, experiential, and intrapsychic factors. As one moves out of the range of tangible advice about physical care and into more abstract matters of how
best to handle situations having to do with child behavior, the resistance
to advice is usually stronger, and the psychological complexities in the parent that may operate against being able to use advice—even when sought—
are much greater. Then the knowledge of psychodynamic factors in both
child and adult behavior and skills in the use of relationships with the
parent to bring about change become increasingly important. Most nurse
specialists other than mental health nurses will not have such knowledge
and skill. Whatever the nurse's particular area of specialization, then, unless she has some unusual combination of other training and experiences,
her skills require supplementation through careful choice of other staff,
should pertinent personal qualities and experience make her employment
as director advisable.

• THE TALENTED APPLICANT WITHOUT RELEVANT EDUCATIONAL PREPARA-
TION   At this point in the evolution of the daycare movement many centers are being directed by people with none of the kinds of education and
training cited above, and unfortunately also by some who have little natural
talent for the work. But in ideal circumstances, should a board consider
applications for directorship from those who have no relevant formal training but who say, for example, "I love little children, I've taken care of
other people's children for years, and I know I can handle the job"? Ad-
mittedly there are self-taught individuals with special talents who could do
an effective job with the help of carefully selected staff. However, our
strong preference would be for a director trained in one of the disciplines
discussed. The reason for this preference is that much of the task of train-

ing other people is the ability not only to know what to do, but why that is the thing to do in a particular situation. In other words, in training staff, the ability to conceptualize and to help them learn to do so is vital. Otherwise, there is little ability to carry over learning appropriately from one situation to another, and instead a great tendency to apply the effective solution for the last problem inappropriately to the next. The capacity to conceptualize what one knows so that it is to some extent transferable to others who want to learn is a skill usually achieved only through a thorough understanding of a formal body of knowledge and supervised experience in its application. The person without relevant educational credentials will generally not have this necessary ability.

We have been referring to necessary roles in running a daycare program and the responsibilities they represent. Someone must be responsible for the various administrative functions; someone must provide the leadership to help a staff become an effective working unit; someone must be knowledgeable about infant care and education, someone about the care and education of older children; someone must be competent in helping parents with both the psychological problems of parenting and with other problems of daily living. These are the major areas of competence—the major roles—needed for high quality daycare. No one applicant is likely to be competent in more than the first two areas plus one other. But as long as all are satisfactorily covered by key staff and/or consultants, it is not vital that the director have specialized competence in one rather than another of the remaining three.

What about academic degrees and amount of experience? Along with others who have written on this subject, we prefer not to be highly specific because latitude is needed for various combinations of academic achievement and practice. We strongly favor the person who has at least a bachelor's degree, plus a significant amount of successful practice. However, we recognize both the supply-and-demand problem and the need for enough flexibility to allow for the very talented and experienced person who lacks an advanced degree.

Qualifications for Other Staff

• THE HEAD TEACHER   Even though the director may be a highly trained teacher competent to work directly with children and to supervise and train other teachers, her administrative duties usually require her to be away from such supervisory activities for significant amounts of time. For that reason it is highly desirable to have as head teacher a person with formal training at the bachelor's level either in early childhood education or in a child development program that has required direct work with children. Several years of practice are usually necessary for a person to carry both teaching and supervisory responsibility. Whether the supervision of the children's program is carried entirely by the director, shared with the head teacher, or the responsibility entirely of the head teacher, we prefer supervision that is based not entirely on observation and later conferencing but on working alongside teachers and assistants. In this way the supervisor not only provides a model but demonstrates her own competence. It might be reasoned that such demonstration would threaten a novice. However, we found that greatly offsetting that factor are the inspiration to learn from someone of obvious skill and the morale-building effect of seeing that the supervisor as teacher is willing to do whatever the situation calls for, just like anyone else, whether changing a diaper, helping to clean up a messy lunch table, or wiping a runny nose.

• OTHER TEACHERS In the beginning phase of a program it is especially important that at least one person in each group except the infant group be a trained teacher. In a program serving mainly children under five, that teacher should have a bachelor's degree with any major plus several years supervised experience in teaching preschool children or a Bachelor's degree in either early childhood education or in child development. Neither the director nor the head teacher will be able to be everywhere at once, and the children will fare much better, staff morale will be higher, and staff learning will proceed faster if one trained teacher is always with the children and the assistant teachers.

• ASSISTANT TEACHERS Many junior colleges now have two-year courses in child development and other relevant subjects leading to an associate degree. Graduates with practical experience before or during this training should make excellent candidates for assistant teacher positions. However, many candidates will probably continue to come from the group that supplied most of our assistant teachers at Children's House—young women without formal training but with practical experience in working with young children. While we believe that in-service training of various kinds—another way of saying continued learning—should be a part of the working experience of every employee, it is obviously of greatest importance for those who come without training.

• NURSE We are referring now not to the nurse as director but as health-care supervisor or consultant, possibly as a part-time employee in the center of average size. A nurse with a bachelor's or higher degree would be our first choice. However, a registered nurse interested in and skillful with children, whether sick or well, should be able to fill this role adequately. She should not be expected, however, to have the knowledge necessary to provide, or train others to provide more than good physical care of infants.

• PHYSICIAN In communities where choice is possible a pediatrician would, of course, be the logical one to serve as part of a nurse–physician health-care consultative team and as the one to be called in emergencies. In communities where such choice is not possible, the general practitioner who includes young children in his practice should be called upon to meet this need.

• LIAISON WITH PARENTS   The most relevant training for working with parents is clinical social-work training. Because a high degree of competence is needed in work with parents of children in daycare, we do not believe the job can be well done by someone with less than a master's degree in the field. Many schools are now offering training leading to a bachelor's degree in social work, but it is unlikely that a graduate of such a program could perform the liaison role without a good deal of supervision. Nor does the educational content of sociology or psychology programs at either the bachelor's or master's level qualify graduates to work with parents without supervision. We recognize that certain services parents need *can* be handled by people with little education and training in social work. However, we have found it much more effective, in helping parents, to establish a real relationship with them, rather than treating them merely as sets of distinct needs vis-à-vis the center. Thus, dealings with a parent should not be divided up between staff who can help with tangible problems and staff who can provide more complex services. A daycare center small enough to need only one social worker would therefore do best to employ a social worker with a master's degree. It may be feasible for two or more even smaller centers to share a skilled social worker, who actively supervises and consults with other staff in their work with parents. Of course, the amount and kind of previous experience of someone with a master's degree in social work will greatly affect performance.

• SECRETARY, COOK, MAINTENANCE PERSONNEL   We shall not attempt to set up any criteria for the selection of these personnel. However, it is important to select people who are not only competent in the technicalities of their work, but whose personalities are compatible with the atmosphere of the daycare center, and whose behavior with children is appropriate. If the center is fortunate enough to select people for these roles who have natural aptitude for relating to young children, these staff members can become very important to the children. At Children's House, for example, a visit to our secretaries' upstairs office was an almost daily treat for the children. The kitchen, where a welcoming cook allowed a peek into the oven and even used "helpers" with lunch or snack, was an auxiliary learning situation for them. Our only male employee, a general handyman, was at times assistant teacher, lunch table companion, special tutor—a kind of therapist to several children and of great importance to all of them.

Child/Staff Ratios

As with staff qualifications, opinions on the number of staff considered necessary to provide daycare in the preschool years vary widely. According to the 1971 survey of state licensing requirements mentioned above, for children *under two years* ratios vary from two children per staff member to ten. For children ages three and four, ratios are from five to fifteen per staff member; for children ages four to five, from seven to twenty children per staff member. Even though some of the ratios are far from what we consider adequate, they probably do not reflect actual practice in 1971 but minimum standards toward which centers had to be working in order to be given a provisional license. However, the ratios do reflect some recognition that child/staff ratios need to vary with the age and developmental characteristics of the children served.

Our child/staff ratio recommendations do not include staff whose primary function is not child care and education. Caregivers, however—especially those caring for infants, who sleep relatively more than older children—may do other kinds of work. For example, either in the room with babies who are awake or within hearing distance of sleeping babies, the caregiver might at times fold diapers or mend clothing and put it away. Because most centers are understaffed, one tends to think of providing enough stimulation, enough child–staff interaction, but babies and young children also need time to themselves, when in the presence of a familiar adult they can play with a toy without the constant stimulation of interacting with another person. It is difficult to give the young child in daycare the experiences he would have in good home care, a situation in which he learns partly by observing his mother doing various household tasks. Thus, if all the necessary "household" tasks in daycare take place apart from the children, they miss important potential learning experiences.

To provide a good program for infants not yet walking we believe it is necessary to have one person available for every two babies, since the infant's ability to tolerate discomfort of any kind is extremely limited. Some other tasks can also be done by the caregivers, but the same person should always be ready to give attention to two babies for whom she is responsible. A backup person whom the babies also know needs to be available in the occasional absence of the primary caregiver.

For children from approximately one to almost three we recommend continuing the same two-to-one child/staff ratio. Active toddlers and runabout children sleep less than during the first year and require more vigilance for safety and longer periods of adult help with learning from play and interpersonal transactions with peers and adults. While there may be short periods during the day when three or four toddlers can be safely and happily in the care of one adult, they are of brief duration, and a one-to-three or one-to-four ratio as the usual plan overtaxes both children and adults.

Young three year olds would probably not do very well in a child/staff ratio of more than three to one, while another group of fairly mature three year olds might manage with a four-to-one ratio. The same variability, of course, also applies to the four and five year olds. While some groups might function successfully with a ratio of five or six to one, others, we feel, would need a four-to-one ratio in order for the program to be of high quality over a full day.

Size of Groups

The daycare literature concerns itself much less with the size of groups than with child/staff ratios. This may be because the size of groups cannot be discussed in isolation from the matter of the number of staff per child. Yet we suspect that anyone whose experience in daycare includes working in groups of different sizes would choose to separate forty children into several groups of varying size, with the younger children in smaller groups, rather than to have two groups of twenty children each. The physical setting of the center—not merely size, but arrangement of rooms and space within rooms—is, of course, a basic determinant of optimal group size, but there are others as well.

Among them is noise, which is a potential cause of heightened stress. A certain amount of noise is a necessary part of any situation in which young children are busily engaged in age-appropriate activities. Yet too much noise can impose unnecessary disorganizing stress on both children and adults. Too many activities and interpersonal transactions taking place in one room can also become confusing and stressful. There is a limit to the number of possible relationships and transactions in which a young child can profitably engage. The teacher's ability to have any sense of the continuity and the quality of a child's experience even for a span of a few minutes depends on there not being too many possible interactions with too many people. Unless the teacher has some idea of what has been experienced by a child during a particular period of time, she will not understand what has led to the child's present situation and will have to fall back on generalities instead of reacting to that child's feelings and behavior in a way that is sensitively appropriate to exactly what has happened.

How much noise is too much? How many activities, transactions, and relationships are too many? Obviously there are no simple or categorical answers. Individual tolerance for each of the factors mentioned varies. The skillful, experienced teacher usually develops an acute awareness of the point at which noise, for example, becomes a disorganizing force within a group, and at which other factors interfere with the sense she and her colleagues can have of what the experience in the group has been for each child during any time segment. In general, though, our recommendations concerning group size are that there be no more than five children under age three to a group, and no more than ten children ages three to five to a group.

Though we shall not discuss here the matter of size and number of rooms desirable for a given population, the above recommendations suggest the desirability of rooms of various sizes rather than the large rooms of equal size found in many daycare centers. Such variety allows flexibility in grouping children, whatever the specific method of grouping chosen.

Considerations of Staff Age, Sex, Race, and Culture

For the young child who spends most of his waking hours in daycare, the experience can be an enriching one if it expands his experience beyond what is available to him at home. One of the ways of broadening the child's experience is by making it possible for him to know a staff that is not homogeneous in age, sex, race, and culture.

We have commented elsewhere on the great amount of energy required to work long hours with young children, and thereby implied the need for youthful stamina. However, energy and stamina do not vary exclusively with age, and it is possible to find people of varying ages who are able to work with young children. Adults of various ages can also be employed as secretary, cook, housekeeper, and in other positions besides that of teacher. Even children who are not in daycare are often prevented as a result of the increasing mobility of the population from knowing extended family members and thus miss experiences with grandparents, aunts, uncles, and cousins. While unrelated persons cannot be completely satisfactory substitutes for these nonexistent or lost relationships, deficits in the child's experience can be reduced through some variation in the ages of people who work with them. A few daycare centers add to the young child's experience through collaborative arrangements with public schools. Boys and girls of junior high and high school age taking courses in family life or in connection with other training come for several hours a week of supervised play with daycare center children, working as assistants to the staff.

Another obvious lack in the lives of many children today in all social groups is experiences with men. While care and education of the young child has not traditionally been the vocational choice of many men, this situation is changing. Even if not many men seek employment in daycare, we suspect that some could be recruited—if not for permanent careers in the field, at least for significant periods of time. A daycare center located in a community that has a college or university can almost certainly work out an arrangement for young men to be volunteers or part-time workers.

In some colleges, child-development courses in which men are enrolled require field work, and daycare centers are a favorite site for such experiences. The use of either volunteers or field-placement students, of course, requires staff time to organize and supervise, and the use of many people who come and stay for brief periods can be confusing to children. But a few workers coming into a well-organized program can provide many opportunities for both the children and the volunteers or part-time workers.

It is easy to say that the child population as well as the staff of a daycare center should be representative of the community in which the center exists. It is not easy, however, to achieve such a goal. In large cities the daycare-center population is likely to be representative of the neighborhood rather than of the community as a whole. In this respect, publicly supported daycare is faced with the same situation as the public schools. If the center is conveniently close to those who need to use it, all too often de facto segregation results, based on long-standing patterns of segregated neighborhoods. We are not unmindful of the fact that some groups prefer the preservation of just such separatism, believing among other things that to preserve their racial or cultural heritage they must have daycare centers attended and staffed exclusively by members of their own group. We respect such convictions and the right of those who have them to work for the development of such daycare facilities, but our own belief is that both children and families benefit from exposure to others of different racial, cultural, and socioeconomic backgrounds. At Children's House, in which, especially during the pilot phase, there was considerable variation in all three characteristics, both children and staff of different backgrounds learned from one another. In a setting where differences are respected, children develop a strong sense of their own race not only through identification but through contrast, through becoming aware of differences. We believe that parents play the basic role in establishing not only the child's awareness of his racial and cultural heritage but also the pride or lack of it in the child. Furthermore, children in daycare will not be able to spend their lives in a separatist world. Many, if not most, will need to work alongside of those who are different from them. We believe that learning about oneself and others can proceed at the same time and cannot begin too early. Thus, while we have no practicable solution to overcoming the same massive problems confronting public-school education, we believe that, ideally, daycare children and staff should be fully integrated. Where this is not possible because of static patterns of de facto segregation and housing, it is still possible in a small but important way to work toward this ideal. For example, a center in an all-white suburban neighborhood can employ an interracial staff; a center in a solidly black or Puerto Rican neighborhood can do the same thing.

The Staff-Selection Process

Before anyone is hired, the sponsoring group of a new center—usually a board of directors—needs to have worked out the general purpose and objectives of the program and the approximate number and age range of children they hope to serve. These factors can make a tremendous difference in what kinds of knowledge and skills must be represented among the personnel chosen. Qualifications need to be agreed upon, especially for the director. They will be determined in part by what specific tasks the particular program will require it director to perform. For example, in a relatively small center the director may be able to supervise the teaching staff. In a larger program, an additional person may be necessary to fulfill that function. Thus, working out what qualifications of education, experience, and personal characteristics a director should have is a necessary precursor to recruitment.

Once a candidate is found who has the required educational and experiential background, whose credentials have been thoroughly checked, and whose personal qualities seem to be acceptable, the board and the candidate must discuss general philosophy of daycare and policies at which the board has already arrived, to be reasonably sure of some degree of compatibility as the basis for a good working relationship. Some flexibility on both sides is of course required—the director should be able to work, for example, within the financial reality confronting the board, and the board, having sought a person of professional competence, should be able in some matters to be influenced in decision making by the director's knowledge of what is and what is not good care and education for young children—but unless at least a basic outlook on daycare is shared, mutual trust will be hard to build.

Once hired, the director should be able to work with the board to determine the number and kinds of staff positions necessary to carry out the proposed program and the qualifications for each position to be filled. The extent to which members of a board's personnel committee take part in actually interviewing candidates probably varies a good deal in practice. However, in harmony with ideas expressed in Chapter 3 concerning administrative structure, we strongly believe that each employee must be responsible first to his immediate supervisor and, through the supervisor, to the director, not to the board. Only in this way can the director be responsible to the board for carrying out the tasks assigned to that position. Thus, in our opinion, the decision both to hire and to discharge employees should be the director's, with the concurrence of the board.

We noted earlier the confusion in daycare guidelines and literature concerning staff qualifications with respect to education and experience. For the board, personnel committee, or director faced with evaluating credentials of applicants, even specific degrees in specific areas of study and exact number of years experience are not completely objective criteria. The quality of the school attended, the content of the particular curriculum, the kind of experience—all must be evaluated. No degree, in itself, and no amount of experience, in itself, guarantees that the applicant will bring a sufficient amount of relevant knowledge to the daycare task. Furthermore, the board needs to check on the authenticity of any candidate's credentials, obtaining confidential letters of reference when possible. We know of one incident in which a person was hired—not by us, we hasten to say—for a high level position in a daycare center on the basis of her statement about degrees and experience that she did not, in fact, possess.

Yet, education and experience are relatively objective matters and are therefore easier to assess than the important personal characteristics. We noted earlier also that various guidelines tend to be fairly consistent as to the recommended personality characteristics in daycare personnel. But a problem that is not dealt with in the daycare literature to any extent is how the person or persons charged with the responsibility for staff selection are to be reasonably sure of making accurate assessments of capabilities and of such intangible qualities as maturity, flexibility, warmth, love of children, and ability to accept supervision. While it is time consuming but not difficult to check credentials and ask for letters of reference, the interviewing process is not only time consuming but very difficult to do well.

Since all employment interviewing is very subjective, more than one person should interview each applicant and the applicant should visit the center more than once. In interviews, information should be both received and given. An interviewer should create an atmosphere in which at some point the candidate feels free to ask questions. It is often advisable to await questions rather than volunteer a good deal of information, since whether questions are asked, what questions are asked, and how they are asked can supply a great deal of information about the applicant. However, at an appropriate point the prospective employee should be given as clear an idea as possible of what the daily work is, what responsibilities are involved, to whom the person would be responsible, and just how the particular position fits into the structure of the center. Otherwise, there can be a failure of clarity about specific expectations.

An effective technique in clearing up expectations is to pose theoretical problem situations to the prospective teacher (What would you do?), and to ask the applicant to plan a typical day for children of a given age group and comment on the rationale for the choice of activities. If the applicant is teaching elsewhere, every effort should be made to observe that person

in action. Similar procedures can be used in filling other daycare staff positions as well. Whether the task at hand is the selection of a director by a
community center's board of directors or the selection of a teacher or
assistant teacher by the director with help from other staff members, many
of the same policies and procedures are indicated.

The applicant should also be prepared for the possibility that the program may change in response to need, that the child-care population may
vary in numbers or age range with consequent change in responsibilities
currently assigned to the position in question. Obviously, information
should be given about personnel practices and about opportunities for on-
the-job learning and promotion. Whether through volunteered information
or through answers to questions, an honest effort should be made to point
out to an applicant one is seriously considering both the advantages and disadvantages of the work and the setting. One helpful practice in a center
already functioning is to arrange for the applicant to talk with a staff
member who is doing the same kind of work the position to be filled involves. Usually staff members have much less resentment about irksome
tasks or frustrating situations if they are told about them before they accept the job. For example, in the event of illness of the cook-housekeeper,
teachers and assistant teachers may have to be willing to help prepare lunch
or do the laundry. At Children's House almost everyone on the staff
helped with every kind of task when emergencies arose. Of course, this
kind of cooperative behavior is in part a matter of staff morale, not just of
employment interviewing policy.

As in filling the position of director, it is also important, through discussion at whatever level is appropriate in view of the responsibilities to be
carried and the training and experience of the applicant, to form an impression of how compatible the general philosophy of child care and education
of the center will be with the applicant's—whether the latter is a profes-
sionally based philosophy or one determined by life experience alone. A
slavish kind of me-tooism is not what is sought, but there should not be
sharp and possibly irreconcilable differences of opinion on basic issues.

Even those who are open and forthright in expressing their views cannot
always act in real situations on the basis of theoretical convictions. One
important consideration should therefore be the applicant's potential for
learning and using what is learned. But the only way to be sure an applicant will make a good staff member is through a trial period of employment. While the terms *trial period* or *probationary period* have frightening and unsavory connotations, the reality is that every kind and level of
employment involves a trial period on both sides, whether or not this
aspect of the situation is made explicit. We suggest that it be made explicit.
It need not be a totally negative process if the employer makes clear that

for the new employee, the job will also be on trial, that daycare is not everyone's métier, so if the decision on either side is to discontinue the association, no disgrace need be involved. In view of the time and care recruitment requires, the employer can with all honesty give assurance that the center's best interest will be served by helping a new staff member function satisfactorily and that there is every intention of providing that support.

Finally, when an applicant is being considered after the daycare center is in operation, it is sometimes helpful both to the interviewers and the applicant to arrange an opportunity for the applicant to observe a part of the program with one of the interviewers. Observing may dispel fantasies about the work to be done, allowing some applicants to discover that the job is really not what they want to do. Discussion of the observation may also help to clarify certain things for the applicant and give the interviewers additional data for their decision. If the staff is fairly secure, the children are used to visitors, and the applicant is not reluctant to do so, going into one of the children's rooms and meeting both children and staff can also be helpful. One such visit at Children's House resulted in a spontaneous invitation from children and staff for the applicant to go along on a little excursion. Before it was over the applicant was interacting with the children and staff as if she was already a member of the group. This bit of experience was probably a more important indication of the young woman's suitability for the work than any amount of discussion calculated to reveal how she might behave with children and other staff.

Staff Development

Once the staff is hired there must then begin a training process or, perhaps more accurately, a learning process, which continues indefinitely. There is frequent reference in the daycare literature to staff training programs. Most often staff training is conceived of as a vehicle for communicating a more or less specific body of knowledge to those with little or no relevant educational background for daycare. The curriculum, along with work experience, is intended to convert the untrained into trained staff. There is a place in daycare for such specific training programs. At Children's House we developed a program for training our assistant teachers that combined reading assignments, informal presentation of various bodies of knowledge by the senior staff, child observation assignments of many kinds, discussion of observations, and informal discussion of all subject areas. The group to be trained took part in developing the curriculum; only a general outline of basic subjects was supplied by the staff committee in charge of the program. Amplifications and additions were made as areas of interest developed, as a result of questions raised both in discussing the content presented and in the ongoing daily work with children. Our program was formulated in response to our particular situation, our particular training group, and their emerging interests as theory and practice came together; to try to reproduce it here would not be helpful to others. Instead, we wish to focus attention on the importance of continuous development on the part of all members of the staff, not just those assumed to have little educational preparation for daycare.

Learning opportunities in daycare are provided not only through specific training programs but through the very process of doing the work, through on-the-job supervision, through being alert to problems as they arise and attempting to find solutions, and through the continuous process of examining all parts of the program and their effectiveness. Each of these potential learning situations existed at Children's House. In addition to the training program and consistent supervision, we all learned from one another through the countless exchanges of ideas, thoughts, feelings, and convictions that took place from person to person and group to group in getting each day's work done. We learned also from exploring together various subjects that were opened up for us because our curiosity was stimulated by some aspect of a child's behavior that we did not understand. From the observation assignments given all staff—not just those without formal training—we came to see, for example, how much there is to know about the individuality of a very young baby. Through our problem-solving staff meetings, when we were concerned about one child and his parents, we learned to bring all the relevant information we had, but at times we discovered how little we knew and how much more we needed to learn. A kind of crossfertilization took place in which the expertise of a person with one kind of training and responsibility in the program added to the knowledge and enriched the practice of those with quite different kinds of training and responsibility. Excellent consultation can be a source of much learning. Perhaps the most important factor in assuring the ongoing development of any staff is an atmosphere of inquiry, of intellectual curiosity, not for its own sake but for its usefulness in advancing problem-solving skills and lessening hardships. For such an atmosphere to develop, zest for continued learning must characterize the consultants, the director, and the others in leadership roles.

CHAPTER 10

The Use of Consultants

We approach the subject of consultation by attempting to put ourselves in the position of the layman elected to serve on the board of a daycare center and of a staff member well trained in child development but new to the field of daycare. How might they educate themselves about the uses of consultation in daycare? Each might have need for a somewhat different kind and degree of knowledge about consultation and how to use it. Our emphasis in this chapter will be on use of consultation by the daycare staff. However, either the board member wanting a quick orientation to the subject or staff member seeking to understand the use of consultation might turn to the literature we mention on this subject.

In our own search of the literature we found very little.* We reviewed Dorothy Kiester's booklet, *Consultation in Daycare* (1969), and Lois Barclay Murphy's paper in *Children* (1968), "The Consultant in a Daycare Center for Deprived Children." Both are excellent, but are written primarily for the use of consultants, though both are of some value to those planning for consultation.

Of the resources we have reviewed, the one that comes closest to dealing with consultation from the user's point of view is a chapter in the Office of Child Development handbook on daycare administration (Host and Heller 1971) entitled "Psychological Services." These services, says the handbook, are usually guided by a psychiatrist or Ph.D. psychologist, who serves either as a part-time staff member or as a consultant. The discussion of the dimension psychological services can add to daycare should be of some help to those new to the field. The authors may not have intended the chapter to be a full treatment of the subject of consultation. However, since nothing about consultation appears elsewhere in the handbook, we must judge that it presents a limited view of the kinds of consultation needed and of who is qualified to supply them. From our experience as community daycare consultants, we believe that there is often need for consultation other than psychological.

---

* This chapter was written before publication in 1974 *Day Care, 3, Serving Preschool Children,* in which Cohen and Brandegee include an excellent chapter on consultation.

Before pursuing the idea of multiple kinds of consultation, we must describe the role of a consultant and the conditions necessary for constructive use of consultants. We like Dorothy Kiester's way of establishing the consultant's role through the use of five "rules" that govern the consultant–client relationship.

> The consultant . . . must explain at the outset the five basic "rules" that will govern their relationship: (1) he is there only at the client's request, (2) for only as long as the consultation seems to both to be productive, (3) to help clarify problems, (4) and help find alternative solutions, (5) about which the client then is free to make the choice.
>
> He shares his expert knowledge but he does not do the changing involved in solutions and he does not *require* the client to do so. He only helps the client find a course of action she can follow in her own efforts to resolve the difficulty. He helps her define her goals but does not impose them; he helps her see ways of achieving the goals but does not enforce them. [p. 9]

From the foregoing it should be clear that the consultant has no authority but that of a particular kind of knowledge. It should be clear also that the consultant–client relationship is a purely voluntary one. The consultant is invited to come and advise, but he may also be asked to go, and his advice may be taken or not, as is best in the judgment of those responsible for the program. The voluntary nature of the relationship is easy enough to assure on the part of the consultant, but it is not always clear that engaging a consultant is voluntary on the part of the client. Board members, for example, may suggest the use of consultation to a director who is not ready to acknowledge the need for help or is resistant to it because the suggestion arouses feelings of inadequacy or competitiveness. Staff members may be eager for more help and this may be threatening to a director. Or a director may be convinced of the need for consultation, but members of the staff may resist the intrusion of an outsider, feeling that their work will be scrutinized and criticized. A wise consultant who is sensitive to some of these expectable human feelings in this situation can do much to allay fears and promote the development of a helping relationship characterized by mutual respect and trust. However, no amount of wisdom on the part of a consultant can enable clients to use help if they see no problem, or if seeing one they have no motivation to solve it or have inordinate need to try to solve it alone. We are not suggesting that a beginning use of consultation must be characterized by a total lack of any but the most positive feelings about the idea and the person chosen as the consultant. Rather, in deciding to use consultation, judgment should be exercised as to when the director and the staff have enough motivation for help, enough recognition of any negative feelings about consultation and enough ability to manage those feelings to insure that the consultant has a reasonable chance of being used constructively. Once the arrangement is begun, a great deal depends on the skill of the consultant in making himself useful in an acceptable way—but the success or failure of the plan does not depend completely on the consultant. In any such relationship there must be a continuing willingness on both sides to be aware of and deal with any impediments or constraints in the working relationship that prevent accomplishment of the primary task.

Helpful consultation is dependent on clear identification of the problem to be addressed. Identification of the problem with which consultative help is to be sought should usually precede the selection of a consultant; as we shall discuss later, the choice of consultants should be determined by the nature of the problem. In some situations, however, the conviction that "things in general are not going well but we don't know why or where to begin" might lead to seeking the advice of an experienced and successful daycare director. Such a consultant might talk to board, parents, and staff, learn the history of the center, its present goals and administrative structure, become familiar with the population the center serves, the physical plant of the center, the staffing pattern, and observe the program in operation, in order to identify the problems, set priorities, and decide which problems require what kind of consultation. A good consultant is realistic about his own competence and does not claim expertise he does not have. Thus the helpful consultant can be counted on to advise about the need for and availability of specialists with consultative skills different from his own.

Once problems have been identified, priorities set, and a consultant selected, the client group's work has only begun. No matter how knowledgeable the consultant, he must have data. He must know all that the staff members know about their own program in the area under consideration and perhaps in others as well. There is no magic by which the consultant draws workable problem-solving plans out of thin air. Consultation that is worth the name is based not only on the relevant experience and knowledge that the consultant has presumably applied successfully in other settings but on detailed knowledge of the particular situation about which his advice is asked. Anyone employing a consultant should be wary of the instant expert who can propose solutions before he understands the problems. The skillful consultant knows how to elicit from staff members more about a situation than they thought they knew.

However, the most fruitful consultative work is based not only on information the staff can contribute—though over time a good consultant will significantly increase staff competence not only in observation of their own program as a whole and of individual children in it but in choosing what observations and information are most significant in a particular context—but also on the consultant's own observations. This means, of course, that the staff must be able to accept some scrutiny of their work. Thus, a certain quality of openness is necessary on the part of the administration and the staff, a willingness to share information and impressions and to risk exploring weak parts of the program if consultation is to be as helpful as it can be.

To be sure, not every daycare center needs consultants. The kind and amount of consultation—if any—needed by a daycare center depends on a number of factors that may vary over time, such as the goals of the program, the characteristics and needs of the population of the center, the variety and quality of staff training and experience, and what kinds of problems do, in fact, arise. But the question of whether or not consultation is needed should not be confused with whether or not need is recognized. Unfortunately, consultation tends to be used more by those who feel secure enough to admit a consultant, and thus it is not always used where it is most needed.

The following are areas in which problems frequently do occur or help is requested in advance to avoid problems developing.

• Program, both initial planning and improvement of an ongoing program. Help might be requested concerning how best to foster each child's growth and development, how to improve curriculum content and methods of teaching particular age groups, how best to use space that cannot be structurally changed, how to group children and deploy staff, or how to provide a program for an age group not previously served.

• Relationship to and work with parents.

• The difficult child: how to understand his behavior and be of help to him in the daycare setting.

• How to recognize the child who is disturbed enough to need professional evaluation; and how to make a referral of such a child for evaluation, including how to help parents understand and accept the need for such a referral.

• Staff relationships: how to identify the nature and causes of staff problems that interfere with the task and how to develop methods for dealing with them.

• Issues involving administrative structure and its implications for everyday functioning. Problems in this area are sometimes due to lack of any clear-cut structure so that lines of authority and responsibility are unclear and role definitions and interrelationships are confused. Problems in this area may be the cause of problems in staff relationships.

• Health, including health-care practices, health education, nutrition, and first aid.

From this list, it becomes clear that needs extend beyond the realm of psychological services.

Who, then, is qualified to give consultation in the various problem areas we have described? Again, categorical answers are not possible; at this time there is no one kind of training or experience that prepares a person to be an expert in all of the areas mentioned. Someone who is excellent in helping with matters of curriculum and teaching methods may have neither interest nor skills in helping to figure out why there is consistent stress and bickering among the staff. A person who provides very astute observations of a difficult child and how to help him on a one-to-one basis may have little capacity for transmitting what he knows into a plan of action that can be carried out in a group situation, especially since there is often insufficient staff for the number of children enrolled. A person who has very sophisticated understanding of the psychological problems of children may be helpful in dealing with behavior but poorly informed about how children learn and how to break down the various steps in the process of learning a particular thing. Someone excellent in advising about how to meet the needs of young children is frequently ill equipped to advise about work with parents. Not only a person's particular training but the settings in which that training has been applied and his special interests need to be evaluated in selecting a consultant to help with a particular problem.

One of the pitfalls to be avoided in selecting a consultant is the acceptance of certain labels at face value without specific information about the individual. There are now specialties within almost every field of study. Thus, for example, it is a mistake to assume that a well-trained and experienced teacher is necessarily an expert in working with prekindergarten children. A pediatrician might be invaluable in consulting with staff about the day-to-day care and emotional nurturance of infants whereas someone equally well trained in another branch of medicine would probably not be. Psychiatrists are not necessarily experts on children and even some trained in child psychiatry have little training, experience, or interest in very young children. Psychologists with relevant expertise are also difficult to select. The Ph.D. alone is no guarantee of applicable knowledge, again because of the many specialties within the field. The psychologist whose Ph.D. is in child psychology should be the most likely prospect, but again the specifics of the person's area of interest and experience are very important. Some child psychologists, like child psychiatrists, have not concerned themselves to any significant degree with preschool children, and some who have confine their work to very specialized areas of research, and their knowledge is not broadly applicable when it comes to working with children in a daycare center. Similarly, because of the many specialities within social work, it is not enough to select as consultant any one who has a master's degree and experience; it is important that the experience be in a relevant field—for example, in settings concerned with the problems of parents and young children.

Perhaps most difficult of all is finding a person who is knowledgeable about and interested in problems related to administrative structure and staff relationships. Yet there is probably no aspect of daycare operation that can more profitably use the relatively objective and dispassionate scrutiny of the outsider. Anyone of those whose qualifications we have just reviewed in relation to other problem areas might out of special interest and previous experience be helpful in these areas also. While there are systems analysts who have made a life study of how organizations work, these studies have been based mainly on huge industrial enterprises. While those responsible for large networks of daycare programs under centralized management might well profit by perusing such studies or even seeking consultation from a systems analyst, the average individual daycare center probably has to make do with the experience of those who have successfully administered programs similar to their own. A good choice for consultant on problems related to confusion about who does what and is responsible to whom might be a daycare-center director who is known to be a clear-thinking person and who is interested in and challenged by administrative problems. A person trained to recognize and deal with feelings and help people cope with them might be the first choice in the area of staff relations; the psychiatrist, psychologist, or social worker already consulting with the staff about other things could perhaps fill this role. If a trusting working relationship has grown up between the staff and the person consulting, say about certain children, that person would probably more quickly than a newcomer be able to involve the staff in the kind of discussion necessary to work out the immediate interstaff problems as well as to develop a method of dealing with similar problems in the future.

In the fields of psychiatry, psychology, and social work there are those who make a study of group process and methods of helping groups work out their interpersonal problems. However, unless the person leading a discussion among staff members keeps the focus on what in the group dynamics interferes with accomplishing the task for which the staff is employed, then the process becomes group therapy. This is a Pandora's box, which is not appropriately opened as part of staff development or of solving the problems of a staff working together. Focus on intereference with specific tasks provides a clear guideline, a kind of boundary for the discussions, which is helpful not only to the leader but to all the participants. Discussion of personal feelings and characteristic behavior are not excluded as long as they clearly interfere with effective task performance.

One form of consultation is the use of advisory groups, as described in the Office of Child Development handbook #7:

> Governing boards of daycare programs will find advisory groups to be valuable adjuncts to the organization. The kinds of advisory groups that day care programs will usually find useful are parent advisory, technical advisory, and policy advisory groups. In addition to serving on the board, provision should be made for parents to be represented on policy advisory groups because they, as consumers of the services offered, can offer invaluable assistance in developing policies and practices that are realistic and effective.
>
> Policy advisory committees help to develop programs, . . . initiate suggestions for program improvement, and act as a channel through which complaints about the program can be made. [p. 15]

We stressed earlier that a consultant's client is free to take his advice or not. A board of directors should also be free to accept or reject suggestions coming from advisory groups it creates. Suggestions coming from such groups would go first to the board and then to the director. Suggestions coming from a specialist consultant to the staff would go to the board, we assume, only if they were in conflict with board policy or the director had reason to think they might be controversial, for obviously much of the work of a staff consultant would involve matters that would not be of concern to the board. Nevertheless, without plans for reconciling advisory group activity with professional consultation, director and staff might be caught between the opposing points of view of a consultant and a board advisory committee. We do not mean to imply that because of such possible difference of opinion the use of either advisory groups or consultation should be avoided. Rather, we wish to call attention to a potential for conflict if there is no anticipation of this possibility, and to stress the need for coordinating the use of advice from various sources.

The potential for problems relating to the use of consultation is even greater in a situation in which several specialist consultants are involved. The need for defining as clearly as possible the specific problem about which each is to be concerned is obvious. The areas we listed as ones in which help is frequently needed are all interrelated, but some are more closely related than others, and especially if several consultants work within the closely interrelated areas, the potential for staff to be given conflicting advice or to think that they had because of communication problems, semantic difficulties, or other misunderstandings is great. Therefore, a group of consultants should confer with one another and, ideally, work as a team. An experiment in such team consultation is reported in *Interdisciplinary Team Consultation in Day Care* (Leach 1972), which describes the collaborative work of consultants in a demonstration project. Unfortunately, what is demonstrated to be successful in such adequately funded projects is seldom feasible in general practice because supportive funds are not available even if personnel is. However, from such demonstration projects, one can extract ideas that, though modified, can prevent unnecessary confusion and conflict and facilitate the most fruitful use of consultation.

CHAPTER 11

Problems of Administration

It is not the purpose of this chapter to give a complete account of day-care administration. Our comments are limited to those aspects of administration not already discussed that we view as presenting particular potential for confusion and conflict.

We begin at the point at which a board of directors, including parent representatives, has been chosen to develop a daycare resource for a given community. The general objectives of the program to be developed have been discussed and agreed upon. Already accomplished are such procedural matters as the drafting of bylaws, the election of a chairman, secretary, and other officers, and the appointment of board committees. Unless a site and funding have already been arranged, the board will, of course, concern itself with finding a site, raising money, and developing an operating budget. After the needs of the population to be served have been determined, decisions will be made concerning the hours the center is to be open, and how many children of what age span the center can serve. Fiscal realities—including estimate of income from fees—will be a major determinant of the scope of the program. In judging how much it will cost for space, equipment, and staff to provide a good program for a certain number of children, the board may either have sought consultation from experienced persons or have given particular weight to the opinion of those on the board who have been chosen because of their experience in daycare. Policies can then be made as to what children will be eligible for admission, how many of what ages can be accepted, and what criteria are to be used in determining fees for service.

The Board–Director Relationship

At what point in its deliberation the board elects to establish qualifications for a director and begin seeking applicants may vary widely from one case to another. While certain matters pertaining to general objectives and policies need to be decided before qualifications can be established, there is advantage in not solidifying too many plans into established policy before the director is chosen. Final responsibility for policy determination rests, undeniably, with the board. To make the best use of the professional competence it is allocating funds to pay for, however, the board should have the help of the director. We have discussed the complexities confronting a board in the choice of a director, presented probable assets and deficiencies of various kinds of candidates, and made some recommendations about qualifications. Here we wish to point out that while the board has the authority to determine admission policy and number and kinds of staff to be hired, the director has the responsibility to advise the board as to whether or not in her judgment it is possible to provide a good program of child care and education (assuming that is what the board wants) in accordance with the board's plan concerning the child population and the staff. If in her judgment it is not a feasible plan and/or would not meet licensing standards and applicable requirements, it is her responsibility to present whatever facts are relevant, as well as her opinion and reasons for it. Perhaps during the process of interviewing a director candidate, tentative board plans can be discussed, so that if there is a wide difference between the board's plans and the candidate's view of what is possible, further discussion can lead either to reconciling views or to realizing that this is impossible.

Before a director is hired, a job description that sets forth with unmistakable clarity exactly what responsibilities the board delegates to her and exactly what her authority is for carrying them out must be established. These responsibilities do not need to be the same in any two situations. For example, one director might have no responsibility for fund raising and another might be charged with substantial responsibility in this area. However, there is a basic responsibility that must rest with the director, and in order for her to accept that responsibility, she must be delegated the authority to discharge it: responsibility for the daily program of the center and how it is carried out by the staff. Only in rare instances will board members have the professional knowledge to determine in detail what constitutes good care and education of young children in a group setting. While there are matters in daycare administration that can appropriately be decided by the democratic process of voting, decisions that should be made on the basis of the authority born of technical knowledge are not among them. Even in the unlikely situation of a majority of board members being daycare experts, one person still must administer the day-by-day program unless the result is to be chaos. Thus, decisions that affect the welfare of children while they are in the center must be made by the person charged with responsibility for their well-being. If during the interviewing process there is enough discussion of basic goals and philosophy of achieving them to insure some degree of compatibility between the board and the director chosen, they can enter into a partnership in which each respects the role of the other in working out problems that arise.

In some situations individual board members with particular expertise can bring to a problem information that ought to modify some aspect of the daycare program. In other situations, the director's ability to explain why certain program procedures are chosen over others can settle arguments and be educational for board members, helping them to understand and, if necessary, defend the program. For example, the director's explanation of how language is taught three year olds all day long in every situation and activity rather than in a specific lesson, might help to bring about greater confidence on the part of board members in the director and the program they are sponsoring. If such efforts in sharing relevant knowledge do not bring about resolution of conflict, then both board and director must fall back on the basic lines of responsibility and authority originally agreed to. When decisions about daily program and procedures are clearly allocated to the director, as we believe they should be, if conflict between board and director arises in this area and neither can convince the other to modify the position taken, then the director has an important question to decide: can she remain and comply with board wishes without compromising not only her own standards of practice but licensing and other standards with which the program must comply? Board members must decide whether they can live with a situation in which they abide by their original delegation of authority but do not like the result in spite of the director's presumed professional competence. Again, we come back to the importance of the board's exploring with an applicant her philosophy of child care and education before a decision is made to employ her and of clarity about the reservation and delegation of authority. Of course, with the best of planning and utmost initial clarity about respective areas of responsibility and authority, many problems will still arise that are not clearly within the prerogative of either the board or the director. Such problems will be infinitely easier to solve if there exists mutual respect and enough flexibility so that each learns from the other.

The Board, the Director, and Responsivity to Parents

Every parent at the point of application to a daycare center should have the opportunity to be fully informed about the program and policies of the center. And every center should have a plan that is known to parents for handling suggestions or complaints they may wish to make while their children are enrolled. When there is an arrangement for each parent to meet regularly with a staff member, suggestions or complaints can ap-

propriately be made in such conferences. Some can be worked out satisfactorily at that level; others may need to come to the attention of the
director. What procedure a director might then follow will be commented
on after we describe another channel for such communication.

In our daycare experience, parents found it difficult to come to group
meetings, and the regular conferences each had with a staff member provided the major opportunity to express their reactions to the program. But
if the time required can be managed, a parent organization can provide
a forum for discussion of concerns. The parent group might choose to
meet most of the time without the director present. If group consensus is
reached about proposing a change, the director can then be invited to meet
with the group to discuss the proposal. And where there is a parent
organization, a staff member in a parent conference who learns of a complaint or suggestion that is not appropriately dealt with at that level can
no only inform the director, but might also advise that the suggestion or
complaint be brought to the group's attention by the parent.

Whether the director learns of the parent proposal from a staff member
when there is no parent organization or learns of it through such an organization, her options are the same. If she is in agreement with the proposal and
has the authority to act on it, no further discussion is required. But if she does
not agree or does not have the authority to make the change proposed, board
action is necessary. Parent organizations usually elect representatives to
the board, and they, then, as well as the director, present the issue in question for discussion and decision.

The particular method chosen to insure responsivity to parent reactions
is not as important as that well-known channels for communication exist
among the parents, the director, and the board.

Board–Director–Staff Interrelationships

Even when employment policy assures that those in authority are persons
of competence and staff members know that they are responsible to the
director, situations can arise in which there is a wish to avoid working out
a problem with the director and instead take grievances directly to the
board. Such behavior is most likely to occur in organizations that have no
established internal procedures for problem solving such as we described
in Chapter 3. If the director is competent in each area of responsibility,
including communication with staff members, there will probably be no
wish on the part of the staff to present issues to the board. Board–staff
contacts, then, might reasonably be limited to occasional joint meetings
for sharing with staff and getting their reactions to proposed changes in or

additions to the center's services. However, there should be provision for communication in certain carefully limited circumstances, for if board members either individually or as a group are permissive about allowing staff to bring problems to them that should be worked out with the director, the temptation is very great during the periods of stress that occur in any organization to do an end run around the director. If attempts to circumvent the director characterize staff behavior and are successful, the inevitable result is destruction of the boundary between staff and board and the director's leaving the program, because if a board allows such a situation to continue, the director loses leadership of the staff, loses her authority over the internal operation of the program, and cannot then be responsible for it. Thus, the board must support her by not allowing direct staff access to it except in the most unusual circumstances.

What can be done, then, to insure that the director's authority to lead is not misused and that the staff has some recourse if really necessary? Let us look first at what happens when director and staff are working harmoniously. Say an issue arises, not having to do with the program, but with personnel practices. The director interprets board policy to the staff, explains why the board concluded that a particular policy must be as it is. Many staff members are still very upset and ask that the matter be reconsidered. The director offers to present the matter to the board. She does so, and the board reaffirms the policy. A significant number of staff members continued to press the issue. The director, having first asked board permission, might ask the staff to choose one or two representatives to appear before the next board meeting, present their own case, hear the response to it, and report back to their colleagues. While the staff representatives might not succeed in their efforts to change the policy, they might be satisfied then that everything could be done had been done. In this example it is clear that direct access to the board comes about only with the specific permission first of the director and then of the board.

In a less harmonious circumstance, staff members might question the director's judgment concerning some aspect of the program. After ample opportunity for expression of views, strong disagreement persists. Some of the staff wish to be heard by the board. The director refuses because decisions about details of the program are not appropriate matters for board action. If staff members go directly to the board either in person or by letter, they should be refused a hearing. If dissension continues in a way that threatens the effectiveness of the daily work, and the director sees no way that the issue can be resolved by further staff discussion, she must take the problem to the board herself. She is then putting her position in the center on the line, asking for a vote either of confidence or of no confidence. If the vote is one of no confidence, she has no choice but to resign. If the board supports her, dissenting staff must either leave or decide that they can carry out the director's decisions in the area of dispute to the best of their ability and with reasonably good grace.

We now come to the unusual circumstance in which direct staff access to the board might be not only appropriate but obligatory. A written request for a hearing stating the reasons for it might responsibly be made by staff members who are convinced, for example, of a director's incompetence. No matter how careful the screening has been, it is possible that a director has been hired whose performance falls seriously below promise. Sometimes credentials are highly misleading and people are hired who cannot live up to their letters of recommendation. Unanticipated events in the life of any person can either gradually or quite suddenly bring about so much stress as seriously to impair functioning. Sometimes physical or emotional illness occurs that was not possible to predict, with the result that functioning, including judgment, deteriorates markedly. In such an unfortunate circumstance, those on the staff in the best position to be aware of the situation, the supervisors or their counterparts, need to take initiative in communicating with the board.

For purposes of simplifying a complex subject we have assumed in some examples a kind of director–staff polarity that in fact seldom exists. It is more likely that groups of any size break up into subgroups that take different views of an issue. The director may have the full support of a part of the staff on one point and lack support from the rest. On another point the configuration of subgroups giving or withholding support may be totally different. Therefore, the situations we have postulated are probably more clear-cut than situations would be in reality. However, the principles reflected provide guidelines for policy making.

Sound leadership is based not on some mysterious charisma that subjugates others and exhorts them to follow blindly no matter in what course. Sound leadership is made up of technical competence, of a strong wish to share learning and develop competence in others, of understanding that every member of an enterprise must be and feel an important and respected part of it. The director who is a good leader involves staff in thinking about changes that should be made and planning for how to meet current and anticipated problems, asks for staff thinking before important steps are taken, invites and encourages suggestions about any aspect of the program, but also keeps staff informed about the realities that necessarily limit what can be done. But she will never confuse the staff about whether she is simply asking their advice or asking them to make a decision. Occasionally matters will come up that she will feel can be determined by a majority vote. Such situations will be clearly distinguished from those in which she is asking for staff reactions before herself making the decision. Once a decision is made, she will inform the staff and will be willing to discuss the reasons for it and its implications. Not all decisions will be popular, but a leader must be able to tolerate not always pleasing everybody.

The directorship carries with it unique potential for influencing the quality of the daycare program and contributing to a smoothly functioning organization. To a large extent, the director's ability as a leader will determine whether the mechanisms set up to structure relationships between and among herself, the staff, the board, and the parents are used gracefully and intelligently or grudgingly and contentiously. The board is responsible for exercising great care in choosing a director, and staff and parents for supporting her, but only she can really serve to meld the groups into a purposeful whole.

CHAPTER 12

Considerations in the Choice of Daycare

Like any community resource, daycare can be used wisely or unwisely. The same program can benefit one child and not another. Some programs are reasonably good for most children. Some that are beneficial for four year olds would be damaging for infants. In addition to variations in quality, there are variations in types of substitute child care. What do those who want to use daycare, those who advise about its use, and those who provide it need to know about substitute care in general, about its use for children of various ages, and about judging the quality of programs? In what follows we describe types of daycare and quality control in each and then discuss factors to be considered in the use of daycare for children of various ages.

Types of Daycare

Daycare facilities may be divided into two major groups distinguished partly by difference in sponsorship: Those sponsored privately by individuals who presumably expect that the fees charged will result in at least a modest income, and those sponsored publicly on a nonprofit basis. While fees may be charged in the second group, part of the cost of service is covered by government funds and sometimes by foundation contributions also.

Proprietary Daycare

In the private or proprietary sector are daycare homes, daycare group homes, and daycare centers. The distinguishing characteristics have to do with the number and ages of children served. When licensing of private as well as public facilities is mandatory, there are requirements as to the number and ages of children who may be accepted. For a daycare home operated by one adult, the upper limit, including the adult's children, is often six. For group homes and daycare centers the limits are higher, but so is the requirement as to the number of caregivers. In each situation licensing also regulates such factors as space and equipment and matters of safety and health.

Compliance with the above regulations, however, is not a reliable indicator of the quality of care given in private facilities that are licensed. Assessment of qualifications for child care in the absence of a good deal of ongoing observation is a highly subjective and speculative process even for the well-trained person, and most licensing agencies do not have enough personnel to provide ongoing observation even when legislation requires it. Thus, evaluations vary greatly with the different people making them. Furthermore, legislation providing for mandatory licensing often does not include specific penalties for failure to make changes necessary to meet minimum standards, even concrete ones involving space and equipment. Licenses are often given on a provisional basis, to be revoked if standards are not met, but there is a strong tendency to continue the provisional license so as not to close down a facility that is much in demand. The most definite benefit to children, then, is the limit licensing places on the number and ages of those who may be accepted for daycare.

Good daycare is costly, even when the standards used are minimal, and the modest fees most parents can afford are ultimately unlikely to make it financially profitable to run a good daycare program. For some good proprietary programs, to be sure, the goal is not to make a profit but to keep the caregiver busy at work she enjoys. But better arrangements may be possible with friends, relatives, or neighbors without any official sanction. A license means that certain judgments have been made by someone presumably trained to make them, but a parent electing to leave a child with a friend can also judge that person's suitability. If the selected person is well and favorably known to the child, the child may feel more comfortable with him or her than with a stranger, and this may offset some deficiency in play space or equipment. Thus a license should not necessarily be the only criterion in choosing daycare.

Also within the private sector but without profit motives are parent cooperatives. They are usually organized by groups of young parents who happen to know one another or are brought together by common need, sometimes under the aegis of women's liberation groups, sometimes as a part of communal living plans. In communal plans, child care is simply one part of the work to be done, which group members share, though often with tasks differentiated according to talents and interests. Many cooperative daycare plans are based on hiring little if any personnel and instead staffing the program almost entirely with parents who use the service

Parent staffed plans deserve admiration for the attempt the sponsors are making to work out their own problems. But in spite of our enthusiasm for the concept of self-help, we have several concerns about cooperatives.

When adults have a fair capacity to be parents, their young children do best when cared for mainly by them. Therefore, it may seem inconsistent that we do not have unqualified enthusiasm for plans that insure more parent care than any other type of group daycare. Multiple parent staffing, however, is not a guarantee of good care even if each participant is a good parent. In the course of just one day the child is likely to be subjected to frequent changes in caregiving persons; and probably no two successive days will be the same with respect to staffing pattern. With such a parade of adults, there is little chance for the child to form a relationship with one or two adults as his special caregivers. Thus, two of the important elements in a child's handling of separation—knowing what to expect in terms of a routine and having someone special to count on—are missing in a program staffed by many parents each working in it a relatively small amount of time. This kind of arrangement is much harder on the young child than some of the informal arrangements made by two or three mothers to exchange child care services regularly within one another's homes, under which each child has fewer other children to cope with, fewer adults to relate to, and fewer changes in the overall gestalt to encompass, and thus can more quickly feel some degree of security during his mother's absence. Another concern, which we shall only mention, has to do with the fact that even with a favorable adult–child ratio, caring for children in groups is quite different from caring for a number of one's own children. There is no assurance that anyone within the parent group has the special knowledge, skill, and leadership ability necessary to plan and carry out a good program of group care and education.

The status of parent cooperative daycare with respect to licensing is not clear at this time.

Public Daycare

In contrast to private or proprietary daycare is public daycare, not operated for profit and usually partially if not largely supported by public funds. Often funding is tied to licensing, and this can be a good arrangement if the standards required for licensing are consistent with sound child-development principles. However, the standards cannot be so rigidly applied as to be unrealistic. Priorities can be established as to which standards must be met at once and which may be regarded as more long-term goals. Deficiencies can be made clear and ways of remedying them suggested. Those charged with licensing responsibility, therefore, should not act as a police force; they should be knowledgeable and skillful people whose responsibility is not to pass or fail the applying center but to help bring practices into conformity with standards. They should act as consultants, suggest other consultants when appropriate, and allow time for change to take place, while pursuing the objective of excellence.

Because the public daycare center is supported by public funds and is thus tightly bound to working toward compliance with standards, it may offer parents the most assurance concerning quality of care. The very fact of public support suggests that what goes on in a center is the concern not only of the staff and of the parents using the service but of the community. Usually the board of directors includes parents, and often there is a professional advisory board as well. All of these factors make for a situation in which the policies, practices, and general quality of the program can be more visible and subject to more scrutiny than is commonly true of any of the other types of daycare mentioned.

But while greater visibility and dependence on public funding can raise the quality of the program, the reality is that we are going through a period of expansion in daycare in which many such centers do not yet provide really good care and education. Often this is not because of disinterest or unwillingness to do so but because of various limitations within which the centers must function, limitations especially of money but also of well-trained personnel at all levels. Standards are thus still minimal with respect to staff qualifications and staff–child ratios. Parents who desperately need daycare may not feel they have the luxury of looking too closely at the center's program. Indeed, if licensing agencies were to close centers for anything but flagrantly bad care, there would probably be a flood of angry protests from those who want the service. Thus the acute need of many parents for daycare and the specific needs of young children may come into conflict in determining priorities.

As with the private facilities, then, the policy of licensing agencies is usually to be patient, to work with staff toward general conformity with minimum standards, allowing time for training to take place on the job. In visiting some daycare centers and serving as consultants to others, we have been most favorably impressed by the high degree of commitment to children and the really valiant efforts being made on their behalf under appallingly difficult circumstances of limited physical space, lack of equipment, shortages of staff, and unfortunately, lack of sufficient knowledge of what is good care and education for children of various ages. Such devotion ought to be supported in every way possible. However, hard work and good intentions in themselves do not result in good daycare.

New Developments

A relatively new plan for delivering child care has characteristics of both private and public daycare. In recent years, social agencies such as family service societies have been active in recruiting daycare mothers and offering training programs and supervision. If training and supervision are good and agencies maintain responsibility for the quality of service through continuing supervision of it, such programs hold great promise. In another new arrangement, a well-established daycare center expands and varies services by recruiting daycare mothers in its immediate neighborhood, bringing them into the center and caring for their daycare children while they are being trained not only through course work but through actual work in the center. This arrangement may—depending on the center's facilities—allow the children in the various daycare homes to come to the center on a rotation basis to use outdoor play space and equipment possibly not available in the individual homes. The center, too, can serve as a kind of storehouse of books, records, toys, and other materials, which can circulate among the daycare homes.

In either of the two plans described, daycare mothers may be recuited as employees of the responsible agency or remain individual entrepreneurs in a voluntary but collaborative relationship to it. Such an arrangement permits ongoing quality control of the daycare homes, encouragement to the daycare mothers and continued training and gradual professionalization of the mothers. As we discuss differential use of daycare below, we shall have more to say about the potential usefulness, for certain children, of family daycare attached to a daycare center or other responsible agency.

Premises Guiding the Use of Daycare

In addition to being familiar with the various types of daycare, parents considering daycare or a person advising parents should have a basis for evaluating a child-care plan for an individual child. Group care, even under the best of circumstances, is stressful for very young children; it can be stressful also for older children, though it is usually less so. Whether or not a stressful situation interferes with a child's development depends upon many factors. Child development theory assumes that stress up to a certain magnitude creates a state of tension that evokes an adaptive response and either influences development in a favorable way or does no harm. However, the needs of the young child for care and protection are so great that the most common danger is that he will be overstressed. Among the factors affecting his ability to deal with the stress of being away from his parents are his age and stage of development, his individual competencies, his resilience or vulnerability, his physical health, his ability to keep the mental images of his parents alive in their absence and his sense of confidence that they will return, his perception of the parent substitutes as trustworthy or not, his ability to make use of what the daycare situation offers in play and social experiences. In general, the younger he is, the more vulnerable to stress he is and the fewer resources he has with which to master stress.

Before discussing what some of the specific considerations are for children of different ages and stages of development, some general premises basic to our thinking about the pros and cons of substitute child care should be stated:

• Healthy personality development depends on the nature of the child's relationship to the most important people in his life, his parents, and in the earliest years, usually his mother. If she is away from him for long periods during his waking hours, this cannot but affect the relationship, though in just what way varies with the specific situation.

• Unless the home care is actually damaging to a prekindergarten child in some way, a short period away from home each day is better for him than a long period—better for his adjustment to the program and better for his overall development. Before the age of about three, children normally learn to best advantage within the family, not outside it. Children of three and four with expanding interests and abilities can profit increasingly from experiences outside the home. However, even five year olds are not expected to tolerate being away from home for more than a half day of school.

• Adjustment to daycare is usually better when the parent can be available to spend some time at the center helping the child both with initial adjustment and with later periods of particular stress that occur.

• When there are choices about whether or not to use substitute child care and about the kind of plan to use, such decisions need to be based on data as carefully collected and assessed as that which goes into making a diagnosis and a treatment plan in a medical or mental health setting. Otherwise one does a disservice to both the child and parent.

In what follows we shall try to be more specific about what factors should be considered in making decisions concerning daycare for children of various ages and stages of development. Chronological age provides only a very approximate idea of a child's functioning, though, so the divisions to follow should be regarded as highly flexible.

The Infant Not Yet Walking—the First Year

The first premise stated above, concerning the importance of the parent–child relationship, is one we wish to stress in relation to the early months of life. We do so not because this relationship is more important then than later, but rather because the belief is so widespread that if a baby is well cared for, who gives the care is not important: "He won't know the difference." Yet careful observation by trained observers tells us that no later than three months of age, and often earlier, an infant is capable of reactions indicating discrimination of the mother or other major caregiver from other people. No later than eight months he shows definite preference for the mother and brief distress when she leaves him. By nine or ten months he is beginning to have an elementary idea of the continued existence of people who disappear from sight, but it is a long time, usually not until about eighteen months, before he can comfort himself—and then only very briefly—with the idea that his absent mother exists and may return.

A relationship requires two people, and thus far we have spoken only of the baby. However, the mutual adaptations between mother and baby, the reading of cues, the getting to know one another—all the manifestations of a developing relationship begin in the earliest weeks of the child's life. Absence from one another during prolonged periods of each day necessarily interferes with this process. Because of the resiliency of most infants, a slowing down in the process of attachment need not lead to disaster, but anything that interferes with the process should be avoided if one expects to optimize development. There is fairly widespread acceptance of the idea that older children going to nursery school or kindergarten usually experience a separation problem. Unless the problem is severe, it is usually viewed favorably, as an indication of the child's healthy attachment to his parents. If we really believe that strong attachment to benevolent parental figures is of crucial importance in a child's development, then we must recognize at what point in the child's life the building of that attachment begins.

To mention just one delay in a child's development that can result from the mother giving little of the daily care: clinical studies of child development have commonly found that language is often delayed when an infant's early vocalizations are not responded to by the mother, when she does not smile at him, repeat his babbling, and talk to him, with all of the pleasure and emotional intensity the ordinarily devoted mother gives her baby. Conscientious attempts to duplicate attentive and pleasurable reinforcement of language in daycare do not, in our experience, achieve as much as quickly as does the average mother. It seems to us a safe speculation that the reason for the difference in result is this: no matter how devoted and conscientious the daycare staff member may be in her efforts, or how fond she may be of her young charge, it is highly unlikely that there is anything like the intensity of emotional involvement between them that exists between a mother and her own baby. This is not to say that all babies receive such stimulation at home, or that for some babies daycare would not offer far more in this and in other ways. During the first ten or twelve months of the child's life the unfortunate effects of separation may be difficult to see, and the separation may thus be easier for *adults* to tolerate, but it is no better a time for a child to be separated from his mother than are later periods of early childhood. If some kind of substitute care during the first year cannot be avoided because the mother must work, part-time will ordinarily be better for the child than full-time.

Many mothers whose need for daycare grows out of a decision to go back to work never come to the attention of any professional adviser, social agency, clinic, or other official body. For many years, arrangements have been made with neighbors or friends, and such arrangements will probably continue to be made. Depending always on the capacity of the friend or neighbor to give good care and on circumstances that allow this— i.e., not too many other children for the friend to care for nor too many other demands on her time—such arrangements may not only provide good care for the baby but may be the most convenient for the mother. However, one disadvantage is that these arrangements tend to be of short duration, and the baby is thus subjected to a succession of different caregivers. This is just as undesirable for the four month old as for the four year old, while, again, the adverse reactions of the baby may not be as obvious. Perhaps the disadvantage of instability in such care can be overcome in agency-recruited and supervised daycare homes. If such services were available and visible in a community at a moderate fee, many parents might choose them over other arrangements.

It is usually easier to provide good group care for children who are not yet walking than it is to do so for toddlers. There are many reasons for this, one of which is the sheer physical exhaustion most adults experience in keeping up with toddlers. Another is that it is easier to find staff who get along with babies, people who find appealing the dependency of early infancy, unlike the growing assertiveness and "into everything" characteristic of children able to get about independently. In addition, it is easier to find staff whose natural way of playing with and talking to babies is good for them than, for example, finding people who deal wisely with the emotional storminess and lability of the toddler. However, the very dependence of the baby that makes him appealing to many also makes it easy to overlook his needs in the face of other demands unless staff members are knowledgeable about how to promote his development and have a strong wish to do so. The baby who is not yet walking can be left in his crib or playpen too much; he can be given toys in a mechanical way and not helped to use them; he can be left alone too much with no one to respond to his social overtures and to his beginning vocalizations or he can be bombarded with stimuli; he can be left wet and hungry beyond any reasonable length of time. No matter what is done against him or what is not done for him, he can do little to protest but cry, and in time he may not even do that. He may, in fact, retreat into apathy or excessive sleep, which may be welcomed by overburdened or unknowing staff who do not perceive the excessive sleep as a symptom. He may, of course, develop more troublesome symptoms, such as inability to sleep, prolonged crying, frequent vomiting, diarrhea, severe rash, any of which may arouse concern but may not be recognized as results of care that fails to be truly nurturing.

Parents or anyone attempting to advise parents about the use of group care should know the characteristics of a program that promotes development rather than impedes it. Having such information makes it possible to ask or help a parent ask cogent questions of a program director—both questions specific as to the details of the program and how it is carried out and general questions concerning the philosophy of child care. How a director conceptualizes the goals of the program and their implementation can be very helpful in evaluating a program for a child of any age. A director or senior staff member should be prepared to enunciate clearly the program's philosophy, goals, and methods of implementation, and to answer simply and directly a good many questions about the program, whether asked by a professional colleague or by parents hoping to use the center's services for infants:

• What is the current child/staff ratio and what may it be in the future?
• Does the way the staff is deployed insure, as much as possible, consistency and continuity of care by one or at most two people?
• What is the record of the center with respect to staff turnover?
• Are there enough staff to insure that if all the babies are hungry at once, no one's age-appropriate tolerance for waiting will be seriously overtaxed?
• What does the program offer besides good physical care? What about it is educational?
• What provision is made with respect to health supervision, and what is done for the baby who becomes ill at the center.
• In the equipment, building, and play yard, what evidence is there of appropriate concern for safety from injury?
• What is the staff's role in protecting a baby from various kinds of hazards, including overstimulation?
• What provision is made for staff lunch hours and other periods of relief from direct child care?
• Is it the policy of the center to allow the parent to be there with the child at frequent intervals and particularly at times of special stress?
• What plans are there for coordinating home care and center care and the experiences of the child?
• What provision is there for the parent to talk regularly with staff about the child's progress or about any problems that may arise?

Answers to these questions plus a visit to sample the atmosphere and to see the program in operation may be more helpful in decision making than information about the educational and experiential qualifications of the director and staff, though these should be known as well.

Also important in evaluating a program for an infant are the kinds of information the director or other staff members ask parents to supply about the baby. Some appropriate areas of inquiry are the baby's present health, past illnesses, a typical day in his life at home, the formula and solids he is taking, his use of a bottle or cup, the amount of self-feeding he is doing, possible food allergies, sleep patterns, favorite toys and comforting devices such as pacifiers, cues he gives as to his needs and feeling states, responses to various ways the parent has of comforting him, and any other individual characteristics. If few or none of these questions are asked, one might be justified in concluding that in the setting being considered, babies of a certain age are all given the same kind of care without respect for individual needs, preferences, and characteristics. One might also be justified in concluding that there will be little attempt to coordinate the infant's home and daycare experiences.

An additional comment about health supervision: one reason group care of infants has not been well thought of has to do with considerations of health. Modern knowledge of infection and its control has greatly lessened the dangers of group care of babies. Even so, the suddenness with which a young baby who appears well can become a baby who is very sick means that someone knowledgeable about signs of illness needs to be always available. Further, that person, if not a nurse, needs to have ready access to nursing and medical consultation.

Finally, the evaluation process is not complete once arrangements have been made for the care of a child. Close attention must still be paid to his reactions. If the baby does not thrive in all aspects of his development, both the parents and those providing his care should look into possible reasons, and together they should plan a remedial course of action.

The Toddler and Runabout Child (1–3 Years)

Most of the questions it is appropriate to raise about quality of daycare for a baby are equally applicable in relation to care of a child who is already walking. Information needed about a baby is also needed about the slightly older child entering daycare. There are, however, additional factors to be considered that are specific to the changing characteristics, capacities, and needs of children between the age at which they start walking and about three years. In the preceding pages we mentioned the exhaustion adults experience in keeping up with toddlers, the difficulty of responding appropriately to their alternating assertiveness and dependence and of dealing wisely with their characteristic emotional storminess and lability. This is not to say that the individual toddler is without assets that can make him a charming companion. He is typically in love with the world, discovering something new that fascinates him every few minutes. His interest in exploring everything he sees, his exuberance at discovering his own physical powers and the powers of words are qualities that make him an excellent learner and in many ways a delight. However, some of these very characteristics make it more difficult to care for him in a group setting than at home.

The toddler's capacity to miss those closest to him without the capacity to keep them figuratively with him in their absence through well-developed mental images makes it especially stressful for him to be away from home and, particularly, away from his mother. We must express disagreement with one opinion we have encountered, that children who are poorly cared for by their mothers do not experience separation anxiety. While we shall not attempt here to document our conviction to the contrary, our research data and the findings of other investigators provide ample evidence to support our belief. Even when care is grossly inadequate or actually abusive, there are almost always some positive elements in the relationship, and clearly the child must feel some attachment to the only parents he has known; hence there is concern about separation. Some abused children, moreover, exhibit acute separation anxiety because they are even more distrustful of strangers than of their parents, who are, after all, not likely to be abusive every moment of the day. The known is usually less frightening than the unknown.

Another characteristic of the one-to-three year old that is relevant to planning for his care has to do with age-appropriate developmental tasks. This concept has to do with what a child at this stage of his life begins to be able to do and is vitally interested in doing, with what the child is ready to learn. The one-to-three year old wants to learn about and is most keenly interested in all the things in an ordinary household, where they are kept and what they are used for. He needs and wants to learn about the everyday activities of the people in an ordinary family. And it is from these ordinary, day-to-day activities that he learns apace. An occasional walk to the supermarket or bus trip to the shoe store provides him with a whole new dimension of life to assimilate. While he is an observer of and even a partial participant in most of the activity around him, not all of it goes on for his special benefit, though he may think so. In the context of getting household tasks done, he is not the center of the universe for even the most loving parent, nor should he be. Yet this very milieu in which the toddler engages in both child's play and the work of the adult world is ideal for him at this stage of his life.

In contrast to the natural family setting and activities, how artificial is the daycare center and what it can provide! It is very difficult to duplicate in the center more than a few of the experiences most appropriate for the toddler, experiences that he could have at home without anyone giving the matter a moment's thought. For this reason, the family daycare home—always having in mind precautions as to its quality—may be a better choice for the child from one to three.

Other characteristics of this age group also point to the desirability of the daycare home, where the number of children in care is usually much smaller than in the daycare center. Although our research data give us reason to believe there is much more social interaction—and interaction of a more complicated kind—among very young children than is reported in the child-development literature, peer relationships are still not as important at fifteen months or twenty-four months as they are later. The child is less capable of coping with them, and his developmental progress is not as dependent on opportunities for play with peers as it becomes later. The child from one to three is not by nature a highly suitable member of a large group, whether of similar or diverse ages, and difficulties appear to magnify as the group increases in size. With his peers, he and they all want the same toy or need the same adult attention at once. In a mixed group he is too frequently an unheeding destroyer of intricate block buildings or a scatterer of puzzle pieces. In either situation, too much frustration is experienced by everybody, noise and excitement mount, and disorganization ensues. The toddler usually does best in a group no larger than four or five with two adults, an arrangement difficult to find in daycare centers. For the child at the lower end of the one-to-three age range, then, a daycare home, if it is a good one, is probably the best choice, whether for a half or a full day. For the child at the upper end of the age range, a family daycare home that is attached, as discussed earlier, to a well-organized daycare center might provide the best of both worlds.

Toilet training, the child's growing sense of autonomy, his more frequent aggressive behavior, and the struggles with adults these developments can arouse are phase-specific issues that become more complicated for child and parent when the child must be cared for partly by others. The parent will need, therefore, to be in particularly close communication with whoever substitutes for her to be sure that there is as little discontinuity and confusion for the child as possible in the way these matters are handled. While it is unlikely that any two adults deal with the same type of situation in exactly the same way, at least a certain compatibility in philosophy of child care between parent and caregiver will ease the complexity and discomfort for both and for the child also, if the philosophy is based on sound child-rearing principles.

We have presented elsewhere our views about age-appropriate, effective, and emotionally healthful ways of dealing with behavior that is not in the best interest of the child or the group. Whether the substitute care is to be provided in a daycare center or daycare home, the parent has a right before placement to know something about policy in this respect. To answer specific questions is no easy task. It is usually not possible to do so in even a beginning way until one knows the child, except to state what one never does, what is contraindicated for any child. There should, however, be willingness to enter into such a discussion. It will be welcomed by the daycare director or daycare mother who has clearly defined principles to guide policies. The parent can be told, though with examples and not in this condensed form, that what is expected of the child and how his unacceptable behavior will be dealt with at different stages of his development will change in accordance with his growing comprehension and capacity for self-control.

Both parents and inexperienced staff may better understand the advisability of knowing what kind of formula a baby is taking and what solids he is getting than of knowing about past events in the family life of a two year old. However, the older the child is when he comes into any kind of substitute child care, the more there is to know about him and the more the staff will be working under a handicap if they know little about him. A child of two has developed many characteristics just as individualized as his eating habits. This is not to say that his characteristics will not change, but at a particular moment in time he carries with him the influences of all his past experiences, and from very early in life those influences are many and highly complex not only in isolation but in interaction one with another. For the one-to-three age group, information about the child and his family important to his care would most helpfully include facts about his eating, sleeping, and toileting, his likes and dislikes, his preferred ways of being comforted, his characteristic reactions to children and adults within and outside the family, his favorite toys and ways of playing, his particular concerns or fears, his experiences, if any, with previous substitute care, and any accidents, illness, hospitalization, or surgery he has undergone. Parents, of course, vary greatly in their ability to give information even in these relatively nonthreatening areas. The daycare staff will also want to know about his reactions to various events of the family life and how his parents have dealt with him around such issues as toilet training, increasing independence, separation experiences, standards of behavior, and ways of dealing with misbehavior. Quite understandably, not all parents are able to give clear, accurate, and undefensive accounts of family events and of their child's behavior and their behavior with him in these crucial areas, especially to one who is still a stranger to them and who may have, as they see it, the power to reject their application. The wise interviewer will, of course, not press the parent to the point of discomfort in trying to develop information that would be helpful but is not essential at a very early stage.

Of course, in all aspects of substitute child care, policy and practice are not necessarily the same. Thus, both the providers of care and the parent must again be sensitively aware of the child's reaction to any plan, not just in the first days or weeks, but over the entire period of the plan's existence, so that whatever change is advisable can be made.

The Child of Three or Four

Again, most of the questions we suggested raising about a program for young babies might well be asked about a program for three-to-four year olds, with some shifts in emphasis. And some of the information we said was important in planning a good program for a child up to age three is equally important in planning for three and four year olds. All areas such as health, eating, sleeping, and toileting need to be reviewed. For example, the child who comes to daycare at three or four may still be having a bottle at a certain time each day; he may be using a pacifier; there may be a particular toy, blanket, or other object that he must have with him at naptime. The period of stress surrounding separation and exposure to a new situation, new adults, and new children is, of course, no time to remove what comforts him. Therefore, those who will be caring for him need to ask about such things, and parents can help their children by sharing such information. They need also to be assured of the caregiver's willingness to have them bring the child's familiar blanket or toy and to go along with habits that might ordinarily be thought of as *not* age appropriate (a bottle or pacifier at naptime for a four year old, for example) until the child can feel safe enough in the new setting to be helped to give up such habits.

Whether we like it or not, some of the vulnerabilities discussed in relation to the toddler and runabout must still be kept in mind with reference to the older child. The human problem over separation from those we love is never quite resolved, though the child at three or four usually has more resources for coping with it than he had at age two. Length of day, also, is still very much an issue, for separation reactions become more acute as the day lengthens and fatigue decreases coping ability. Toilet training may or may not have been accomplished by age three or four, so it, too, may present either a normative kind of stress for child, parent, and caregiver, or a problem of some magnitude, depending on the previous history of the training efforts. Discussion of standards for child behavior and methods of dealing with unacceptable behavior is thus highly important.

A matter that in our view is not *more* important at three or four than at one or two, but that may well be to many parents, is the educational aspect of group care. At Children's House we did not conceive of care and education for young children as separate from one another, but rather saw care that is really nurturing as having many educational components and education as not existing apart from good care. Thus, the "curriculum" included elements of both. But there are many reasons why one hears more references to what a child should learn in daycare at three or four than to what he should learn at earlier ages, though we know that his ability to do well when he gets to public school is greatly affected by what he has learned from the beginning of life, that each stage lays the foundation for later learning. First, it is simply easier for many people to conceive of a curriculum for three and four years olds than one for younger children. This is partly because a child's normally more varied and complex capacities at three and four allow him to be interested in and to work for increasing periods of time at pursuits that can be recognized as learning activities by everyone. Second, the closer a child approaches the age for entry into public school—in many communities five years—the more parental concern there is about his readiness to do well there. Daycare administrators may also contribute to this tendency, for the accumulated experience of many teachers over the years with three and four year olds in nursery school may make it easier for administrators to talk about a curriculum for this age group than about a curriculum for younger children.

One of the dangers we see in the emphasis during the past decade on pre-kindergarten learning lies in the tendency, as it was expressed many years ago in another educational context, to teach subjects, not children. Therefore, careful consideration should be given to any part of a program for three and four year olds specifically identified as educational. Our hope is that not only those operating daycare centers and those helping parents make decisions about substitute care but parents, too, will concern themselves not just with what is taught but with how teaching is done. During the recent years of emphasis on cognitive functioning many young children in this country have been subjected to situations in which a series of subjects is Taught—now we'll learn our colors, now it's time for language stimulation—situations not greatly different at least in plan and attempted execution from the old plan of an arithmetic lesson, then a language lesson, and so on, characteristic of the least creative grade schools. Often such situations in daycare are imposed by supposedly qualified curriculum consultants, or they result from buying packaged curricula from companies commercially exploiting the headstart and daycare movements. Such packaged plans can have little to do with individual children who make up a group, each perhaps at a different level of learning readiness and at different levels of readiness in each learning area. Often the staff struggling valiantly to carry out such sterile methods of prekindergarten education have little knowledge about the necessary conditions for learning in the early years to guide them. Earlier chapters deal at length with matters relating to curriculum content and methods of teaching three and four year olds that are based on such knowledge. Here our intent is simply to emphasize the importance of being sure that the daycare center bases its educational program on principles that are consistent with what is known about how young children learn.

We believe that ideally even the four year old should not be more than a few hours without his mother or other familiar family member. However, because of the child's increased abilities of many kinds, it is a little easier to provide him with experiences in the daycare center and its environs that are like some of the experiences he would have if he were spending most of his day at home. If the child first comes to daycare at age three or four, he may already have had the benefit of learning those things which are the center of interest for toddlers and can best be learned in the average home. However, whether he has or not, he will be interested in doing with his teacher, the cook, and the handyman some of the things he might otherwise do at home with his mother or father or big brother: cooking simple foods, helping prepare snacks, putting play equipment away, learning to pound a nail in a board, helping to wash the sandbox utensils, holding the hose to fill the wading pool, going on an errand in the neighborhood, taking a bus trip with a small group of staff and children to a park or zoo, and occasionally having the experience of buying the afternoon snack at a nearby bakery or soda fountain instead of having it come from the center's kitchen.

Especially for the child who is in daycare for many of his waking hours, experiences like these are important for several reasons. He not only learns from them but he also needs the change of pace involved in a more casual, relaxed, "after-school" atmosphere. He needs relief from those aspects of the daily program that are more nearly the forerunners of later school learning. He also needs experiences that are not entirely child-centered but are related to the adult world. In a small daycare facility where some of the housekeeping chores are done by those who also teach and care for the children, he learns from discovering that "we can't go for our walk yet because we have to put the laundry in the washing machine first" or "on our walk we're going to stop at the store because we ran out of milk," and it is important that he has some part in these activities. Now and then he can go to the laundry room and really help put the towels in the washer, and he can carry one of the cartons of milk part of the way "home" if he wishes.

Our discussion of three and four year olds in daycare thus far has emphasized developmental characteristics that make it easier to provide a good program for them than for one-to-three year olds. However, by the time a child is three or four all those aspects about him that add up to his individuality are a bit more pronounced. He has had a little more time to have experiences with people, especially with parents, which have helped to determine how he feels about them, and those experiences will largely determine what his expectations are of the daycare staff. His experiences, if any, with siblings and other children in the past will partially determine his feelings about and expectations of children in the center. Whether or not he has had previous daycare placements, he may have learned to expect kindness and consideration from adults, to see them as helpful and comforting, or he may have learned to fear them, to avoid contact with them as much as possible in order to be safe, to expect neither help nor comfort. With respect to children, he may have had little or no experience or too much; he may see them as potential playmates and friends or as natural enemies.

Any real child is likely to reflect a more complicated, less clear-cut and extreme combination of feelings and attitudes than these. We wish to emphasize, however, that the strongly entrenched habits, feelings, attitudes, and expectations that a three or four year old can bring may create great stress for him and for everyone else. Perhaps not immediately but in time he will usually attempt to recreate with all staff or with the member who is the most meaningful to him the same kind of relationship he has with the most important person to him at home. Thus, if he and his mother are engaged in a retaliatory kind of fighting with one another, he may do his best to engage staff in the same kind of skirmishes. If his care at home has not taught him that he is valued, he may repeatedly put himself into situations of potential danger, requiring the utmost vigilance on the part of staff in order to protect him. If he has been flagrantly discriminated against in relation to a sibling, his jealous rages at the center may be out of proportion to expectable feelings of rivalry with other children for staff attention and affection. And because of the deeper entrenchment of the older child's problems, the most exemplary behavior on the part of the staff may not quickly cause the problems to lessen or disappear. Working them out usually requires not only skillful work on the part of the staff but collaboration of the parents in this effort.

When a community provides daycare services that are geared to the needs of children and parents, choices can be made that are, indeed, supportive of both. Parents and their advisors can evaluate services both for their general quality and their suitability for a specific child.

CHAPTER 13

The Challenge of Daycare

We come now to our hopes for the future of daycare. The basic requirements for quality daycare were listed in Chapter 1 and their implementation has been the subject of all the intervening chapters. Our conviction about what is required grew out of five years of experience in trying to meet some of the needs of the children and parents who came to us. We are fully cognizant of the difficulties encountered by those who try to find funds, space, and trained personnel to carry out good programs, but ways must be found to increase the quality of services.

Overcoming Obstacles

There have been and will continue to be obstacles in the way of excellent daycare that have less to do with lack of funds than with other issues. We shall mention only a few of them. One is the potentially self-defeating tendency to turn what is ostensibly a program to serve certain needs of children and their parents into a program whose primary aim is to provide employment for adults. There is undeniable need for employment opportunities, most of all perhaps in the very areas where the most citizen planning and control of daycare services now exist. However, if goals are confused and people are employed in daycare centers simply because they need employment and not because they are qualified for the work to be done, the result is almost certain to be poor service. Of course, every public service institution—every hospital, social agency, or clinic—must guard against the ever-present danger of becoming an establishment whose policies and practices are determined more by the convenience and needs of the staff than by the needs of the group it was created to serve.

Another obstacle to achieving services of good quality is related to what can most tersely be described as antiprofessionalism. For many complex reasons, antiprofessionalism has characterized the last decade. The long overdue social revolution of the sixties and seventies could not have come about without some degree of antiprofessionalism. New methods had to be found to create and deliver services tailored to the specific needs of people who have been neglected by traditional institutions, and such efforts were resisted by many professionals. Many who did not resist entered into well-intentioned planning efforts, but often mistakenly thought they knew all the answers about the needs of people they proposed to help. The demand for decision-making power about services by the users of those services is an inevitable and necessary part of the process of achieving the self-determination that characterizes any democracy. Further, professional people have sometimes been ignorant and unmindful of cultural patterns and therefore have not only planned unsoundly but antagonized those they proposed to serve. Justifiable anger over being ignored by various "establishments" for generations caused many minority groups to want to shut out all but their own members, to shut out even the professionals within the group, to do everything for themselves.

We wish to make clear that the antiprofessionalism we have in mind is not a racial issue, though that issue is sometimes involved. While many traditional agencies, threatened with being judged irrelevant, scrambled to employ minority-group staff with professional training, those professionals were often not sought by their own ethnic groups for consultative or leadership roles in newly funded programs. Even when they were, many complex factors, including suspiciousness of professionalism, often created obstacles to working together as great as those sometimes attributed to racial or cultural differences. Sometimes the failure to work harmoniously within a homogeneous racial group was due not to antiprofessionalism per se, but to the fact that racial origin alone does not determine identity. Thus, some program planners who found professional leadership within the predominant ethnic group to be served also found that they had employed a person whose thinking, feeling, life experience, and life style were hardly distinguishable from those of other professionals in the same field.

Some professionals, of various racial origins, sympathetic to these understandable reactions, simply tried to wait out the beginning period with its inevitable errors and successes, knowing that those doing it all themselves would find their work unimaginably difficult, the results often disappointing, and might, having become secure in their control, ask for professional advice about some aspects of their task. Other professionals, however, equally sympathetic to the wish for self-determination, attempted to deal with the situation by virtually repudiating their own professional knowledge and standards and aligning themselves with those whose credo seemed to be "Anyone can do anything." Brief training courses given by such professionals to those with no previous relevant preparation except knowledge of their own neighborhood supposedly turned them into their neighbors' mental health consultants and therapists.

We strongly believe in the ability of those without previous experience in a particular job to bring to it valuable insights out of their life experience.

An important part of our own program was based on that belief. However, we believe with equal conviction that there are identifiable bodies of knowledge and skills that can be learned only through prolonged and arduous professional education, a belief that is widely accepted in relation to medicine. For those who know how complicated human behavior is, the thought of turning the group care and education of large numbers of young children over to daycare personnel who are not given both training and ongoing supervision by those with sound professional preparation is almost as upsetting as contemplating surgery by a layman. To be sure, laymen, in the position of parents, have been doing a reasonably good job of child rearing for generations. But as we have stressed, care of groups of children away from home by those who are initially strangers to them is not at all the same thing as care of children within their own homes by their parents.

Another obstacle—widely acknowledged—is the expense. The major cost in any daycare program is for personnel and there is no doubt that the numbers of staff needed in order to create and maintain high quality daycare makes it expensive beyond the capacity of parents and the usual sources of support. The solution to this problem does not reside with local, state, and federal government alone, though government has a vital role to play. The question of how daycare will be supported is part of the larger question of whether and how our country will provide an environment and services that enhance the quality of life for all its citizens.

This book has not addressed the complex economic, social, and political issues involved; nor do we have the expertise to do so. However, one approach to the problem of the high cost of good daycare is to use those who give their time and interest without financial reward to supplement and enrich a basic program. In an earlier day many of the psychological support systems and tangible services needed for child rearing were provided by extended families, neighbors, and friends. While to some extent this still occurs, such support systems are much less available now. The growing need for daycare is one of the indicators of that condition. However, the volunteer spirit is still very much alive. There are many people of both sexes and all ages for whom the satisfaction of a piece of work well done, the gratification of being valued or needed, and the pleasure in developing a relationship with a child or parent are ample compensations. We believe, then, that more systematic and creative use of volunteers is not only desirable but probably a necessary step. Volunteers can include students at junior high, high school, and college levels desiring a practicum experience in relation to school courses or trying daycare to help with a career choice; interested men and women without children or whose children are grown; persons with talents and interests in music, drama, arts, and crafts who enjoy sharing their knowledge; and trained persons such as teachers, nurses, and social workers who are not seeking regular employment but who want to stay in touch with their professional selves.

The benefits of the participation of volunteers can be realized only if an atmosphere is created in the center in which volunteers can work successfully and smoothly alongside hired staff: Those responsible for the program must first of all make certain that volunteers are selected because of their ability to work well with children or parents. This means that not everyone who offers can be accepted. There are well-intentioned, generous persons whose gifts do not lie in this area and the selection process must take this into account. One professional staff member must then be responsible for the supervision of the volunteers' work. She should be able to help them use their time in a way satisfying to them and helpful to the program. The number of volunteers in any one day or week must be limited so as not to create confusion for the children. The purpose of added help will be defeated if the proportion of constant to inconstant staff is unbalanced. One implication of this is that volunteers should be seen as adding to the quality of the program by supplementing paid staff, not by replacing them. A good volunteer program should not be seen as a way of avoiding the development of paid positions for the key staff basic to a sound program. Finally, the procedures discussed elsewhere in the book for staffing, administration, and working together are applicable also to this task.

Another obstacle to achieving high quality daycare is the low priority our society gives to services for children and the consequent downgrading of those who provide such services. Despite overwhelming evidence to the contrary, the belief appears to persist that because many parents do a good job of rearing their children, any child placed in any kind of institution can be effectively cared for by any "decent person" who wants a job. If there were more public awareness of the skill required of a child-care worker in any kind of setting, there would be more respect for that role and more compensation for it, and it would be more attractive as a career. In many fields not everyone can be or needs to be a professional in the academic sense of that term. Not everyone in a construction company, for example, needs to be an architectural engineer. But unless professional engineering knowledge determines the construction plan and the plan is carried out by skilled workers whose special abilities are respected enough that they are compensated accordingly, the skyscraper will fall down.

One obstacle in the way of what could be a most enriching aspect of daycare is the belief on the part of some that racial or cultural identity can be preserved only in a social environment made up entirely of members of one racial or cultural group. Certainly there should be sufficient staff from the ethnic groups of the children in a daycare center to help the children develop self-respect and awareness of their ethnic identities. But we believe parents play the primary role in encouraging such development in very young children. Furthermore, the ability of any adult to support such development is determined by much more than his racial origin. We therefore believe that the benefits of integration make it a worthwhile goal to pursue.

Our preference is that the child population of daycare centers not be racially homogeneous. In the relatively small community of New Haven, services organized within neighborhoods need not be. However, in large cities homogeneity tends to be the pattern and will continue to be if centers are located, as they should be, conveniently close to the neighborhoods of those who use them. But even if the child population in many instances must be ethnically homogeneous, the staff need not be. Black and white staff at Children's House worked together on a peer level with black and white children, and at no time did a problem arise from behavior based on the preference of a black teacher for black children or a white teacher for white children. A great many rich opportunities for learning would have been lost to both children and staff in our program if we had had children and staff of only one ethnic group.

Daycare as a Nuclear Service

In recent years there has been much emphasis on finding more effective ways of organizing and delivering human services. The prevalence of articles on this subject in professional literature has reflected awareness that traditional ways of providing many social and health services are not effective in reaching large segments of the population. Many program administrators have had to reexamine and modify their ways of working. Some outreach programs and other methods of making services more visible and easily obtainable by those who need them have emerged. Another trend has been greatly increased citizen participation in decision making both within traditional agencies and in methods of service organization such as Model Cities. That those who need various services should have an effective voice in determining what they are to be is no longer a new idea. Nor is it a new idea that within large cities there are discrete neighborhoods often having quite separate and distinct needs. Thus planning based on complexes of services within neighborhoods has grown. It is an eminently sensible idea that services identified by a group of people as the specific ones they need should be available to them within a reasonable distance of where they live.

If one could magically reorganize all the human services needed in a community or neighborhood, one could undoubtedly centralize services and coordinate them in such a way that neighborhood residents would not have to have almost superhuman persistence and motivation, plus the ability to travel miles within a city, in order to use them. Such a neighborhood center could include services related to public assistance, medical care, housing, job training, employment, and legal aid. It could also include a daycare center, a family-service organization, and services now organized either separately as child-development, child-guidance, and adult-psychiatry clinics or under the umbrella of mental health clinics. In such a neighborhood service center one might still need help in finding one's way around. Upon applying to a central admissions office each applicant could be assigned one person who would initially become his enabler, perhaps at times his advocate, to see that he was not buffeted about, that he got whatever services he needed in the least difficult and most efficient way possible.

We believe that daycare can serve as a nuclear service, around which the delivery of a whole array of social services can be arranged. People tend to seek the service they are aware of needing. If use of daycare also provides the opportunity for contact with one person whom the parents see regularly and come to regard as "their person," many other needs emerge as they come to feel respected and to develop trust in the worker's integrity and concern for their welfare. Where the "felt need" can be met, the greatest opportunity exists for the kind of relationship to develop that allows people to reveal other needs and problems; where trust exists, people can most easily accept help with their problems, both internal and external. Referrals to other agencies are possible, if such facilities exist. But such referrals mean the whole process of getting information from clients, making diagnoses, and especially of establishing trusting relationships must be repeated—a costly and exasperating imposition on the client. If a daycare staff member already known to a family can work with a team of specialists in the context of a central service organization, much reduplication can be avoided, for information can be readily shared among the specialists in different areas. For the daycare program, such a structure provides a built-in consultative staff.

When we introduced the possibility of reorganizing services on a neighborhood basis, we invoked the power of magic. While something close to magic may be needed to bring such a change about, we believe that the change will ultimately have to be made, that such carefully planned systems of delivering services will be far less costly than our current arrangements, which are not even adequate in what they attempt to provide. But such changes will begin to be made only when we reorder our nation's priorities, realizing that social services cannot be treated as fringe benefits or stopgap measures, but are essential to our society's health. And among top priorities in social services is support for parents in protecting and nurturing their children's potential for development into competent, healthy adults.

Appendixes

Résumé of Arrangements for the Program at Children's House

Children came to the center Monday through Friday for care and an educational program that was planned to fill their developmental needs. We did not at first fully appreciate quite how stressful a whole day in group care would be for young children. We came to believe that ideally no child should be in the center for the entire nine hours it was open, if he could be cared for by a familiar, responsible person. Since we were committed to the idea that the plan had to be the best we could make for each child and parent, we were able to shorten the length of day in several instances. It was necessary, however, for some to be there the entire time the center was open. The full day included breakfast for those who needed it, morning and afternoon snacks, lunch, and a nap or rest period.

Our clinical social-work staff saw parents at home or at the center twice a month, or oftener if they could use and were agreeable to more frequent contacts. Central to the study was the hypothesis that we would be unable to help the children substantially or to have any abiding influence on their development unless we could form a partnership with the parents.

Staff pediatricians examined the children thoroughly at the time of admission, and saw them at the center when they were ill. During the second phase there was even more frequent involvement of pediatricians, since the project provided complete well- and sick-child care, including house calls.

Each child had his special person assigned to be his major caregiver and teacher, a role carried by nurses and paraprofessional child-care workers as well as by those specifically trained as teachers. All those working directly with the children in the daycare center gradually learned to help in planning the daily program as well as in carrying it out. They also developed helpful relationships with parents. Morning contacts were usually brief, but in calling for children in the afternoon, parents often lingered to talk with the staff.

Children began arriving at around eight o'clock, and most stayed until four-thirty or five. A few children went home just before or after lunch, and for them the morning was very much like what they would have experienced in a good half-day nursery school program.

They were received by a familiar person in one of the playrooms or in the playground. The parent or other family member who brought the child and the child's teacher had an opportunity to exchange a few words at that time, though no time for extended conversation. We considered it important that we be informed about the child as he came to school. At first, these exchanges with parents around a child's arrival were only with the head teacher. Later, as parents and staff knew the children and each other better, such conversations took place with other teachers as well. Throughout, of course, these communications were augmented and facilitated by the social worker assigned to each family.

Parents were encouraged to stay at least long enough each day to help the child make the transition from home to the center. As one would expect, the need to have parents remain varied both among individuals and, in the same child, at different times. Staff were asked to make parents feel welcome, which, after some awkwardness early in the program, they were able to do. But frequently parents were in a hurry to depart and considerable effort was spent in helping them understand the importance of their role in the child's settling in and the importance of saying good-bye instead of disappearing when the child wasn't looking. For more details on this matter, see Chapter 5.

Some of the young infants needed to be fed immediately on arrival or to be put down for a nap. Their daily program was organized first in accordance with their individual needs for feeding, being changed, bathed, given naps, and so on. As they grew older and there was more waking time independent of being fed, bathed, and changed, more time was spent in play or other activities, such as being taken out in the carriage or stroller, placed on the floor or a mat outdoors to play, and taken into the room with the older children.

Beginning, on the average, when toddlers were around eighteen months old, they were received into a large playroom containing familiar toys and helped to say good-bye to their parents, and to find an activity or an attractive toy or a place on someone's lap if they needed it. Each child gradually learned, as his awareness permitted, that he had a cubby for his clothing and other things he might bring from home. As other children and staff arrived, other rooms were opened to keep the groups small, and around nine o'clock breakfast, or snack for those who had had breakfast, was served. The young toddlers ate in high chairs; when they were old enough to sit in small chairs at tables they did so (usually at about sixteen to eighteen months). Mealtime was always considered an important social experience, and children usually ate in the company of one or two other children and one or two adults, who sat at the table with them. Occasionally, a child who was unusually upset was fed in a room away from others.

While children were eating, the staff not with them were setting up the rooms for the activities of the morning. For infants, planned but mostly quite informal learning experiences occurred throughout the day. For the toddlers and older children, from about nine-thirty to eleven each morning we organised, indoors or outdoors, certain activities and experiences important for their learning. Plans for these activities and choices of materials were made each week for the week ahead, in meetings in which all the children's staff participated.

At around eleven in the morning children were cleaned up for lunch, which was served around eleven-fifteen or eleven-thirty. After lunch they were made ready for naps.

Some went to sleep fairly promptly; others, only after considerable delay. Some slept as long as two to two and a half hours; others were awake after forty-five minutes. The young child's need for rest, as well as his need for the reassuring presence of a familiar adult, was acknowledged and planned for.

Children were up from naps at varying times and were dressed for the afternoon. Some were called for around three o'clock, so there was little time for play. Partly because of the varied departure times, but largely because of the effect of the length of day they spent in our center, we learned to keep the after-nap activities informal and individualized. This often was the time for a walk around the neighborhood, perhaps to a nearby grocery store, or a ride on the shuttle bus. Indoors the time might be spent with one child hearing a story, another singing songs, another playing with small toys or puzzles, another going along as clothes were washed or folded. It was also a time when we asked that specific individuals spend time with a child who had a special need.

Afternoon snack was given some time after all the children were up from nap and dressed. Rather than simply handing out juice or milk or fruit or ice cream, we tried to make this activity too one in which toddlers and their caregivers could enjoy something together and from which the children could absorb knowledge. For example, a teacher might sit down in the midst of the children and peel oranges or apples, talking about the fruit and what she was doing. On a neighborhood walk a few children might be taken into a store where their snacks were purchased and eaten as they continued their walk or came back to the center to join the others. Another time, crackers might be (quickly, of course) spread with cheese or peanut butter as the teacher talked with the children. As they grew older, there was more frequent use of the kitchen, where a few at a time, children participated in preparation of pudding, cookies, or other snacks. Staff came to regard snack time not merely as a time to feed the children but as an activity that could be used to expand the children's experience and knowledge in various ways.

Departure time was variable within the group, but predictable enough for each child usually to allow for adequate staff coverage. Most children began looking wistfully for their parents or, as they had the language to do so, to ask about them long before departure time.

Children were called for by mothers, fathers, uncles, grandparents, and friends. Parents understood that we would not release children to a person we did not know except with their specific permission. Reunion behavior between parents and children was variable. Sometimes children were obviously relieved and happy to see parents. At other times, while just as eager underneath, they might cry, ignore their parents, become provocative. Usually parents had more time at the end of the day to stay for a few minutes' talk with the staff, which we encouraged within the limits of the child's tolerance. This time was used to exchange information about the child or whatever else parents wanted to talk about. While the children were, at the end of the day, quite ready to leave, their parents often tended to linger.

Children who were picked up late, either by plan or unexpectedly, had a more difficult time than others as the day wore on. They learned to know, through cues such as the pattern of activities and probably some perception of their own rhythms and feelings, about when they should leave. References to mother and other family members increased; they went more often to look out the window. Those who were regularly called for at five or five-thirty seemed to find the end of the day at the center quite difficult.

The Criterion Model for Preschool Curriculum

BY JUNE PATTERSON

OUTLINE FOR WRITTEN SUMMARIES ON CHILDREN

Name of child: Date of report:

Age at time of report: Reporter:

Date of first entrance to school:

A. General description of the child (physical description and summary in a "nut-
   shell," which provides an introduction of the child to the reader). This general
   description should be written after the specific summaries are completed *but* should
   appear as *A* in the final written report. It should include the following information:
   (1) the child's strengths, interests, and areas of greatest satisfaction
   (2) Are these appropriate for his age and experience?
   (3) his limitations and/or areas of vulnerability (areas where he needs a great
       deal of help or has had particular difficulty)

B. Attendance (days absent and reasons, i.e., illness, separation problem, family
   away, other).

1 Relationship to Self

   1.1 *Personal Tasks*
        For each of the following personal tasks write a summary statement about
        the child's ability and the quality of his performance.

   1.11 Taking shoes and socks off
        from: pulling shoes and socks off
        to: unbuckling or untying shoes, pulling off shoes and socks and placing
               socks into shoes, putting shoes into locker or in a particular place
               where he can locate them when needed

   1.12 Taking outdoor clothing off
        from: making no attempt to undress himself; easily distracted from un-
               dressing; lacking body adaptations when adult is helping him

to: removing cap, mittens; unzipping or unbuttoning jacket; removing jacket and sweater; removing boots or rubbers and snow pants; may need some help with difficult rubbers, snow pants, and zippers

1.13 Putting socks and shoes on
from: making no attempt to put socks and shoes on; lacking adaptation of foot when adult does it for him
to: straightening out sock to locate heel and putting the sock onto his foot with heel underneath; orienting shoes to right and left feet; putting shoes on proper foot; tightening and tying laces or buckling shoes; usually independent in this task

1.14 Putting clothes on
from: making no attempt to dress himself; lacking body adaptation when adult is helping him
to: orienting clothing (pants, underpants, shirt, etc.) with regard to front and back; putting on clothing in order (e.g., underpants before pants; snow pants before boots, etc.); usually independent in dressing

1.15 Toileting
from: expressing physiological discomfort by body movements; needing an adult to go with him to the toilet
to: going to the toilet when he feels he needs to go; managing his own clothing; wipes, flushes toilet, and washes his hands without adult help; generally independent in toileting

1.16 Washing
from: watching others; playing with water, soap, and paper towels
to: pushing up sleeves if needed; turning on water himself; washing hands with soap and water by rubbing palms of hands together and palms over backs of hands, rinsing off soap and drying hands with same action; turning off water, putting towel in wastebasket; washing and drying hands independently whenever needed

1.17 Caring for personal property
from: identifying personal belongings as his, but not assuming responsibility for them
to: putting sweater, jackets, rubbers, etc., in his locker; putting toys he brings from home in his locker unless used by him or on loan to others; putting object he has made during the morning which he wishes to take home into his locker (or into the outdoor basket); checks his locker (or outdoor basket) for his belongings at end of day

Some questions to guide your thinking:
- Is he competent for his age and experience?
- Is he responsible? Does he ask for help?
- In response to what situational variable do you find resistance, helplessness, dawdling, wetting himself, other?
- Does he take pleasure in caring for himself?
- In regard to personal tasks, what are the outstanding qualities and characteristics of the child?

- What are the outstanding changes in his behavior (thinking, feeling, acting) related to personal tasks since he entered school and/or since the last written summary?
- What teacher behavior and/or learning opportunities have been most helpful?

1.2   *Speaking Capacity*
Write a summary for each of the following (i.e., articulation, structure, and usage); utilize examples to amplify your summaries.

1.21 Articulation
from: using speech comprehensible only to one familiar with his speech pattern
to: speaking clearly enough to be understood by any listener; articulation of uncommon consonants or consonant blends may still be immature

1.22 Structure
from: using pronouns, nouns, verbs, and some adjectives only in making statements; questions expressed by intonation—e.g., "Outside?"—questions asking what, where, how used only in specific familiar situations—e.g., "Where daddy?"
to: using simple sentences with modifiers; using a series of sentences to convey a sequence of events; questions asking what, where, how, why used in mature word order—e.g., "Why can't we go outside?"

1.23 Usage
from: using words and denotational gesture or physical contact rather than speech to communicate
to: using connotational and denotational words, inflections, and gesture discriminately to name and describe events, things, express ideas, ask questions; using plurals and conditional words correctly

Some questions to guide your thinking:
- How does he use language?—to influence others, to get information, to get help, to get attention, to recall experience, to think with, to play with the sounds of words (rhyming), to make plans, to solve problems, other?
- How is his speech best described?—conventional, inventive, original remarks, sense of humor, pleasure or interest in new words, leaves out important details, precise words?
- What characteristics of his thinking are reflected by speech?—rigid, flexible, spontaneous, good memory, other?
- What is the quality of voice?—tone, pitch?
- Changes from predominate pattern in response to what? How?
- Is he competent for his age and experience?
- With regard to speaking capacity, what are the outstanding characteristics of the child's language?
- What kind of information does he have about himself (e.g., his name, address) and the functions of people and objects (e.g., doctor, mailbox)?
- What kind of physical and social knowledge does he have?
- What are the outstanding changes in his behavior (thinking, feeling, acting) as reflected by his speech since he entered school/or since the last written summary?

• What teacher behavior and/or learning opportunities have been most helpful?

1.3   *Moving Capacity*
For each of the movement capacities given below, write a precise descriptive
statement of the child's freedom, control, and use of skills; give examples
where relevant.

1.31 Control of basic movement
from: using a narrow range of joint motion in attempts to bend, stretch,
twist, crawl, squat, sit, spin, push and pull; movement cautious, jerky,
or sudden, and/or lacking in control
to: usually agile in the use of speed, force, and space; using his body
in a variety of different ways with different bases of support freely
and skillfully ("skin the cat," somersaults); having more than usual
skill in one or more activities; utilizing verbal directions that are
kinesthetic cues as well as visual models when attempting a new action, e.g., "move lightly," "be round," "get set," "give with it"

1.32 Patterning of walk
from: walking with feet flat on the floor and with a wide base of support;
little action in the knee joint; may toe in or out
to: walking with a smooth easy transition in the heel-toe progression;
using the foot as a rocker to receive and give impetus as he progresses forward, backward, and sideways; the length of the stride uni-
form in the forward direction

1.33 Patterning of run
from: modified run in which the sole of the foot contacts the floor, legs
stiff or little knee bend, uneven length of stride
to: running using the foot with heel-toe progression; even, smooth stride;
arms and legs in opposition for balance; control in starting, stopping,
turning, and variations in speed

1.34 Patterning of jump
from: stepping down or forward in jump motion
to: jumping up from the floor with force and control; jumping and
landing from a variety of heights, maintaining balance and spreading
impetus over ankle, knee, and hip joints

1.35 Balancing
from: balancing on a wide base of support close to the ground with arms
moving at random; movements heavy or jerky
to: balancing on a narrow base of support at varied heights using cross-
extension reflex to counterbalance; balancing at a variety of heights
and on unstable surfaces of varying widths

1.36 Paterning of hop
from: hopping once or twice on dominant foot maintaining momentary
balance
to: maintaining balance hopping on either foot with variations in distance, timing, and direction

1.37 Patterning of gallop
from: using a gallop rhythm while walking, running, leaping, or in combination
to: maintaining a gallop pattern with same foot lead, with variations in distance, levels, tempo, and force

1.38 Paterning of skip
from: moving in a skip rhythm but not with a skip foot pattern
to: maintaining a skip pattern (step-hop) with variations in distance, level, direction, tempo, and force

Some questions to guide your thinking:
- How well has he mastered his own body in basic patterns in terms of his age and experience?
- What is the quality of his movement?—limited, light, hesistant, aborted, restless, scattered, disorganized, rigid, tight, free, persistent, extreme caution, reasonable caution, accident prone?
- Does he take pleasure in his growing skills and abilities?
- What is his energy level?—low, great deal of energy expanded moving, other?
- How much space does he use? What levels of space?
- How would you characterize his movement?—agile, clumsy, well coordinated?
- What are the outstanding characteristics of the child's movement?
- What are the outstanding changes in his movement skills since he entered school and/or since the last written summary?
- What teacher behavior and/or learning opportunities have been most helpful?

1.4 *Patterning of Affective Expression*
Write a summary of the child's affect.
from: showing almost no variation in mood as indicated by facial expressions, body tension, and movement; little external expression of feeling in situations where most children would smile, laugh, cry, squeal, hug, flee, shrug, wiggle, etc.; or expresses feelings in ways difficult for others to understand, e.g., laughs when hurt
to: generally communicates affect spontaneously and has a variety of moods, e.g., brash noisiness to absorbed stillness, sober thoughtfulness to responsiveness, justified anger to tender sympathy

Some questions to guide your thinking:
- What is his characteristic way of handling strain, anxiety, disappointment, anger?—understands the situation, tries to handle it himself, becomes active, asks for help, realistic behavior, inappropriate affect, appropriate affect, lets off steam in violent action, turns on adult, withdraws to recover, withdraws to simmer, plans or plots revenge, denial, masturbation, thumbsucking, nail biting, other?
- What is his response to the frustration, disappointment, or anxiety of another child?
- What is his response to fatigue and/or illness?
- Is it difficult for him to shift moods or is he flexible in moods?
- How does he recover from upsets?—quickly, slowly, other?

• What are the outstanding affective characteristics of the child? Give salient examples which illustrate his characteristic responses.
• What are the outstanding changes in his affective expression since he entered school and/or since the last written summary?
• What teacher behavior and/or learning opportunities have been most helpful?

1.5 *Situational Responses*

1.51 Decision in making a choice
      from: wandering from place to place without selecting a task; watching others
      to: choosing new as well as a variety of familiar activities
      Write a summary statement regarding the child's ability to make choices from alternatives presented in the school situation. Support your statement with examples of typical behavior and/or situations in which his behavior varies from the usual.

   • What teacher behavior and/or learning opportunities have been most helpful?

1.52 Approach to problem solving
      from: deferring to others when faced with a problem; may leave situation; may or may not act on a specific suggestion for a solution
      to: attempting increasingly complex as well as different kinds of problems; varying initial approach to task, situation, or person, and trying alternative approaches when first action not successful; requesting assistance with some problems; usually finds solutions or partial solutions
      Write a summary statement about the child's developing ability to solve problems in (1) social situations and (2) with materials. Support your statements by specific examples of behavior which are typical and/or situations in which his behavior varies from the usual.

   • What teacher behavior and/or learning oportunities have been most helpful?

1.53 Persistence in a task
      from: pursuing a task for a few minutes, then leaving, or may remain but drift into semi-involvement in the task at hand
      to: sustaining effort in a variety of selected tasks even though pressured to leave by a friend; work usually is sustained over long periods of time, sometimes leaves and returns to a task; needing support in pursuing new tasks which require new skills
      Write a summary statement about this child's initiative and his growing ability to pursue a task to completion. Support your statement by specific examples of typical behavior.

Some questions to guide your thinking:
   • What are the outstanding characteristics of the child in regard to situational responses given above?
   • What is his general action pattern?—free–flexible, free to become involved, free to question, complains, tight organization of behavior or limited action, disorganized behavior, adaptive or nonadaptive behavior, disruptive behavior, other?

- What is his general approach to solving problems?—only approaches problems when success seems certain, attempts tasks too difficult, usually finds solutions, asks help from children and/or adults, gives up easily, perseveres, inflexible when looking for alternatives, adaptive flexible behavior?
- When working at a task is he distractible, reflective? Are tasks often aborted, left and returned to later, completed? Does he persevere at the same task in non-adaptive ways or does he work in adaptive ways toward mastery?
- Can you suggest a pattern in these interdependent behaviors?
- What are the outstanding changes in his making choices, solving problems, and being persistent since he entered school and/or since the last written summary?
- What teacher behavior and/or learning opportunity has been most helpful?

2 Relationships to Adults

2.1 *Adults as Supporters of Self-Regulation*
from: complying without question to limits imposed by adults or frequently breaking limits and safety regulations
to: questioning authority and limits by asking reasons for policy, procedure, or adult's response; listening and responding to reason; may express dislike of reasons

Write a summary statement of the quantity and quality of the child's interaction with the adult regarding his ability to utilize the adult as a supporter of self-control. Give specific salient examples which illustrate your statements.

2.2 *Adults as a Resource for Assistance and Evaluation*
from: not contacting adults; moving away from adults; making excessive contact with all available adults including strangers
to: contacting an appropriate adult for conversation, information, companionship, assistance, evaluation; usually can wait a few minutes for adult help or attention

Write a summary statement of the quantity and quality of the child's interaction with the adult regarding his ability to use the adult as a person helpful to his learning. Give specific salient examples which illustrate your statements.

What are the child's outstanding characteristics regarding his relationships to adults? Are these consistent for all adults?

Some questions to guide your thinking:
- How does he accept the adult as a supporter of self-control?—rigid clinging to limits, excessive testing, understands logic of adult's reasons, free to question, healthy defiance, clear sense of reality, passive behavior, tells adult off, other?
- How does he utilize the adult as a resource?—asks questions, asks for help, avoids adults, asks for more help than is needed, seldom asks for help, relies on the adult to "read him," other? Does he seek out adults rather than children?
- What are the outstanding changes in his relationships to adults since he entered school and/or since the last written summary?
- What teacher behavior and/or learning opportunities have been most helpful?

3 Relationships to Children

   3.1 *General Interaction* (cross-situational)

   3.11 Quantity of interaction
       from: leaving area when others enter; not going into an area occupied by others; interaction (physical contact, proximity, verbal contact) only when others interrupt
       to: interacting frequently with three or more particular children, sustaining contact for a long period of time; interacting with a variety of children in teacher structured activities and routine tasks; working independent of others on particular tasks for a sustained period of time

   3.12 Quality of interaction
       from: responding to others by voicing objections, turning away, leaving situation, making intrusive physical contact
       to: varying mode of interaction with different people in different situations —e.g., gives and receives help, makes suggestions which are accepted, acts on ideas of others, pursues mutually acceptable resolutions of conflict; sustains interaction and at the same time responds to other people and/or events with verbalization and gesture
      Write a summary statement about the child's developing ability to interact socially with particular children including (1) the amount and (2) the quality of interaction. Give specific examples which illustrate your summary.

   3.2 *Situationally Specific Interaction*

   3.21 Conflict resolution
       from: not taking verbal or physical action when conflict arises; actively joining into any conflict; watching others who argue, defend themselves, etc., from a distance; may express concern verbally, crying, and/or by body tension when he sees or hears others in conflict
       to: usually able to resolve conflict in mutually acceptable ways with three or four other children who can also do this; usually asks for help when working with others who are less able to resolve conflict then he; after he has tried discussion and debate unsuccessfully is able to defend himself verbally or physically
      Write a summary statement defining how the child resolves conflict with other children. Give specific examples to illustrate your summary and which are representative of his behavior.

   3.22 Taking turns and sharing
       from: not waiting for a turn (either attempts to take material or place from another or leaves situation); does not share (either attempts to take all material or space for himself or gives up all to others)
       to: usually waits for his turn in a variety of situations with four or five others who have also learned to take turns; may explain how to take turns to others; may make "fair trades" by mutual agreement with several other children; shares with a variety of others; may devise through play ways to use materials with others
      Write a summary statement defining the child's actions in situations where

taking turns or sharing is called for. Give specific examples which present the child's ability to share and take turns.

Some questions to guide your thinking:
- Who are his particular friends?
- Does he seek certain children without success? Why? Successfully? Why?
- Are there antipathies with particular others?
- Does he avoid a particular child?
- What are his favorite activities with his friends?
- Does he choose to be or work with different children in different situations?
- What portion of his time does he spend with a child, children, independently?
- How does he join others at work or play?—accepts their advances, makes advances to others, watches, watches and joins, follows, leads, balance of following and leading, reciprocal relations?
- Is he demanding, aggressive, controlling, dependent on others for ideas and actions, asserts own intentions, reciprocal sharing, other?
- Does he retreat from conflict? Go out to find it?
- How does he respond to the conflict of others?
- Does he take pleasure in another's achievement? Does he show sympathy in another's dissappointment?
- What are the outstanding characteristics of the child in regard to his relationship with children?
- Can you find a pattern in his behavior?
- What are the outstanding changes in his behavior toward other children (thinking, feeling, acting) since he entered school and/or since the last written summary?
- What teacher behavior and/or learning opportunities have been most helpful?

4 Relationships to Groups

4.1 *Basic Responsibilities*

4.11 Care of school property
    from: watching others who replace materials to shelves, cupboards, baskets, etc.; watching others wash paintbrushes, roll and wet clay, etc.; responding to the ideas of care and working beside a teacher for a part of the task
    to: assuming responsibility for and having well-organized ideas about setting up and retoring order to areas within the room and yard; working along with a teacher and several other children to accomplish a variety of tasks, e.g.—cleaning the bunny cage, watering plants, mixing paint, cleaning brushes, setting the table for snack or lunch; using a variety of materials in a variety of ways safe for himself and for others, and preserving the materials
    Write a summary statement defining how the child assumes responsibility for school property. Give specific examples which illustrates this and are representative of his usual behavior.

4.12 Respect for property owned or in use by others
    from: helping himself to material which belong to another or are in use by another; watching others use materials
    to: asking another child if he can use materials or equipment owned or

in use by him; making reciprocal agreements with another child about the use of materials; having well-organized ideas about property rights and respecting these rights even when he strongly wishes to use specific materials

Write a summary statement defining how the child assumes responsibility for property owned or in use by others. Give specific examples which illustrate this and are representative of his behavior.

4.13 Observation of space boundaries

from: wandering out of the boundaries of the yard; running away from the yard; follows another out of the yard

to: requesting permission of the teacher when he wishes to go to an areas outside of the yard; understanding the reasonableness of staying in a safe place; may raise questions about the reasonableness of limits

Write a summary statement defining how the child is able to cope with the freedom and flexibility within his group. Give specific examples where relevant.

Some questions to guide your thinking:
- Does he demonstrate an awareness of the privileges and/or responsibilities related to being in a group?
- What is his response to group limitations, privileges, and responsibilities?— fair play, taking turns, destructive, disruptive, seems removed, active participant, watches, minimal participation, other?
- Is his behavior appropriate for his age and experience?
- Does he resist, comply? Is he compulsive, adaptive, flexible, self-assured, self-assertive?
- What kinds of information, knowledge, and understandings does he have which come out in his assumption of such responsibilities? Are there illustrations of how this information is organized?
- To what extent does he see situations from his point of view and to what extent can he see it from another's point of view?
- What attributes, functions, or properties does he note as he encounters the materials?
- Does he habitually bring materials to school? How does he use them? Are there clues to why he brings them?
- What are the outstanding characteristics of this child in regard to basic responsibilities?
- Can you find a pattern in his behavior?
- What are the outstanding changes in his behavior regarding his responsibilities as a group member since he entered school and/or since the last written summary?
- What teacher behavior and/or learning opportunities have been most helpful?

4.2 *Participation in Group Activities*

4.21 Story groups

from: responding by gesture, expression, or comments to a book looked at with him, read to him, or a story told to him and one or two other children to: responding to a story-discussion for 15 to 20 minutes; taking turns for comments; expressing relevant and related ideas and/or raising questions without excessive tension or hesitation; taking part in simple dramatizations of stories recalling sequences, lines of the part being taken, and expressing affect appropriate to the character, taking turns being an actor and being a part of an audience; telling a story which becomes a play for a group time; leaving and joining a group in such a manner that it is evident other's interests are taken into account

Write a summary statement regarding the child's behavior during story time, his particular interests, and significant changes over time. Give specific examples which support your statements.

4.22 Music groups

from: spontaneously singing along as accompaniment to his actions, e.g., singing, "Mary goes up and Suzie goes down" while swinging; listening to a variety of music; attending to (i.e., seeing, hearing, using) a variety of simple instruments—e.g., drums, bells, tambourines; attending to a variety of different instruments, e.g., flute, violin, piano

to: singing a variety of songs; matching tones with variations in loudness and duration of tone; singing different words to the same melodies, i.e., ones child makes up or ones known in general; identifying music which consists of melody or melody and harmony; identifying musical instruments as they are played; identifying musical instruments as a class by seeing or hearing them; clapping or beating time to a variety of tempos, creating rhythmic patterns; responding to the mood of a wide variety of music

Write a summary statement regarding the child's behavior during music times, his particular interests, and significant changes over time. Cite specific examples which support your statement.

4.23 Movement activity groups

from: observing a movement activity group; joining a group at times holding a teacher's hand or with a particular child, or for a particular movement

to: usually attempts all modes of moving explored; may watch first; often active throughout the time (20–25 min.); suggests variations within activities; asks for and accepts adult help with patterns not mastered; observes safety procedures and may suggest other ways "to do it safely"

Write a summary statement regarding the child's behavior during movement activity time, particular interests, and significant changes over time. Cite specific examples which support your statements.

4.24 Trips

from: expressing fear or concern about leaving the yard; breaking out of bounds easily or having little control

to: practicing appropriate behavior and safety rules in familiar places; adjusting behavior quickly in new places or with unexpected changes; knowing purpose of trip and attending to details

Write a summary statement regarding the child's behavior during trips and significant changes over time. Cite specific examples which support your statements.

4.25 Snack groups

from: helping wash tables for snack; being helped to organize himself at the table by an adult; keeping his crackers in hand or on his napkin; drinking his juice; helping with spills; talking about when is on the table or people there; focusing on self-help skills; staying at the table until finished; putting his cup and napkin in the wastebasket; helping wash the tables and sweep floor if needed

to: washing tables for snack; counting people and matching cups, napkins, chairs, to the number of people; organizing himself at the table; pouring his juice; helping himself to crackers; chewing with mouth closed; having social conversation with others; cleaning up after himself; cleaning tables and sweeping floor as needed

Write a summary statement regarding the child's behavior before, during, and after snack and significant changes over time.

Some questions to guide your thinking:
- What is his response to group activities (story, music, movement, trips, snacks)?—sharp attention, attention to detail, long or short attention, content of response, spontaneous response, ability to take turns, recall, inventive ability to assume and follow through on responsibility?
- How does the group respond to him?—sought after, avoided by, threatened by, unnoticed, other?
- What are the outstanding characteristics of the child's behavior regarding his ability to function in teacher-structured situations engaged in by the group?
- Can you find a pattern in regard to his ability to function at group times?
- What are the important changes in his behavior in group situations since he entered school and/or since the last written summary?
- What teacher behavior and/or learning opportunities have been most helpful?

4.3 *Conduct During Transitions*

For each of the following transitions, write a summary statement about the child's conduct and the quality of his behavior.

4.31 Arrival at school

from: coming into the school accompanied by his mother

to: coming into the school independently, greeting his teacher and friends, becoming involved with materials and/or other children; utilizing a teacher as a support when he is angry, physically hurt, or fatigued

4.32 Organized change in activity

from: watching others; following a specific routine; needing an adult's help to get organized

to: assuming and carrying out responsibilities in a well-organized way during transitions (i.e., reorganizing materials, preparing for snack, getting dressed to go outside, choosing a specific activity); suggesting and accepting variations in routines with ease

4.33 Dismissal from school
    from: resisting leaving school or being compliant about leaving school
    to: being matter-of-fact about leaving school; gathering up his personal belongings; anticipating something he plans for tomorrow; telling his friends good-bye

Some questions to guide your thinking:
- With whom does he come to school? What is his response to deviations in the usual pattern of arrival?
- How does he come into the classroom? What are his characteristic ways of coming into the classroom? In what situations does he deviate from his usual response?—comes directly into the room, hides outside the door, sits in his locker, talks to teacher, seeks a particular child, goes directly to materials, watches others, stands alone, other?
- What is his conduct during transitions?—organized, disorganized, tests limits, destructive, seems to understand the sequence of events, other?
- If he is disorganized, what seems to help him most?
- What are his characteristic ways of parting with his father? With his mother? —warm, matter-of-fact, contactless, clinging, vascillating, other?
- What is the adult's characteristic way of parting from him?—quietly interested, anxious, help with clothing, talking with teacher including or excluding the child, other?
- What is his usual time of departure?—early, late, on time? What is his usual behavior at departure?—eager to leave, reluctant to leave, matter of fact, wants to show parent something, testing limits, dawdles, cries, other? What is his response to deviations in the usual pattern of departure?
- In what situations does he deviate from his usual departure behavior?
- What is the parent's characteristic behavior at departure time?—patient, vascillating, firm, sure, angry, other?
- What are the outstanding characteristics of the child's behavior during transitions? Can you find a pattern in these interrelated situations?
- What are the outstanding changes in his behavior during transitions since he entered school and/or since the last written summary?
- What teacher behavior and/or learning opportunities have been most helpful?

5   Relationship to Objects and Ideas

5.1 *Objects Manipulated as Body Extensions*
    For each of the following (objects manipulated as body extensions) write a summary statement about the child's skill, ability, and the quality of his performance.

5.11 Riding a tricycle
    from: sitting on the seat of a tricycle; may place feet on pedals and hands on handle bars; may move legs in a rotary motion when pushed; may propel himself forward in a walking motion
    to: riding and guiding tricycle with control of force and direction using pedals to brake, can back up; using this skill in dramatic play with others

5.12 Throwing a ball (6–8-inch ball)

from: sitting on floor with legs apart and rolling ball in the direction of others; standing and swinging arms with underhand pattern in direction of toss; some inaccuracy in timing of release or force causing errors in direction and distance

to: throwing ball accurately with force appropriate to varied distance; bounces ball for at least three consecutive bounces; throws ball up and catches it; tosses ball at a variety of targets; keeps his eye on target

5.13 Catching a ball (6–8-inch ball)

from: sitting on floor with legs apart, trapping ball with legs, arms, or hands; handles ball

to: moving forward toward ball, catching it firmly, bringing it in against his chest; keeping his eyes on the ball in flight; may respond to flight of ball by moving forward, sideways, or backward as necessary to make a catch

5.14 Using a pencil (pastel, felt-tip pens)

from: grasping pencil in fist

to: using thumb and two fingers in opposition and the arm as support in handling pencil; using the pencil with the preferred hand (right or left?) and the other hand for keeping paper in position

5.15 Cutting with scissors

from: using two hands on scissors to snip paper; using one hand on scissors for random snipping into edge of paper

to: using scissors in a preferred hand (right or left?) with other hand supporting the paper; cutting with thumb and fingers in opposition; making a smooth accurate cut in a straight line; may not be accurate when cutting around an irregular figure

5.2 *Objects Shaped or Reformed*

For each of the following (objects shaped or reformed) write a summary statement about the child's skill, ability, and the quality of his performance.

5.21 Working with clay

from: patting, rolling, flattening clay; rolling balls in palms of hand, breaking, bending, stretching, making holes, etc., in clay

to: combining simple three dimensional forms which fit together, accomplished by moistening and blending surfaces with thumb and fingers, using simple tools to vary texture; looking at what he is doing from different directions and making changes and adaptations from visual cues; using many words indicating actions, qualities, and relations of the material; taking care of the tools, media, and his products

5.22 Working with finger paint

from: using tips of fingers or whole hand to spread paint; using the media tentatively; using the media for smearing; possibly verbalizing and/or responding to the media as "icky" or "messy"

to: using a variety of hand and finger motions in order to paint; attending to mixing colors, experimenting with textures, lines, and shapes; looking at the finger painting and making decisions about designs, colors, textures, and relationships; using many words indicating actions, qualities, relationships of material; with help from adult, cleans up self and area after painting

5.3   *Objects Used for Construction*
For each of the following (objects used for construction) write a summary statement about the child's skill, ability, and the quality of his performance.

5.31 Block building
from: building simple rows, towers, and bridges
to: building three dimensional structures which reflect his ideas about his environment; selecting sizes and shapes for a particular purpose; making adaptations with multiples and particular cuts of blocks to his purpose; using buildings for play; saving structure over time for adding complexity and for play

5.32 Structuring building-game sets
from: fitting pieces together or pulling pieces apart
to: fitting pieces together to make a design or replicate objects in his environment; working with a plan which he may or may not verbalize; making adaptations to the potential and limitations of the materials

5.33 Woodworking (hammering and nailing)
from: pounding a nail, started by a teacher, into soft wood using the hammer in either hand, attempting to use other hand for support keeping board steady; responding to cues such as "Watch the top of the nail," or "Hold the board with his hand."
to: starting nail himself, pounding it into the board with his preferred hand and using the other hand to steady board at a safe distance; using nails to join board together, joining spools, wheels, etc., to boards; working with a plan which he may or may not verbalize; combining nailing, sawing, and accessory materials for his particular purpose

5.34 Woodworking (sawing)
from: watching and/or helping teacher put wood into vise; using saw to make short, erratic strokes in a groove started by the teacher
to: putting wood into vise; sawing wood with long, even, firm strokes; choosing, measuring, and cutting wood for a particular purpose

5.35 Pasting and gluing (paper or wood)
from: spreading glue or paste on paper and objects to be pasted; spreading paste all over paper and then attaching object; applying paste over objects pasted
to: using paste and glue in a variety of ways to attach objects to paper or wood; using paste or glue for special effects; choosing particular materials to accomplish his purpose, combining materials, shapes, and colors in unusual ways

5.36 Puzzle working
from: dumping puzzle, attempting to assemble at random, e.g., one piece

to: in all places or all pieces in one place; assembling one-piece cutouts using picture content, shape, color, and size as cues to assemble puzzles, rotating pieces to test fit; working puzzles which contain 25 pieces (jigsaw or inlay puzzles)

5.4   *Drawing and Painting Activity*
For each of the following drawing and painting activities write a summary statement of the child's skills, abilities, and the quality of his performance.

- What are the characteristics of the child's use of color, line, texture, and design?
- What colors can he name? Mix?
- Does he draw a human figure? If so, what parts does he include?

5.41 Drawing with pastels, felt-tip pens, charcoal, soft pencil
from: making scribbles, dots, and lines of color; making several drawings; repeating schemata
to: choosing and blending colors with sureness and discrimination; using a variety of line, shape, color, and texture to accomplish intent of drawing; drawing a variety of symbols representing the same object, idea, or feeling; using the pastel in a variety of ways, i.e., like a pencil, on its side for a mass of color, blending color with finger

5.42 Easel painting
from: making blobs, dots, and lines; usually attending to color, line, or texture
to: choosing and mixing color with sureness and discrimination; making elaborate pictures combining colors, or placing colors side by side, or by combining schemata; painting a variety of symbols representing the same object, idea, or feeling; using whole or parts of the paper in ways visually pleasing to him; handling the brush with agility, rotating it in his hand to change angle of brush

- What are the outstanding changes in his use of materials since he entered school and/or since the last written summary? What materials has he chosen repeatedly?
- What teacher behavior and/or learning opportunities have been most helpful?

5.5   *Language Activity*
For each of the following write a summary statement of the child's skills, abilities, interests, and quality of performance.

5.51 Attending, observing
from: responding through action to a single direction; exploration and interest in sand, water, soil, and animals
to: responding to several directions which involve a sequence of acts; relays a message to a third person; testing properties of the physical world and the objects in it; verbalizing observations of simple machines, liquids, gases, sound, heat, light, magnetism, electricity, animals, and plants; discriminating fine differences in auditory, visual, and tactile stimuli

5.52 Writing symbols

    from: drawing loops, zigzags, wavey or jerky trailings

    to: writing many upper and lower case letters from memory; writing his name, names of members of his family, his friends and many commonly seen words from memory; copying words he needs for work or play; writing with a preferred hand (left or right); asking teachers to write words for him

5.53 Reading

    from: looking at books and/or pictures, naming objects and people

    to: looking at books from front to back, left to right, top to bottom; following pictures in a book to tell a story in sequence; reading pictographs and arranging sequences correctly; naming upper- and lowercase letters; saying the sounds of the letters; reading by sight many common words; reading new words "by sounding out the word"; showing interest in written words outside of books, e.g., teacher-made charts and lists

- What are his particular interests which are evident by his observations?
- What kinds of inferences and generalizations does he make from his observations?
- How effective is his memory, recall, attention to detail, and questioning? Can he repeat a sound sequence? Can he look at a group of objects (5) and when one is removed name the object removed?
- Does he ask adults to show him how to write letters? Words?
- What letters does he recognize? What words does he recognize?
- Does he know the sounds of letters? Which ones?
- Can he group objects on the basis of beginning sounds?
- Does he look at books or read as a self-selected activity?
- What are the outstanding changes in his language activity since he entered school and/or since the last written summary?
- What teacher behavior and/or learning opportunities have been most helpful?

5.6 *Dramatic Play Activity*

Write a summary for each of the following (i.e., player interaction; properties, place; and role structuring); utilize examples to amplify your summaries.

5.61 Player interaction

    from: imitating important others in solitary play (e.g., mother, father)

    to: participating in interactive role play with three or more other children; a great deal of language and gesture used to act out complex relationships (e.g., two mothers, one visitor, a daddy, and two babies; a fire chief, an assistant chief, and two firemen)

5.62 Properties and place

    from: handling objects that have significance in terms of adult role behavior, or replications of such objects (e.g., carries a doll around; wears a man's hat while working puzzles)

    to: using very few properties; speech and gesture indicate a variety of imaginary props (e.g., hands used for telephone, places built or designated as needed to sustain play)

5.63 Role structuring

    from: reproducing discreet actions of adults (e.g., bathing a baby, putting on tie and hat)

    to: increasing the complexity of a role repeatedly chosen, or plays a variety of roles within a sequence logical to the cultural subgroup of which he is a part: conflicts usually resolved by adaptation or compromise of role behavior content and continuous action is maintained

Some questions to guide your thinking:

- Is he able to engage in dramatic play? Does he engage in dramatic play spontaneously? What does he play? Are these flexible?
- Are there disruptions in this play? In response to what? Are there persistent themes? Are there persistent roles?
- Does he show a wide range of affect in play?
- What kinds of information, knowledge, and understanding does he have which comes out in play? How is this information organized and categorized? —stereotyped, flexible, reflecting reality, other?
- What attributes or properties does he note as he encounters objects and materials in play?
- How effectively does he label properties and attributes?
- What kinds of inferences and generalizations does he make?
- To what extent does he see situations from his point of view and to what extent can he view it from another's point of view?
- How effective are his memory, recall, attention to detail, questioning, and problem solving utilized in play?
- What are the outstanding characteristics of the child's dramatic play?
- What are the outstanding changes in his dramatic play since he entered school and/or since the last written summary?
- What teacher behavior and/or learning opportunities have been most helpful?

5.7   *Concept Usage*

    Write a summary statement about the child's thinking in regard to the ideas below. To support your statements, give examples of what he does, says, and with what relevant materials. Do not generalize from one specific instance.

5.71 Causation

    from: pondering "how come?" and "why?"

    to: inferring causes on the basis of his observations, showing awareness that observer's viewpoint influences observation; explaining and predicting the consequences of his own and others' actions, and natural phenomena; testing his explanation and predictions

5.72 Seriation

    from: ordering 3 familiar objects on the basis of one dimension (e.g., size: largest to smallest)

    to: ordering a variety of materials or objects (from 6 to 10 elements) on the basis of any one of a variety of dimensions (e.g., size, brightness, texture); using words related to seriation (e.g., largest, middle, next to the smallest, darker than)

5.73 Number
    from: chaining numbers 1 to 10; naming the cardinal numbers 1 and 2 for sets of significant objects (e.g., 1 nose, 2 hands, 2 cookies)
    to: counting (i.e., by ones up to 25) a variety of objects in a variety of situations; verbalizing "more than" when objects are added to a set and "less than" when objects are taken from a set without physical correspondence; verbalizing cardinal numbers, 0 to 10, in a variety of situations and with a variety of materials; using a variety of quantitative words (e.g., big, many, few) in a variety of situations with a variety of materials; using language which relates parts to whole (e.g., half, quarter); combining numbers that total 1, 2, 3, 4, and 5

5.74 Space (map)
    from: locating significant objects and places in familiar space
    to: locating objects in unfamiliar space; locating objects by spatial directions which are given verbally; placing objects in relation to one another as seen from other perspectives; using words which convey ideas about position, perspective, proportion, and distance (e.g., top, through, middle, corner, center, straight, curve, smaller than, near, far)

5.75 Time (calendar)
    from: referring to time in the present, now
    to: telling how old he will be next birthday; telling time of his bedtime; telling the sequence of his activities in a regular schedule; telling the days of the week in regard to significant events, naming the days of the week; naming the present season with regard to significant events; using yesterday, today, and tomorrow; using the names of objects for measuring time (e.g., clock, calendar)

5.76 Description and classification of objects by functional or formal properties
    from: identifying an object as belonging to a particular set (e.g., given a picture of a bird places that picture with pictures of birds when alternative placements might be with fish, cats, etc.); matching and sorting objects comprising a simple set by one functional or one formal property (color, shape, size, texture, odor, material)
    to: taking the whole class apart to find subclasses and making comparisons of "all" and "some"; abstracting the common property of a class and extending the class to include all objects possessing that property; explaining the rationale for his classification

5.77 Measurement
    from: using the word "measure" as a global idea (e.g., "We measured the rabbit"); using the general terms of "bigger," "smaller," "more than" for most measurement ideas
    to: showing understanding of the unit-iteration principle in his application of invented units (e.g., six large rocks balances 20 small rocks; the table is 7 hands long); utilizing common instruments for measuring (e.g., ruler for length, scales for weight, cup for volume, thermometer for temperature); utilizing correct names for measuring instruments and the units of measurement

- What are the outstanding changes in his use of the concept given above since he entered school and/or since the last written summary?
- What teacher behavior and/or learning opportunities have been most helpful?

A Teacher Observation Report

Lynn Rogers entered Children's House the first week in October 1967, when she was 2 years 8 months old. She had been known to some of the adults since June of that year, for she played on the sidewalk alongside the corner house that was to become our daycare center. As we went back and forth to make decisions about or note the progress of the remodeling, Lynn would appear alone or with several other children. At first she watched through the fence, and would look at us and then scamper away with a big smile. Later she announced, "I'm comin' this school." After a few weeks of brief conversations with her, she was often at the corner as if on the lookout for us, waving and calling as we came closer, "Where you goin'?" or "What you doin'?" We noticed that she often made trips to the corner store with Jean, her six-year-old sister, to purchase bread, milk, pop, potato chips, or popsicles. They usually offered neighborhood children and us some of whatever they had to eat.

In September, after the older children had started school, Lynn often played alone, climbing on the fence or steps of her house, making up games of running, hopping, or riding a tricycle along the block on which she lived. It seemed that she was allowed to go to the corner in both directions from her house, but not allowed to cross the streets or go around the corners alone, and she stayed within these limits. During this time, she reasserted daily that she was coming to this school and our conversations continued.

By the middle of September, teachers were in the yard and garage opening cartons of toys and equipment and Lynn was a daily visitor. It was striking that she watched and talked to us, but was never intrusive. She seemed lonely without the other children and we provided some diversion and companionship. Teachers were delighted when a social worker told us that all her siblings but one had been to nursery school and that her mother wanted Lynn to come to Children's House for the morning program. We knew by this time that if Lynn didn't come to our school all of us would be sorely disappointed.

When Lynn entered school she was described by a teacher as a small, tightly knit girl with a round face, big wide-open eyes, curly eyelashes, and sparse hair done in many tiny pigtails. Her skin was a medium brown color, somewhat darker over the forehead, behind the ears, at the back of her neck, and an uneven color on her cheeks and the rest of her body. Her skin was dry and scaly from eczema and particularly so on her forehead, scalp, neck, shoulders, elbows, and knees. Her clean clothing was often too big or too little and usually very worn. Slightly longer acquaintance revealed a friendly, responsive, generous little girl with a low husky voice and a contagious laugh that suggested a wellspring of delight within her. In the first week of school, our impression of her as a child with a zesty, self-directed involvement in familiar situations was confirmed. We also found her to be a child with quickness to feel hurt or rebuffed by actions or comments intended as statements of fact, not criticism.

After the first eight weeks in school a teacher, using the Criterion Model, summarized Lynn's school behavior from notes recorded in the daily log in order to formulate a body of knowledge so that an educational diagnosis and prescription could be made for her. Following the report, we have included a brief review of the general process used to individualize the educational program with reference to the specific decisions we made regarding Lynn.

Relationship to Self

Personal Tasks Lynn was very competent in personal tasks. She was quick to learn routines and within the first week learned to put her personal belongings in her cubby. For example, she often brought a jump rope to school and placed it in her cubby after she and other children played with it. Her cubby was a special place at school, as evidenced by her placing anything she made there in it to "take home with me" and by her using it as a place to escape from disappointment or anger, or just to sit in for a moment.

She undressed herself with ease and when dressing needed help only with difficult fasteners, finding the back and front of T-shirts and pants, and orienting her shoes correctly. She quickly learned where her towel and washcloth were located and only needed an adult present to help her with her sleeves and for conversation as she washed. She was less competent in toileting and was dependent on adults "reading her" or on routines to get her to the toilet on time. During the end of October, she wet her pants several times. These accidents occurred in the late morning outside and were discovered by a teacher; Lynn gave no indication of distress that we could recognize. (See also "Conduct During Transitions.")

At lunch Lynn ate with three other children, a teacher, and an extra helper from the research staff. By lunchtime (11:15), she seemed to have exhausted her capacity to be independent. At this time she was apt to need help in remembering which table was hers and to attend to eating, although she handled a fork and spoon well. If an adult fed her for a few bites she usually could finish a meal on her own. However, by about noon, when she left for home, she looked quite sleepy, sucked her thumb, and cried if anyone other than her oldest sister, Alice, or her mother came for her. She looked and sounded much younger than the Lynn of nine o'clock in the morning. (Again, see also "Conduct During Transitions.")

Speaking Capacity   Lynn usually spoke in simple sentences, putting nouns, verbs, and objects together. Her articulation varied from situation to situation. For example, when she played with children or named objects in a book spontaneously, she articulated vowels and even some difficult initial consonants clearly enough to be understood by the listener ("I got ah ribbon," "Where's dat doll?"). However, she mumbled or used incomprehensible or infantile speech when asked by an adult a direct question that required recall over time on her part, when asking a teacher for help or permission, or when in a new situation. Her speech was also less good structurally at these times—i.e., she used one word ("dat," "him") with gestures, or fragmented language ("dat doll") with gestures, in place of complete sentences. Frequently, her comments, needs, and requests were understood by teachers only in context, or by guess, intuition, or familiarity. In general, Lynn's language was concrete and nonspecific—"I got one," "Give me dat." She used language most vigorously to accompany her actions (see "Moving Capacity") and to ask for attention. Although her vocabulary was still quite limited at this time, the number of words heard at school had increased considerably over the nine-week period. She knew and used the names of most toys and materials with which she played, of some parts of her body, and of most of the children and all of the regular adults. She had a rich vocabulary of gestures.

Moving Capacity   Lynn was free and easy in most tasks that required body movement. She was also free in her use of space and her movements were generally well coordinated. For example, she pushed, pulled, turned, twisted, and spun about, using a full range of joint motion. It was easy for her to support her body weight by her arms and swing herself on the horizontal bars. From this position, she quickly learned to pump herself back and forth to gain momentum and to lift her legs at just the right moment to hoist them up on the horizontal ladder bars. She then learned to support her body weight with her knees bent over the bar and with her head down and to swing back and forth in this position. She seemed quite comfortable upside down and used her body in a variety of ways with different bases of support. She ran, climbed, hopped, galloped, and jumped rope with ease.

She smiled, laughed, and produced a great deal of clear, spontaneous language around movement activities. However, she was unable to use the teacher's verbal cues or instructions for performing physical skills. Rather, she learned best by being put in the correct position or by imitating other children.

Patterning of Affective Expression   Lynn usually expressed positive feelings (joy, contentment, or pleasure; sympathy and affection) in much the same way with variations only in intensity: smiling and laughing contagiously. For example, on completing a puzzle she would smile or chuckle gleefully and look at the adult and back to the puzzle. If it had been an especially hard task she would clap her hands and often repeat the task.

Her negative feelings (anger, hurt, disappointment, fear) were all expressed in about the same way and with the same intensity: she hung her head, protruded her lips, and cried. It was difficult to know what had happened to sadden, disappoint, hurt, or anger her, or to know the depth of her feelings. At this point, the cause often escaped the teachers. Lynn was often unable even to confirm or deny the cause of her upset by nodding her head when asked.

Situation Responses

Decision in Making a Choice   Lynn made choices among alternatives, choosing new as well as familiar activities. During the first few weeks of school she learned that each day there were several alternatives available indoors and outdoors. Although she often came to school saying, "I wanta worka puzzle" or do some other activity she had done the day before, perhaps as a way of reestablishing her presence, she carefully looked around and made choices independent of teachers or other children. Without teacher help or suggestion, and often withstanding strong urging by other children, Lynn helped herself to many available materials. She did not ask for materials or toys that were not immediately available or that were out of sight.

Problem Solving   Lynn's approach to problem solving is considered here in three parts because her ability to solve problems varied so much in these three common situations.

• PROBLEMS CONCERNING HER BODY IN PHYSICAL SPACE   Here she tried one or more alternatives when the first action was not successful; she revised the sequence of action when necessary for a final solution. For example, walking up the cellar door slide, Lynn found her path to the top blocked by another child. Carefully maintaining her balance to avoid slipping down again she gradually maneuvered herself to the other side, which was not blocked. Again she started up the slide, only to find a child above her again. She chuckled and grasped the side of the slide with two hands, moved her legs over the side of the slide, and dropped to the ground. She then climbed the ladder and came down the slide. Marvelously capable in this kind of problem solving, she did less well in others.

• PROBLEMS OF CONFLICT RESOLUTION   During the first few weeks of school, when Lynn faced a conflict she hung her head and cried or gave way to others. A few weeks later, while she continued to cry, she was able to respond to a teacher's question with "Tim hit me," or "Annette took my doll." Also she was beginning to act on specific suggestions given by a teacher, if the teacher who had seen the incident supported her and supplied the language.

• PROBLEMS ENCOUNTERED WITH MATERIALS   Lynn approached problems with materials in a concrete, piece-by-piece way, and was easily defeated. For example, solving puzzles she used one cue, shape, to attempt a solution. If she was not immediately successful, her very precise fine motor skills became rapid and less precise as she rotated the piece quickly, trying to make it fit the same place without stopping to look and reevaluate the task. Teachers found that verbal support alone did not seem helpful to Lynn; she needed active help from them through demonstration of the use of the material or help in readjusting her approach.

Persistence in a Task   Lynn was usually able to sustain effort in two tasks: dramatic play and active physical play. With teacher support, she could persist in other activities: art, table games, looking at books, and working puzzles. With encouragement and time she could return to a task she had abandoned earlier because of lack of skill. She was not reflective about tasks unless strongly supported by a teacher. For example, she attempted to force puzzle pieces in at random; only when a teacher said, "This is the girl's arm. Where does her arm go?" could she look and locate the position.

Relationship to Adults

Lynn's relationship to adults at this time could be characterized in three predominant ways: she was responsive, agreeable and wanted to please; she was mildly teasing when she wanted attention and affection; and she was quick to feel hurt or rebuffed.

Adults as Supporters of Self-Regulation   In the first few weeks of school Lynn complied with limits, requests, and suggestions made by a teacher without question and with a watchful, wary look. She seemed to feel the need to be very careful not to do anything that might be disapproved, that is, she was excessively compliant and careful. By the end of the second month, there entered a teasing quality in her contacts with teachers when the teacher was working with Lynn in a small group. Lynn would, for example, refuse to take off her boots or to eat, or attempt to tip her chair backward and say, "No, no," with a smile and a twinkle in her eye. Saying to her, "It looks like you want some help," "I know you're here and I can think about you when I'm serving Tim's plate," or "I care too much about you to let you tip your chair and get hurt," and giving her a pat or a hug would elicit a chuckle and a quick affectionate response from her. Teachers were left with the impression that friendly, caring, and affectionate contact with the adult was what Lynn was asking for in this behavior and that when it was supplied she could expand her relationships.

Adults as a Resource for Assistance and Evaluation   Lynn's primary contact was with one teacher. She watched AZ and imitated many of her actions—tilting her head to one side in a pose of thoughtfulness, putting her left hand on her hip as she surveyed a situation—her language—"Now, let me think," "Hello, Annette," "You are fun"—and was beginning to laugh at herself as did AZ when she made minor mistakes, such as starting to put her sweater in the cubby adjacent to hers. She was soon able to contact many adults for conversation and for help with her clothing, and looked attentive as they talked about process, products, and situations. She could wait a few minutes for help if she knew it was forthcoming. She was friendly and responsive to all teachers and most often elicited a smile and a friendly contact from the adult.

All teachers found Lynn difficult to comfort when she cried, when her skin itched because of her eczema, or when she seemed sleepy. But they found her fun and rewarding to work with at other times.

Relationships to Children

Quantity of Interaction   During the first few weeks of school Lynn made frequent contacts with Annette. These two children had previously been in each other's homes and played together while their mothers visited in the afternoons and on weekends. Lynn made many contacts with other children in outdoor play and teacher-structured activities. By mid-November these contacts were frequent with most children in a variety of situations. She avoided several aggressive, unpredictable boys.

Quality of Interaction   Lynn had several ways of interacting with children: (1) She could simply join an ongoing group and work beside one or two children. For example, Sandra and Jennifer, two older children, were packing a suitcase for a "trip." Lynn went into the doll corner, got a pot and a spoon and began "cookin' breakfast." She played beside them about ten minutes. (2) She could give a child something he was looking for or seemed to want. For example, Annette could not find a pair of high heels and Lynn gave her the pair she had been wearing and helped herself to a large pocketbook. In another situation, Cindy wanted another cracker at the same time Lynn reached for one. She immediately passed the basket with one cracker in it to Cindy. There was often this quality of genuine generosity in her contacts with other children. (3) She cried or backed out of situations that called for aggressive behavior on her part as described under "Problem Solving."

Conflict Resolution   See "Problem Solving" and "Quality of Interaction with Children."

Taking Turns and Sharing   From the very first at school, Lynn could wait for a turn if a teacher said, "After Cindy, it will be your turn," and if the waiting was brief and not competitive. Often in a situation where taking turns involved competition, she cried. For example, there were only two swings and on several occasions three children raced to the swings. If two looked as if they would get there before Lynn did, Lynn gave up, dissolved in tears, and needed considerable reassurance and physical contact from her teacher before she could accept the waiting.

Lynn could share with most children from a small stock or often gave up something she was using to a number of other children. She avoided three boys and one girl who were often aggressive, competitive, and acquisitive.

Relationships to a Group

Participation in Group Activities   Group activities during this time were limited to story group, snack group, music group, and walks with several others in the neighborhood.

Her story group was composed of three girls, Lynn the oldest. At this point they enjoyed picture books and were learning to turn pages, to name objects, and to make the sounds animals make. Books were new to her and she often carried them around in a doll buggy or brought one to an adult to "read me," which meant to talk about the pictures and ask her the names of objects. She was not yet able to listen to a short story.

At music time the whole group was together just before lunch. Lynn was often the first one there and often had a suggestion for a song to be sung. She imitated the teacher's gestures that went along with songs as well as the adult's facial expression or movement unrelated to the singing.

Her senses of melody, tone, and rhythm were excellent. She sang clearly the words of very simple songs such as "Swinging, swinging; Lynn goes up; Rusty goes down." More complicated words were often garbled— "Where oh ho is hosome, Stanley?" ("Where oh where is handsome Stanley?") On many days by the end of ten minutes of this late morning group activity Lynn snuggled up next to an adult, scratched her eczema, or looked tired and sleepy.

By mid-November, trips were simply short walks around the neighborhood. Although she lived in this neighborhood, Lynn was unable to tell us or point out the directions of the public school, the neighborhood store, or the playground. Yet we knew that she had been to all three of these places many times starting from home. Lynn walked along, talking to a teacher and holding onto a teacher's hand. Her behavior seemed appropriate and safe, yet several teachers remarked that Lynn did not particularly enjoy these short trips and often seemed apprehensive during them. Nor did she talk about what she had seen on return.

Snack was usually a pleasant time for Lynn. She liked milk, juice, fruit, cheese, cookies, and crackers. She liked to play games centered on naming the children, the food, body parts, or articles of clothing. If a teacher did not immediately initiate such a game, Lynn would drink her milk or juice and begin the game herself, "What is dis, Miss K?" (or Callie or Annette) and others would pick up the game. Lynn quickly learned to pour her own juice, help herself to food, and put her cup and napkin in the waste basket. She enjoyed working along with a teacher washing the tables before and after snack and would hold the dustpan for crumbs or sweep alongside a teacher. She often wanted to exchange her broom or sponge with the teacher, as if the one the teacher was using were better.

Conduct During Transitions   During the first eight weeks of school Lynn's behavior went through a series of changes regarding transitions from school to home and home to school.

Mrs. Rogers brought Lynn to school the first time for a short visit the last week in September. They came with Annette and her mother and stayed about an hour. A teacher showed the children the playroom, play yard, and their cubbies, and they played in each area for a while, used the toilets, and located their towels and washcloths. Lynn seemed at home exploring the whole place and taking the lead with Annette. The two mothers watched the children and talked to a teacher. We had the distinct impression that Mrs. Rogers felt very pleased to see Lynn so independent and sure of herself. Mrs. Rogers took the lead in asking questions about time, daily schedule, whether the children needed a change of clothes, and about the school.

On the following Monday morning, Mrs. Rogers brought Lynn to the play yard, handed a teacher a bag of clothing, and stood and watched Lynn while talking with a teacher. Lynn helped herself to a tricycle and began to ride looking back at her mother from time to time. After five minutes or so Lynn returned to the gate and her mother told her, "Good-bye." Mrs. Rogers also told the teacher and Lynn she would be home if Lynn needed her and just to call. It seemed clear that her mother thought Lynn independent enough to manage without her. This seemed true for the first two days and there was little or no indication that separation was hard for her.

On the third day, she called her mother and Alice, an older sister, several times on the housekeeping-corner phone to report what she was doing: "Hello, Alice, you at school?" "Hello, Mommie, I had snack." By lunchtime she began to scratch and seemed very tired and sleepy, sucked her thumb, and was glad to go outside and wait for her mother at 11:45. When Mrs. Rogers came Lynn ran to her and they walked home holding hands, Lynn looking very alive and talking quite spontaneously.

The fourth day was very much like the third except that Lynn cried before lunch and her mother was called to pick her up early since she seemed so tired and sleepy. Her mother came immediately. At twelve o'clock that day, Lynn was observed on her own tricycle riding up and down the street, not at all droopy and looking like her lively nine-o'clock self.

For the next few days she seemed fine during the morning, though from time to time very tired and sleepy at lunch. Twice she cried when she saw Jean, another sister, coming to get her, and once she cried when her mother came. Again each day by twelve-fifteen we saw her at play in front of her house jumping her rope or riding her tricycle.

On the ninth day of school she cried easily over small frustrations, called her mother and Alice on the toy phone during the second half of the morning, and, when asked, "Lynn, do you need your mommie?" cried and said "Yes!" We called Mrs. Rogers and she was not home. Lynn seemed satisfied that we had tried and went on to play until lunchtime, when she almost fell asleep at the table. When Margaret, her middle sister, came for her at noontime, Lynn hit her and cried. She did not nod her head when the teacher commented that it seemed as if she needed her mommie, but just continued to cry as they left.

The next day Mrs. Rogers seemed genuinely sorry that she had not been home the day before, and stayed and watched Lynn in the play yard for about twenty minutes. Lynn had a very good morning, ate her lunch, and went home directly afterward with Alice.

On Monday morning of the third week of school, Jean, Lynn's six-year-old sister, said she had a holiday that Friday. AZ asked Lynn if she would like Jean to visit our school on her holiday. Lynn was delighted, asked Jean to come, and the next morning Jean came by to say she'd like to visit. Lynn anticipated this all week, and Friday was a very pleasant day.

The next five weeks Lynn came to school with seeming ease, usually brought by her mother or her older sister, Alice. At noon, when it was time for her to leave, she often seemed sleepy, scratched her arms, and appeared ready to go home. (See "Personal Tasks.")

During an organized change of activity, such as moving from outside to inside, Lynn needed to be told ahead of time, "Soon we will go inside," or "After you finish your cake, I'll help you put the sand toys away, and then it will be time to go inside." She was beginning to be able to follow a specific routine, which enabled her to cope with transitions.

Relationship to Objects and Ideas

Lynn used many of the materials and pieces of equipment available at school, doing almost everything there was to do. During one indoor play-time, for example, she colored with pastels, worked puzzles, watched children working with clay, played in the doll corner, wrote with a pencil, and cut with scissors. She stayed with each of these activities an adequate, though not a long, amount of time. Active participation was usual, watching others and inactivity were rare.

Lynn's skill with materials and the complexity of her work with them had increased in the eight weeks since school began, although she needed considerable help to think about what she was doing. The following are examples of such progress.

• From grasping a pencil crudely in the palm of her right or left hand and scribbling to holding a pencil between her thumb and index finger and drawing firm dots, loops, and hooks.

• From being unable to hold scissors to accurate cutting with scissors— not to cut something out, but simply to cut and turn the position of the paper.

• From simply pounding and squashing clay to using acquired skills that involved pounding clay in order to flatten it, breaking it apart and sticking it together again. She also learned to repeat words the teacher used to describe the clay—"wet," "sticky," "dry," and "hard."

• From building simple towers and rows with blocks to building bridges and more complex towers, which she decorated with small colored cubes, and rows that were used as roads.

• From trying to fit puzzle pieces randomly to rotating the pieces, testing the fit, and using shape as a cue in solving puzzles.

• From using one color when easel painting to using several colors and beginning to mix color on her paper. Also from making only vertical and diagonal strokes to making swirls, loops, daubs, and lines in a variety of directions. At this point, color and line were the two variables she was most likely to use, and she was beginning to look at her work as she did it.

Language Activity   Lynn was able to respond to a single direction—"Ask Miss G for a shovel," and two directions when she was highly motivated—"Let's wash the tables, and then you can ask Mrs. A for the snack tray." She would then get a sponge, help clean the table beside a teacher, and then lead the way to the kitchen for the snack tray.

Although she was more action oriented than reflective, she was beginning to verbalize her observations of clay, look at her paintings as she mixed color on the paper, watch an anthill near the sandbox, then block the patch of the ants and chuckle and look at the teacher as the ants went around the stone or over the twig, break open mushrooms found in the yard and try to separate the tiny folds. Her attention to detail had to be focused and directed by a teacher, and she could sustain interest and attention only as long as the teacher supported her.

Lynn was beginning to be interested in looking at books and naming the objects and people in them (see "Story Groups"), but her interest in books could be sustained for a few minutes on her own.

Dramatic Play Activity   Lynn usually played beside another child without interaction. Only Annette would she invite to assume the role of another mother. She used real objects and imitated adult roles. For example, she dressed up in skirt and high heels, put on a scarf to "go to the store," put her baby in the doll carriage, "wrote" a list, called the store on the phone, and prepared a meal. Her dramatic play was independently initiated and sustained but minimally elaborated. From day to day it was repetitive and concrete.

Concept Usage

Causation   Lynn could anticipate the responses of her favorite teacher (see "Relationship with Adults"). She seemed to be able to anticipate what would happen if she worked or played near several aggressive children (see "Relationship with Children"). She was unable in most situations to understand the causes of her own feelings (see "Affect"). When teachers pondered why with her she seemed thoughtful, but did not suggest reasons.

Seriation   Lynn used the word *first* only in highly personal ways, e.g., "I'm first."

Number   Lynn could chain one, two, and three accurately. She could take
             two crackers, say she had one nose, two eyes, one mouth, two
hands, and two feet.

Space   Lynn used her body in space well, and could locate objects in the
             room and yard by action. She did not yet use many prepositions
and sometimes the ones she did use were incorrect. After demonstration
she could then follow the verbal direction, "Put the basket on the bottom
shelf."

Time   Usually time was *now* to her, but she was beginning to learn *after*
            in relation to routine times—"After we clean the tables, we will
have snack." She was beginning to use this word correctly herself, meaning
right after. It was very difficult for her to delay strong wishes and the
minutes after lunch before going home must have seemed a very long time
to her. When her third birthday was coming up soon, with considerable
practice she began to recall that she was two years old and would be three
on her birthday.

Description and Classification   Lynn used many objects in appropriate
                                      ways—a bowl and spoon for stirring, a
bag to put groceries in. She could match colors and knew the names *red,
blue,* and *green,* but did not correctly attach these colors to objects. For
example, when asked what color her dress was she responded with the
name of a color, but not the color of her dress. She was aware and enjoyed
the texture of materials, but rarely used any language related to texture.

Measurement   Measurement was a global idea to Lynn, and she used the
                    words *big, bigger, little* and *more than,* though not always
correctly. These words were also used in highly personal ways, e.g., "I got
more dan dat," "I ain't little."

On completion of this summary profile of Lynn's school behavior for
the first eight weeks, some of her strengths and areas of vulnerability could
be clearly delineated. Her areas of strength were:
• her competence and pleasure in most personal tasks
• her ability to speak clearly and spontaneously while engaged in movement activities
• her unusually skilled use of her body
• her ability to solve practical problems that involved herself, others, and
  objects in space
• her good practical memory

- her willingness and pleasure in the use of a wide variety of materials coupled with her ability to make independent choices and to persist and return to tasks difficult for her
- her ability to use a model for learning, as illustrated by her imitation of her teacher's actions and language
- the pleasure she took in the number of contacts she made with a wide variety of children in varying situations
- her ability to initiate and sustain dramatic play and to play out a sequence of events
- her growing pleasure in books and her good sense of melody, tone, and rhythm
  Areas where Lynn needed help were also quite clear:
- her strain over separation from her mother
- her concrete and nonspecific language and her use of gestures in place of language
- her poor memory in certain situations, as evidenced by her inability to guide us or point out the local school, store, and playground with which she was familiar in another context
- her reaction to strain, conflict, and disappointment, expressed all in the same way and with great intensity
- her concrete, piecemeal way of solving problems and her tendency to become active and slapdash rather than being able to delay action in order to think
- her great need for adult attention and approval
- her avoidance of aggressive children and her giving up when aggressive action was called for on her part

This kind of careful determination of a child's strengths and weaknesses is basic to establishing priorities for the child's learning, for individualized teaching means building on the child's own strengths and helping him overcome his weaknesses. Decisions on all aspects of the program depend on such careful assessment, and cannot rely on haphazard observation. To be sure, observations were made by all team members and were communicated in many informal ways, but one hour of each day was spent by the teaching staff consolidating the information for each of the children, evaluating the teaching–learning process, and adapting plans on the basis of these evaluations. Regular case conferences were also scheduled, for review of all data on a particular child. These conferences, as well as providing a forum for the discussion of specific information, served to underscore the individuality of each child and his family.

A case conference about Lynn occurred the week the teacher's summary was completed. There were several summaries of contacts with Mrs. Rogers by the social worker, a summary of a developmental and physical examination, and the teacher's summary, which had been circulated before the conference.

CC, the social worker assigned to this family, had the impression from her contact with Mrs. Rogers that Lynn needed more nurturance at home in the form of physical contact and allowances for feelings to evolve and be recognized. She reported that Mrs. Rogers said Lynn looked forward to school and talked about children, teachers, and activities at home; that Lynn imitated others more at home since she had been in school, sang songs, had learned many new words and phrases, spoke more clearly, and could talk about her experiences better. Lynn's mother talked freely about her wetting and crying. Lynn had cried before coming to school and had several toilet accidents at home, too. Mrs. Rogers had demonstrated that she was available and would try to cooperate in any way she could that would be helpful to Lynn, but it appeared that, at this point, Mrs. Rogers was not able to talk with Lynn about her mixed and probably perplexing feelings, nor to provide directly the special consideration Lynn needed. But she was a conscientious mother who sought opportunities for her children that she could not herself provide.

Some particularly relevant information that came up at this time was that Mrs. Rogers had been hospitalized shortly before school began. Lynn had been very concerned and anxious about her mother's absence from home and had needed constant reassurance about her whereabouts and when she would return. Mrs. Rogers still did not feel well, and this in itself could stir up some anxiety in Lynn about separation.

The pediatrician noted that there was no physical reason for Lynn's being tired and sleepy and wetting, and it was reasonable to assume that this behavior was in response to stress.

Teachers thought the comparatively restricted physical environment of the school and yard—that is, a yard with a fence and gate—might well seem strange and confining to a three year old used to going outside and back to her mother as she needed to.

MK, the developmental examiner, confirmed our perceptions about some aspects of Lynn's functioning. For example, Lynn was described in the testing situation as not being reflective; she tended to respond so rapidly that sometimes she either failed to consider the relevant aspects of the stimulus or lost track of the idea of the task. On the other hand, her performance with the pegboards was slowed down by her seeming to function with the notion that each peg had a special hole, rather than simply putting them in across the board. Lynn had asked the examiner to look at her and called attention to herself by a contagious, pleased laugh, by smiling at the examiner, or by clapping her hands and smiling when she completed a task. Lynn's spontaneous verbalizations were better articulated than her responses to direct questions, and she was easier to understand in the second testing session than in the first. She was found to be interested in the test materials and persistent even with difficult tasks. It was also noted that Lynn was not helped by verbal instructions, but that demonstrations were more meaningful to her.

We were then ready to set up an individualized way of working with Lynn. Our plan was as follows.

• We thought Lynn's stress reactions around separations required consideration. We decided to encourage Lynn to use both the real and play telephone to provide a connection with her mother. We would talk with Lynn about how children sometimes want to come to school and at the same time miss their mothers. We would continue to feel free to call Mrs. Rogers to come early when Lynn needed her. We would help Lynn to learn the sequence of her morning at school so she could anticipate the day. We would tell her stories about herself, what she did at school, when she went home, and what we saw her do after school in order to develop a greater sense of continuity. We would observe her further and try to determine if there were specific situations in which she had toilet accidents.

We did not know if napping at home occurred in reaction to specific stress, but Lynn did fall asleep at school when teacher attention was focused on a group and preparation for lunch. We decided to involve Lynn in lunch preparation so that she would not feel alone or abandoned at times and see if this would help her.

• Lynn's lack of reflectiveness interfered with problem solving and learning. We decided to use her interest in the materials, her need for adult attention and her ability to learn by imitation to help her become better able to think. AZ, the teacher Lynn had the deepest attachment to, would work directly with her as a model. She would involve Lynn using materials jointly with her. She would talk about them but more importantly would demonstrate. She would show Lynn how to stop what she was doing and look at the materials, taking Lynn step by step through the process. She would show her how to recognize and think about correcting an error. We had already found this effective in helping Lynn solve problems with children. Since Lynn was not able to use verbal instructions alone, teachers would demonstrate in action, gradually diminishing the use of actions as she could use verbal instructions more effectively.

• Since Lynn particularly enjoyed dramatic play, we would continue to provide opportunities for her to extend and enrich dramatic play with other children. We would particularly observe the themes and content of her play in order to extend and enrich it, as well as to gain insight into Lynn's thinking.

• We decided to make storybooks with the children in Lynn's story group, since she and the two other children also often engaged in spontaneous play together. The teacher would draw pictures with the children of the children themselves engaged in daily activities. Such activity could provide an impetus for enjoying books, help provide language for experience, and help Lynn and the others recall and organize their thinking about their day at school and what they were learning. It would also provide an opportunity for teachers to ask questions of them about subjects on which they had something to say.

• We decided that Lynn's avoidance of some children at this time was wise and that helping her to build realistic skills with materials and language would gradually increase her competence and support her self-confidence so that she could cope with them more comfortably.

Bibliography

Argyris, C. (1962), *Interpersonal Competence and Organizational Effectiveness,* Homewood, Ill.: Richard D. Irwin, Inc., The Dorsey Press.

This book describes a research project with a group of executives who began the process of increasing the effectiveness of their work relationships. The results suggest a new concept of responsibility that increases internal commitment, creativity, flexibility, and cooperation.

Benedek, T. (1959), Parenthood as a Developmental Phase. *J. of the Am. Psychoanalytic Assn.* 7: 389–417.

Subtitle: A Contribution to Libido Theory.

A psychoanalytic presentation to demonstrate that personality development is a continuing process that includes parenthood.

Beyers, P. and Beyers, H. (1972), Nonverbal Communication and the Education of Children. In: *Functions of Language in the Classroom,* C. B. Cazden, V. P. John, and D. Hymes, eds. New York: Teachers College Press, pp. 3–31.

This essay compares and contrasts the verbal and nonverbal components of communication. The point is made that in order for children to become competent in communication, they must be taken seriously in direct human involvement.

Bibring, G. (1961), A Study of the Psychological Process in Pregnancy and of the Earliest Mother–Child Relationship. *The Psychoanalytic Study of the Child.* New York: International Universities Press.

Report of data from a psychoanalytic study of the psychology of pregnant women and of mothers with very young infants. Particular emphasis is placed upon pregnancy and early motherhood as a developmental crisis.

Boguslawski, D. (1966), *Guide for Establishing and Operating Day Care Centers for Young Children.* New York: Child Welfare League of America, Inc.

A practical pamphlet for professional use in producing good daycare programs from an organization experienced in evaluating children's facilities.

Braun, J., and Lasher, M. G. (1970), *Preparing Teachers to Work with Disturbed Preschoolers.* Cambridge, Mass.: Nimrod Press.

A detailed description of a three-year training program for preschool education specialists to work with disturbed children (Tufts University).

Cazden, C. B. (1971), *Child Language and Education*. New York: Holt, Rinehart and Winston.

The development of language and much of what is known about children's speech is extensively and logically presented. Some implications for teaching may be found.

Chapman, J. E., dir. (Nov. 1971), *A Review of the Present Status and Future Needs in Day Care Research*. Washington, D.C.: Social Research Group, George Washington University.

Subtitle: A Working Paper.

Prepared for the Interagency Panel on Early Childhood Research and Development. The title speaks for the content.

Cohen, D. H., and Stern, V. (1958), *Observing and Recording the Behavior of Young Children*. New York: Teachers College Press.

This pamphlet provides help for teachers in observing and recording children's behavior. On-the-spot running records of the child's behavior during routine times, when using materials, when relating to others, and when involved in a group activity are thoroughly explored. The sections on descriptive language for recording are very helpful to teachers who are learning to observe and record behavior of children.

Cohen, D. J., and Brandegee, A. S. (1974), *Day Care, 3, Serving Preschool Children. Washington,* D.C.: Government Printing Office. Department of Health, Education and Welfare Publication No. (OCD) 74-1057.

One of the series of handbooks on daycare from the Office of Child Development, this volume covers all major aspects of daycare specific to the needs of children from ages three to five. It includes many helpful references.

Committee on the Infant and Preschool Child, W. B. Forsythe, chairman (1971), *Standards for Day Care Centers for Infants and Children under 3 Years of Age*. Evanston, Ill.: American Academy of Pediatrics.

This manual outlines the basic standards for quality daycare for children under three years of age. It does not give details of implementation.

Costello, J., and Binstock, E. (1970), *Review and Summary of a National Survey of the Parent–Child Center Program*.

Prepared for the Office of Child Development, U.S. Department of Health, Education and Welfare.

The first year of operation of thirty-six parent–child centers was surveyed, and a national reporting system was devised. The survey is reviewed and summarized, and evaluative statements are made.

Day Care Consultation Service, Bank Street College of Education (no date), *Toward Comprehensive Child Care*. Washington, D. C.: Day Care and Child Development Council of America.

In this paper the need to enhance family relationships is seen as the central issue of daycare. A historical perspective is presented and existing family-centered programs are discussed.

Dittman, L., ed. (1973), *The Infants We Care For*. Washington, D.C.: National Association for the Education of Young Children.

The Commission on Infancy of the NAEYC considers the issues and programs for infant group care with a view to what is optimal for the development of the child and his family.

Duckworth, E. (1972), The Having of Wonderful Ideas. *Harvard Educational Review* 42: 217–31.

Relying heavily on Piaget's theory of intellectual development, the author presents a powerful case for teachers seeing the world from the particular child's point of view. She conveys a profound respect for children's thinking and feelings and commitment to helping children increase their repertory of actions and thoughts. Having the first wonderful idea is viewed as increasing the probability of continuing to have wonderful ideas.

Erikson, E. H. (1950), *Childhood and Society*. New York: Norton.

The first of many of Erikson's unique contributions to clinical and theoretical psychoanalytic concepts, and the social significance of childhood.

Erikson, E. H. (1959), Identity and the Life Cycle. *Psychological Issues* 1 (no. 1). New York: International Universities Press.

Subtitle: Selected Papers with a Historical Introduction by David Rappaport.

A monograph that outlines the psychosocial theory of ego development.

Escalona, S. K. (1968), *The Roots of Individuality*. Chicago: Aldine Publishing Co.

This book, while reporting findings of a particular study, also contains a valuable summary of the history and current trends in child-development research. Normal patterns of development in infancy are described.

Espenschade, A. S., and Eckert, H. M. (1967), *Motor Development*. Columbus, Ohio: Charles B. Merrill.

Substantial normative data relating to motor performance and development are presented in chapters six, seven, and eight. The descriptions of patterns of movement are of particular use to teachers of young children.

Fraiberg, S. H. (1959), *The Magic Years*. New York: Charles Scribner's Sons.

This is among the best of all the books about early childhood. Discussions of theories and facts about development and child care are presented in a style that is highly readable and practical without oversimplifying complex issues. It is especially vivid in its picture of the mind of the young child and is a valuable guide to understanding and dealing with him.

Freud, A. (1965), *Normality and Pathology in Childhood*. New York: International Universities Press.

This summarizes and synthesizes a wealth of data and clinical experience from psychoanalytic studies of infancy and childhood. Of particular usefulness to teachers are the chapters on the relevance of child observation and the concept of developmental lines. The presentation of the concepts of psychological normality and pathology is clear and should be of great help to all students of child development.

Freud, A., and Burlingham, D. (1944), *Infants Without Families*. New York: International Universities Press.

This is a valuable documentation and discussion of reactions of very young children to separation from their families. It includes both practical suggestions for substitute parents and psychodynamic explanations.

Hartmann, H. (1958), *Ego Psychology and the Problem of Adaptation*. New York: International Universities Press.

This is a translation of Hartmann's 1939 essay, which was a landmark in the development of ego psychology in psychoanalysis. Among the many influential ideas proposed are the role of learning in adaptation and the importance of the interaction of inborn and experiential factors in development.

Host, M. A., and Heller, P. B. (1971), *Day Care, 7, Administration*. Washington, D.C.: Government Printing Office. Department of Health, Education and Welfare Publication No. (OCD) 72-20.

A handbook for organizing and administering daycare programs in the Office of Child Development series.

Huntington, D. S., Provence S., and Parker, R. K. (1971), *Day Care, 2, Serving Infants*. Washington, D. C.: U.S. Government Printing Office, Department of Health, Education and Welfare Publication No. (OCD) 73-14.

The first in the Office of Child Development's series of nine handbooks, making explicit different aspects of child-developmental needs for good infant-care programs.

Isaacs, S. (1933), *Social Development in Young Children*. New York: Schocken Books.

Observations are presented that support the social and sexual aspects of the child's egocentric state: his friendliness, cooperation, hostility, and aggression.

Kamii, C. K. (1971), Evaluation of Learning in Preschool Education: Social-Emotional, Perceptual-Motor, and Cognitive Development. In: *Handbook on Formative and Summative Evaluation of Student Learning,* B. S. Bloom, J. T. Hastings, and G. F. Madaus, eds. New York: McGraw Hill.

This presentation offers the reader concise illustrations of formative and summative evaluation in a Piagetian cognitively oriented preschool.

Keister, D. J. (1969), *Consultation in Day Care.* Chapel Hill, N.C.: Institute of Government, University of North Carolina.

A manual that distinguishes the role, function, philosophy, and practices of daycare consultants.

Keister, M. E. (1970), *"The Good Life" for Infants and Toddlers: Group Care of Infants.* Washington, D. C.: National Association for the Education of Young Children.

Subtitle: Report on a Demonstration Project, University of North Carolina, Greensboro.

This description of a demonstration project for quality child care includes comparative test scores of center/home pairs.

Keyserling, M. D. (1972), *Windows on Day Care.* New York: National Council of Jewish Women.

Subtitle: A report based on findings of the National Council of Jewish Women on Day Care Needs and Services in their Communities.

This data on daycare needs and services was collected in 1970 from 431 centers in 176 sections of the country. Statistics are tabulated and recommendations are made.

Landreth, C. (1972), *Preschool Learning and Teaching.* New York: Harper Row.

This book gives precise explanations of what makes children learn, what they can learn, and what teaching is all about. The discussions are well grounded in research findings and reflect sensitivity to the teaching–learning process.

Leach, L. B. (1972), *Interdisciplinary Team Consultation in Day Care.* West Hartford, Conn.: Greater Hartford Community Council.

A report of a demonstration pilot project in consultation to daycare centers through a poll of six specialists from different disciplines acting as a team. A critical evaluation of their experiences is included.

Mallum, M. A. (1970), *California Children's Centers Curriculum Guide.* Hawthorne, Calif.: California Children's Centers Directors and Supervisors Association.

Subtitle: Goals and Growth Experiences for the Early Years.

A guide for curriculum planning with eight areas of development and their respective goals identified. This guide was issued by a statewide committee of the California Children's Centers Directors and Supervisors Association for use in the in-service training of teachers.

Murphy, L. B. (1968), The Consultant in a Day Care Center for Deprived Children. *Children* 15 (no. 3): 97–102.

Individual problems in daycare centers and the role of the consultant in fostering constructive attitudes are discussed.

Murphy, L. B., and Leeper, E. M. (1973), *Caring for Children*. Washington, D.C.: Department of Health, Education and Welfare.

A series of ten guides for use in establishing and operating daycare centers.

Naylor, A. K. (1970), Some Determinants of Parent–Infant Relationships. In: *What We Can Learn From Infants*, L. Dittman, ed. Washington, D.C.: National Association for the Education of Young Children, pp. 25–47.

How well the developmental tasks of parenting can be accomplished depends on multiple influences, among them the quality of care the individual received as a child, and the particular characteristics of the infant. Two cases of parent–child problems are presented.

Naylor, A. K. (1972), Work with Parents, Team Collaboration, and Problem Solving (in Day Care). In: *Social and Health Needs in Childhood and Adolescence*, J. F. Gorman, ed. Berkeley, Calif.: School of Public Health, University of California, pp. 61–70.

From the Child Development Unit of the Yale University Child Study Center Daycare Research Project, experiences are related concerning the problems of collaboration in a multidisciplinary staff.

Neubauer, P., ed. (1974), *Early Child Day Care*. New York: Jason Aronson.

The papers presented in this monograph are from a two-day Institute on Issues in Early Day Care held by the Jewish Board of Guardians. The papers deal with issues about children *at risk*, the selection and training of daycare staff, the need for work with parents, treatment of infants and toddlers in a therapeutic setting, and the special problems of the child under three in daycare.

North, A. F. (1971), *Day Care: Health Services—A Guide for Project Directors and Health Personnel. Child Development*. Washington, D.C.: Office of Child Development, U.S. Department of Health, Education and Welfare Publication No. (OCD) 73-12. Government Printing Office.

This guide was written for directors, physicians, and any who are concerned with the health of children in daycare. Services, administration, and technical considerations are described.

Patterson, J. M. (1971), Analyzing Early Childhood Educational Programs: Instructional Procedures. *Educational Leadership* 28 : 802–05.

This article presents a brief discussion of the decision-making process related to materials and equipment, adult roles, the use of space and time, and provisions for individual differences.

Piaget, J. (1936), *The Origins of Intelligence in Children*. New York: International Universities Press. 1952.

In this volume Jean Piaget introduced his seminal theory of the development of intelligence in children. His delineation of the stages of sensorimotor intelligence and his theory that mental faculties develop through being used have exerted profound influence on the child-development field. A brilliant summary and synthesis of the work of Piaget and his colleageus is available in Piaget, J., and Inhelder, B. (1969) *The Psychology of the Child*. New York: Basic Books.

Pizzo, P. D. (1972), *Operational Difficulties of Group Care*. Washington, D.C.: Day Care and Child Development Council of America, Inc.

This paper is a description of the major differences between daycare and nursery school and the difficulties for daycare operations stemming from the lack of recognition of these differences.

Prescott, E., and Jones, E. (1972), *The "Politics" of Day Care,* vol. 1. Washington, D.C.: National Association for the Education of Young Children.

This study of variously sponsored daycare programs was conducted in South California. The monograph is illustrated with case histories and includes information on regulations and licensing.

Prescott, E., Jones, E., and Kritchevsky, S. (1972), *Day Care as a Child-Rearing Environment,* vol. 2. Washington, D.C.: National Association for the Education of Young Children.

This report is of a study begun in 1964 that evaluates group care by the range of experiences provided, the responses of the children, and the match between the developmental needs of the child and his family and the program offered by a particular center.

Provence, S. (1967), *Guide for the Care of Infants in Groups*. New York: Child Welfare League of America.

Written for those who plan and provide care for infants living in institutions, this guide presents information on the developmental tendencies and needs of infants and recommends ways of meeting those needs.

Provence, S., and Lipton, R. (1962), *Infants in Institutions*. New York: International Universities Press.

This report of an observational study of the development of a group of infants living in an institutional environment compares their learning experiences with those of family children and measures their developmental progress by tests. The absence of adequate mothering is described in terms of concrete variables.

Read, K. (1976), *The Nursery School: Human Relationships and Learning*. 6th ed. Philadelphia: W. B. Saunders.

For the past twenty-six years this text has served as a handbook for nursery school teachers. The recent, revised edition has about the same outline and the same strengths as the earlier editions, while the examples, pictures, references, and content take into account changes in thinking about young children and new knowledge. Its main strength remains: a consistent and humanistic point of view about children and teachers.

Rice, A. K. (1965), *Learning for Leadership*. London: Tavistock Publications Ltd.

Subtitle: Interpersonal and Intergroup Relations.

This is a report of what participants of a study group learned about the problems of leadership, defined as controlling the transactions between internal and external environments. In the process of examining their own behavior, the group evolved new conceptions of leadership, which will aid in meeting the demands of increasingly complex organizations.

Ruderman, F. A. (1968), *Child Care and Working Mothers: A Study of Arrangements Made for Daytime Care of Children*. New York: Child Welfare League of America, Inc.

This project, which ran from 1960 to 1964, was designed as a resource for data as well as an instrument for action to promote the goals of those concerned in the planning of daycare programs.

Sale, J. S., and Torres, Y. L. (1971), *I'm Not Just a Sitter. A Descriptive Report of the Community Family Day Care Project*. Pasadena, Calif.: Pacific Oaks College.

A booklet on family daycare written from the point of view of the worker, about her attitudes, responsibilities, and care-taking activities. Many photographs document the text.

Social and Administrative Services and Systems Association and Consulting Services Corp. (1971), *A Survey of State Day Care Licensing Requirements*. Washington, D.C.: Child Care and Child Development Council of America, Inc. Child Care Bulletin no. 4.

With a preface: "Licensing—What It Is and What It Isn't."

This bulletin is one of a series (nine in all) on child care in answer to the need for concise information. It synopsizes state licensing procedures and requirements.

Southeastern Day Care Project, N. E. Travis, dir. (1974), *How to Do Day Care: Some Shared Experiences*. Atlanta: Southern Regional Education Board.

This is not intended as a complete manual on daycare, but a wide variety of experiences and many aspects of daycare are covered. The information was obtained from eight daycare center directors and their staffs.

Steinfels, M. O. (1973), *Who's Minding The Children?* New York: Simon and Schuster.

Subtitle: The History and Politics of Day Care in America.

A book that delineates the complexity of the movements giving rise to the demand for daycare. Examples of current daycare practices are given and the sociological implications for the future shape of daycare are made explicit.

Yarrow, L. (1964), Separation from Parents During Early Childhood. In: M. L. Hoffman and L. W. Hoffman, eds., *Review of Child Development Research,* vol. 1. New York: Russell Sage Foundation, pp. 89–136.

This review article summarizes many of the studies on separation, discusses their implications, and proposes a conceptual framework for future studies.

Sources of Information about Child Care and Programs for Children

Bank Street College of Education
69 Bank Street
New York, N.Y. 10014

Black Child Development Institute
1028 Connecticut Avenue, N.W.
Washington, D.C. 20036

Child Study Association of America
9 East 89th Street
New York, N.Y. 10028

Child Welfare League of America
67 Irving Place
New York, N.Y. 10003

Day Care and Child Development
Council of America
Suite 1100
1401 K Street, N.W.
Washington, D.C. 20005

Educational Resources Information
Center (ERIC)
Clearinghouse on Early Childhood Education
University of Illinois
805 West Pennsylvania Avenue
Urbana, Ill. 61801

Government Printing Office
Washington, D.C. 20402
(Many documents published by various government agencies and departments can be obtained directly from the GPO.)

National Association for the Education of Young Children (NAEYC)
1834 Connecticut Avenue, N.W.
Washington, D.C. 20009

National Council of Organizations for Children and Youth
1910 K Street, N.W., Room 404
Washington, D.C. 20006

Office of Child Development
U.S. Department of Health, Education and Welfare
Box 1182
Washington, D.C. 20013

Index

Administrative structure, 25–28

Adults, relationships to, 184–85; role of teachers in helping children build, 153–56

Age-specific competencies and vulnerabilities, and child's ability to cope with separation, 61, 65

Aggressive behavior, 119–23

Aid to Families of Dependent Children, 48

Andrus family, 55–60

Antiprofessionalism, 238–40

Argyris, C., 32 *n*

Atmosphere of daycare center, enriching affective, 83–84

Baird: family, 50–52; Yvonne, 75–76

Banks, Curtis, 78

Bath and dressing, 141–43

Behavior: aggressive, 119–23; expectations for child's, 88–89; imitative, of infants, 99–100

Board of directors: interrelationships of, with director and staff, 217–20; relationship with director, 214–16; responsibility of, to parents, 216–17; and staff-selection process, 201–03

Capello, Stanley, 21–22

Children: attributes of healthy, 179–81; central role of human relationships in development of, 6–7; importance of developmental approach for, 4–5; problem of separation for, 9, 62–67; ratio of staff to, 196–98; at risk, illustrated, 14–23

Children's House: daily operation of, 89, 247–50; perception of, by parents, 43; Phase I of, 11–12, 14–23; Phase II of, 11, 12–14

Complaints, staff members' responses to, 46–47, 216–17

Confidentiality, 29–30

Consistency of environment, 85–86

Construction activities for toddlers, 114–15

Consultants, 205–09; advisory groups as 212–13; problem areas requiring use of, 209–10; qualifications of, 210–11

Contrast in environment, 86–87

Cook in daycare setting, 196

Cooperatives, parent, 222–23

Criterion Model for Preschool Curriculum, 178–79, 181–86, 251–70

Cultural gap, 45

Davis: Jennifer, 22; Linda, 22, 75

Daycare: basic requirements for high-quality, 9–10; family, 224–25; new developments in, 224–25; as nuclear service, 242–43; obstacles to high-quality, 238–42; premises guiding use of, 225–34; pressure for, 2–3; proprietary (private), 221–23; public, 223–24; types of, 221–25

Developmental approach, 3, 4–6, 80

Director, 205; choice of candidates for, 189–94; constraints on, 26; as consultant, 211; interrelationships of, with board and staff, 217–20; qualifications of, 188–89, 201–02; relationship with board of directors, 214–16; responsibilities of, 25–26; selection of, 201–02, 203. *See also* Staff

Dressing: infants and toddlers, 141–43; older preschool children, 158–59

Eating. *See* Mealtime

Economic need, as source of pressure for daycare, 2, 3

Educational diagnosis and prescription, 185–86

Educators, early childhood, as daycare directors, 189–90

Edwards, Cindy, 18–20, 151

Environment: consistency and repetition

299